Stolen Land – Stolen Lives:
and the great con trick
of DEBT!

by

Shirley-Anne Hardy

*

CONTENTS

PART I:
THE LAND QUESTION –
ITS HIDDEN GOLD

PART II:
RETURN JOURNEY

PART III:
KALEIDOSCOPE

Author's Preface

T *he land question* is the great unresolved riddle of civilization. How indeed could it *not* be, when every naked infant born onto this earth depends upon land for his very survival here? Yet the great mass of humanity are born as outcasts, having – due to corrupt institutions of human invention – no right to this Earth whatsoever - *no birthright in the land.*

In this, humankind is in a dangerous position, having set its judgment above that of the great Giver to us of the gift of this Earth; and from our misjudgement in this, economic, social, political and environmental turmoil have followed. But humankind does not see the danger of its position.

Henry George, the American who devoted his life to the resolving of this great matter, referred to it – in the opening chapter of his book "Progress and Poverty" – as "the riddle which the Sphinx of Fate puts to our civilization, which not to answer is to be destroyed". How true his words have proved! – for in the 130 years since his book came out, our civilization has progressed to the point where it is destroying not only itself, but the Planet as well.

My own discovery of Henry George's work more than half a century ago – solving the puzzle which had been with me since childhood, as to why some were so rich in our society, and some so poor – was, as many others have also described it, a 'Damascus' experience, for it has shaped my life ever since.

Already well into 'senior years' when "Birthright in Land – and the State of Scotland Today" was produced in 1999, I was convinced at the time that its over six hundred pages formed my final say on the matter. However, as it has turned out – something remained yet to be said!

*

Acknowledgements

O n this all-important question of *Acknowledgements* – where I owe so much, both for the special support I have received in the making of this book, and for the encouragement, over long years, of many dear and precious friends – I have found myself compelled to ponder deeply an article, written by the Editor, which appeared in the January 2011 issue of *Comment*, our excellent local monthly publication, which we in Highland Perthshire are so fortunate in having.

In delving once more into the "perennially raised" issue of anonymity, the Editor spells out "the major hurdle to appearing in print and being identified locally by name" as being that 'contributors' housing tenure or employment could be put at risk, if stated views did not concur with those of landlords or employers. Equally, their relatives or children might be subject to discriminatory acts or remarks, or spiteful sanctions taken against them ... Although employment patterns have changed over the past 30 years, the deterrent of sanctions being brought to bear for 'speaking up' remain just as pertinent today ..."

The above matter raises of course the extremely vexed question of what meaning is left at all to the term 'democracy', which we have been so successfully and dishonestly drilled into using to describe the system we live under – a matter that I am glad to say is dealt with within the pages of this book. (See Part III ch.2)

But to return: this is a very radical book – and of far more than "local" reference of course. Having seen a great deal more deeply into the whole LAND issue in the twelve years since the publication of my previous book, ("Birthright in Land – and the State of Scotland Today" in 1999), it is a great deal more radical than that book was. It is moreover unthinkable to me that I should jeopardise, through the thoughtless mentioning of a name, the well-being of any of those I care for, however much I would like to express my gratitude openly. Such are the thoughts, therefore, that have prompted my resolve to place the names here, of the many to whom I owe so much, rather in invisible than in visible ink; upheld by the thought that they are recorded also in those more etheric 'akashic records' from which they can never be erased. And so – a heartful of thanks to each and all of you.

Of more specific acknowledgement, I would record a big indebtedness to John Smith for the abundance and diversity of the reading material with which he has supplied me over the past two decades, the fruitage of his own investigations – as a devourer of books at such a rate and on such a range of subjects that it is no wonder he is known to some of his acquaintances as "the Library"!

I would also make special salutation here to the memory of the late William Smith, founder and director of Injustice by the Law, who dedicated his time, his energies and his great spirit to helping the many so cruelly suffering under the injustice of our deeply flawed economic system. His presence remains with me – a shining and inspiring memory.

I must now express my indebtedness to the two lots of friends who, separately and on separate occasions, gave me the first two parts of the title of this book, which marry so perfectly. (The third part is my own addition, prompted by insights gained in the early days of preparing this work.)

I would next like to thank my Readers, who could not have been of more help in every way, and to whom I owe a lasting debt of gratitude, including for their patience in bearing with me, over this somewhat prolonged journey.

I must next thank my Typesetters, and here I must first express my deep indebtedness to Christina Bayne, who set out so excellently in 1981 my original booklet, "The Land Question", and who gave me a most helpful start also with this one. However, a time-break then occurred, after which the idea of the book took a different turning, and I had to start again from the beginning. For this setting out therefore my deep gratitude goes to Trish Crawford, not only for her highly professional work – (and the incredible speed of it!) – but because of the way she has proved, too, an almost magical finder of 'solutions' along the way – solutions that have decidedly eased my path! Here I can at last set down my thanks to Trish also for her wonderful setting out of the List of Contents for "Birthright ..." – thanks which could not appear in that book, since it was snatched back from its first day at the printers to accomplish this!

I would thank warmly also Vicky Petrie of Danscot Print Ltd., for her help in every way in guiding this book through the printing process.

For more general help with my work over the years, I must express special gratitude to Comment of Aberfeldy for finding space for many articles by me, which has helped to spread their message. Several are reprinted here – (see Part III ch.1), where I have allowed myself some altering of titles and some minimal editing, for a wider audience.

I am much indebted, further, to both The Georgist Journal (USA), and Good Government (Australia), who have each reprinted several of these articles. It has also been a special happiness to me to find favour for my articles with The Permaculture Activist(USA), since the Permaculture movement is one I warmly support. (One is republished here in full, along with an extract from the other – see again Part III ch. 1.)

Of those many overseas friends, with *all* of whom I value contact in this movement for radical land justice, I would express my special appreciation to Richard Giles (of Good Government), with whom I have on several occasions been grateful to consult, for his deep understanding of the land question and of the writings of Henry George; also to the Henry George Institute of America, under the directorship of Lindy Davies, both for its outreach work to America's grim prison scenario, and also for its educational courses which have inspired such a movement in Africa – (land whose sun first blessed my life); and further, to Alanna Hartzok, founder and co-director of the Earth Rights Institute and tireless worker for land justice, from whom I have also received much valuable material.

This book would not be complete without an expression of much gratitude both to the Highland Health Store in Perth, and to the Scottish Deli (Food for Thought) in Pitlochry, for their many kindnesses in keeping me supplied during the most intensive stages of this journey. And finally, I would warmly thank Alan and Isla Robertson of Pitlochry for the provision, in their welcoming store, of their masterly photocopying machine, at which I have been so regular a visitor over many months.

*

I would acknowledge with gratitude to the publishers permissions for extracts from their publications, as follows:

The International Biogenic Society – from the work of Edmond Bordeaux Szekèly, and also for his image.

The Robert Schalkenbach Foundation, (90 John St., Suite 501, New York, NY10038-3202, USA.

Website: msullivan@schalkenbach.org/schalkenba@aol.com) – for extensive quotations from "In Quest of Justice" by Francis Neilson.   Also for the picture for my chapter "Stolen Land – Stolen Lives."

Constable & Robinson Ltd. – from "We Want Real Food" by Graham Harvey.

Unity House Publisher (www.unity.org) – from "The Symphony of Life" by Donald Andrews.

Permanent Publications – from "Through the Eye of a Needle" by John-Paul Flintoff.

The C.W. Daniel Co. Ltd. (1939) – from "The Restoration of the Peasantries" by Dr G.T. Wrench.

Faber & Faber Ltd. – from "Reconstruction by Way of the Soil" by Dr G.T. Wrench.

Collins (1945) – from "The Wisdom of the Fields" by H.J. Massingham.

I trust the above list is complete, and offer my sincere apologies if there are any oversights.

*

I should like to place here a special acknowledgement to the publishers Pluto Press, for the interest of their book "The Real Rights of Man" by Noel Thompson, although I did not manage to refer to it within these pages.

From this book I learned of the exceptionally clear grasp of the land question by Thomas Spence (1750-1814), explained by the fact that, although always listed as a Newcastle man, his parents, from Aberdeen and Orkney, only moved to England in search of work. Unlike the better known Chartists of the mid 19th century whose vision, as Noel Thompson points out, was essentially Fabian and Socialist, (seduced as they were by the blandishments of centralized power) – Thomas Spence was of the true lineage of Scotland's radical thinkers on this matter, not least in seeing clearly that monopoly capitalism would be fully sufficiently dealt with, in getting rid of the underlying *monopoly of land*.

*

Images

Paperlink (2010) – for the cartoon by Steve Best on "Whisky Galore".

The Robert Schalkenbach Foundation – see above.

Harold Lane – for his 'Pons Asinorum', the Tumbling Mountain Torrent, the Permaculture Garden, Tree and Daisies. Here is the place where I can at last acknowledge the many fine drawings contributed by Harold Lane to "Birthright in Land ...", which for some inexplicable reason escaped acknowledgement in that book – for which my apologies indeed. Among these were the Mountain Torrent and the Permaculture Garden reproduced here. I am deeply indebted to Harold for all that his artistic skills have contributed to my work.

Skye Isaac – for the Olive Branch (from their garden in New Zealand). Also for the Thomas Berry quotation.

The Georgist Journal – for the Land Monopoly cartoon.

Shanti Sadan – for the seated figure.

I would also acknowledge with gratitude the small black-and-white reproduction of "The Christmas Carol Singer" to the work of the artist, William Wier and to the Trustees of the British Museum.

*

Other useful addresses:

For Social Problems by Henry George: Dove Scotland, c/o Dr A. Hardie, 24/7 Greenpark, Edinburgh EH17 7TA. For Progress and Poverty and other works by Henry George: Shepheard-Walwyn Ltd., 107 Parkway House, Sheen Lane, London SW14 8LS, www.ethicaleconomics.org.uk. Works by Henry George are obtainable also, along with those of Francis Neilson, from The Robert Schalkenbach Foundation, USA – see Acknowledgements above.

The Nockian Society, 42 Leathers Road, Fort Mitchell, Kentucky 41017, USA – for Our Enemy the State, by A J Nock.

Henry George Institute, 121 East 30th Street, New York, NY 10016, USA (www.henrygeorge.org) – for online classes in economics.

Some Vital Messages at the Start!

1) No Aspersions Cast

At the end of one of my articles reproduced in this book (see Part III ch.1) is placed the following statement:-

> The above article casts no aspersions upon any individual, no matter what may be their position within the present system. It is the structure of our society that is at fault, and no individual is to blame for that. It is a joint responsibility in which we all share, and the united efforts of us all are needed to re-structure it aright.

The same thought is expressed at least once elsewhere within these pages, but in a book which has much to say about the rottenness of the structures now barely holding our sinking society together, I place it here also, at the start, to make fully clear that – neither does this book cast any aspersions upon any individual; and for the same reasons as given above.

Further: many there may be, working within the present system, who in fact long for a freer life and better use of their energies; but being trapped in such a situation the question of anonymity – (see preceding ch. *Acknowledgements*) – deters the voicing of their views. Fortunately beneath all such constructed falsities we are equally, all of us, simple beings belonging to the human race – a recognition awaiting equally those who, in the present system, play the less fortunate role of wielders of power.

In this lies our hope.

*

2) 'Sexist' Vocabulary

As stated on this question, at the start of "Birthright in Land – and the State of Scotland Today" – (hereafter referred to as "Birthright in Land ...", or sometimes simply as "Birthright ..."): so far as I am concerned, I go for SIMPLICITY!

I understand that 'man' in any case may originally have been used in our language as a generic term, specifying no particular gender, but simply a human being. If it was not, then we certainly need to grant it this additional meaning, as appropriate – for there is no proper substitute.

Thus in so far as linguistics are concerned, in my vocabulary – *man embraces woman*!

(See further my published letter on this in Part III ch.1.)

*

I am happy to be able to add here some support for my above stance, from the fascinating *Ringing Cedars of Russia* series of books – (see reference to which in one of my published Letters, in Part III ch.1). For here John Woodsworth – who has done such an excellent work in translating these books into English – faced with the same problem in the Russian language, resorted to restoring to their word 'chelovyek', (today used as our 'man') – a possibly more original meaning in Russian, likewise generic, signifying both man and woman.

Mention of this *Ringing Cedars of Russia* series provides an opportunity for me to add, concerning these extraordinary writings, that it has been well said in one of the books (I believe I am right – by the translator?) that if Anastasia, whose wisdom teachings are the substance of the series, is not a real person, then it must be conceded that her creator, Vladimir Megré, is a creative genius of the stature of Leo Tolstoy.

More importantly – Anastasia's teachings are something we must surely be glad to discover for the challenging times ahead. In particular, there are in Book I her careful instructions as to how to go about the sowing of seeds for edible plants, so that they will bestow the blessing of whatever healing may be sought, upon their sower. Moreover, where other plant-life is succumbing to adverse weather conditions, these plants have proven their ability to maintain themselves in a flourishing state.

This series of books is of interest at so many levels; and of course the Russian people, from their recent peasant past, retain ever a profound sense of connection with their 'Earthly Mother'.

*

3) A Movement – *not* an Organization!

The timely arrival from America, in the last days of April, of the quarterly *Georgist Journal,* prompts a reminder of something

I had intended for this book – but several bits of interesting material had in the end to be abandoned if the third printing deadline (which I was resolved not to miss) was to be met.

The following is an extract from the editorial by Lindy Davies in the Spring 2011 issue of the Journal just received:-

> "A movement is a spontaneous, aggregate phenomenon. It is very different from an organization. An organization functions under conscious direction and a specific mission statement – and when its Directors fail to guide an organization competently towards its mission, it can be said to have failed. But a movement cannot fail. It can only either happen or not happen. If it does happen, it is because some critical number of individuals and groups care enough about it to make it happen. If someone were to try to turn a movement into an organization ... it's very likely that the movement would be weakened ..."

What an excellent summing-up of what a movement is!

In "Birthright in Land ..." there is included an article entitled "Imprisoned Ideas" which similarly points this distinction – between those working to spread an idea who became 'Prisoners of the Organization' and those who remain true to it as 'Servants of the Spirit'. The point is made that "the idea having embodied itself in an organization, the organization then proceeds gradually to slay the idea which gave it birth."

The article, by W.J. Brown, MP, first appeared in The Spectator of 19th September 1947, and having come into my hands in the early 1950s, I can no longer remember its exact provenance. But it has been so great an educator in my life that I placed it, in "Birthright ...", in a section entitled "Three Fundamentals", (along with Chief Seattle's statement and an extract from *The*

Essene Gospels). The article brings out that it is of the nature of organization to betray the idea it was formed to serve, since the preservation of the organization gradually takes precedence over the serving of the idea.

In this connection I recall that, on the writing-paper of the Nockian Society, (founded in memory of A.J. Nock, author of "Our Enemy the State" – of which more in this book), there is a delightful note at the top right-hand corner: "No membership – No Committees – No Dues". (I hope I have remembered it exactly? Some such notice anyway!) The Nockian Society has soundly defended itself in advance against the dangers of organization!

Let us then, in Scotland at any rate, ensure that our work to bring forward this essential reform does so, with the same wisdom, as a movement which eschews organization; in every part of the land the people taking it upon themselves to MOVE things forward in their own chosen ways.

Warm thanks to the Georgist Journal!

*

Finally I must quote, in closing, the following from the American environmentalist, Thomas Berry, which I have just come across. For it speaks so beautifully and profoundly of the emergence of the true man, rooted in the wisdom of the land – that child of Gaia who alone is capable of taking forward the *movement* essential to the establishing of justice, and so – peace on earth.

"The depths of the soul emerge from the human world because the inner form of the mountains and the numinous quality of the sky have activated these depths in the human being."

These words convey the essential message of this book: the recovery, after so long a dispossession, of our original *land-rooted wisdom and being*.

4) Unattributed Items

Any unattributed items in this book are by the Author, myself, Shirley-Anne Hardy. (In some places my name is given in abbreviation as SAH.)

*

Opening Thoughts
from Others' Writings

*

A nd while some danced happy and carefree with songs and music, others shed tears which no hand could wipe away ... How did this happen? How could such a gulf have opened out? ... Why is it that some words, even though spoken distinctly and out loud, are incomprehensible to some human beings? The words fade away and disappear like water – without taste, without colour. Without a trace.

(Solzhenitsyn)

*

The plowman plows, the sower sows,
The repear reaps the ear,
The woodman to the forest goes
Before the day grows clear;
But of our toil no fruit we see,
The harvest's not for you and me:
A robber band has seized the land
And we are exiles here.

(Edward Carpenter, 1844-1929)

*

Let others labour,
    We shall own the land;
They'll work for bread –
    And place it in my hand.

(B.C. Mollison)

Truth is violated by falsehood,
but it is outraged by silence.

(Author unknown)

*

Introduction

B orn into a world in which all land in already owned by someone, we usually see land first as simply – the essential living-and-working space that we are in need of, but of which we (most of us) unfortunately possess none; and that we are therefore faced with – burdened with – a demand for payment from some 'landowner' for access to it.

This view of land instils in us the belief that, as it is something that is *owned*, so it must be a form of *capital* – just as other capital goods are owned; (and indeed, this is precisely what is taught in our schools and colleges). Consequently – that there is a *natural capital price* for land – (students are never asked to figure out where it comes from) – from which there follows inevitably a *rental demand* for access.

Nevertheless, at some level of our being it may be there lingers a feeling that this whole picture is not quite right.

The natural Law of Rent invites us to see the picture another way round, giving us a different view – a different understanding – of land ... and in doing so, discovers the *great con trick of DEBT!*

*

Part I

The Land Question –
its Hidden Gold

*

Somewhere, in one of the ancient Hindu scriptures, it is written – that man walks over the gold he does not see under his feet.

How strangely applicable, these words!

*

Chapter 1

Introducing the Hidden Gold:
The Natural Law of Rent

*

Introducing the Hidden Gold: the Natural Law of Rent

*

B eyond the well-known Bridge of Sighs – in Venice, I believe – in another realm, another dimension, lies a certain other, less well-known bridge. This one is called 'pons asinorum', or 'the bridge of asses'.

The following interesting account of it, kindly sent me by a friend, is owed to the book "True and False Economics" by the late W.A. Dowe of Australia:-

"In political economy 'the Law of Rent' was commonly called 'pons asinorum' by analogy from Euclid, in which the fifth proposition was called 'the bridge of asses', because if the student didn't master it, he could make no further progress in geometry and fell over the bridge of failure into the river. It is a very good analogy. As George Bernard Shaw said, not to understand 'rent' precludes any progress in economics." *

Further insight into the scope and depth of this beautiful natural law – enabling us verily to skip across that 'bridge of asses'! – is provided unexpectedly by a somewhat smaller creature, a cat. The story follows – but first let us be introduced to this natural law itself, as set out overleaf in useful pictorial

6

form. ** For simply a brief study of this will enable one already to firm-foot it onto that asses' bridge!

---

* The reference to George Bernard Shaw is to his entry in "Everybody's Political What's What?" (1944, p. 22). I quote it here mainly for the interest of its closing sentence. However, to make its meaning fully clear one surely needs to read "and Socialism built *in its place*" – for Socialism has never had any truck with the Law of Rent! – (as indeed GBS himself indicates).
"Finally I must insist that the crux of the land question is the classical theory of Economic Rent, dubbed by Lassalle the Iron Law of Wages. Like the roundness of the Earth, it is unfortunately not obvious. It is the pons asinorum of economic mathematics. Our politicians cannot draw their conclusions from it any more than Shakespeare could draw his from the okapi or the axolotl: they simply do not know of its existence. Karl Marx, by an absurd reference to it in 'Das Kapital', proved that he did not understand it. John Ruskin, after a very promising beginning as an economist by his contrast of exchange values with human values, was stopped dead by it. Yet Marx and Ruskin had more brains and keener interest in social questions that three or four million average voters. It is the rock on which Liberal Cobdenism has been broken and Socialism built in the struggle between plutocracy and democracy."

** While generally known as *Ricardo's Law of Rent*, after the man believed to have first formulated it, to my great interest a foot-note in the unabridged version of "Progress and Poverty" – (the seminal work on this natural law by the

American, Henry George) – states that it was first formulated by Dr James Anderson of Edinburgh, (of whom I recently came across further interesting mention in the brilliantly researched "History of the Working Classes in Scotland", by Tom Johnston, circa 1929 - better known as author of "Our Noble Families"). This would not surprise me since, from evidence I have already set out in "Birthright in Land", it is clear that the Scots have a long history of an unusual grasp of *the land question*!

The pictorial version of this Law of Rent one does not often come across. But ever since first seeing it, (either as published in the movement's "Land and Liberty", or perhaps as given out to us at the Henry George School of Social Science in London, of fond memory, which I attended in the 1950's?), it has seemed to me a treasure – and it naturally appeared in both my earlier books. For it is surely an incomparable aid to understanding the drastic implications for us of the long and ongoing suppression of this great natural law.

[Note: It was only in January 2011 that – on searching an old file for something quite different – I came upon an earlier version of this natural law than that used in my previous two books. This one included two definitions, and four notes on the diagrams which helpfully highlight the robbery of the people which has taken place under society's transgression of this natural law. It also included the word "iron" – clearly inserted upon that prompting from GBS/Lassalle, (see previous footnote).

Why did I omit these helpful additions in 1981 ("The Land Question")? – and so also just twelve years ago ("Birthright in Land . . .", 1999), by which time it seems I had forgotten their existence. Perhaps I hesitated to add anything to the original diagram issued by the movement for this reform?

While I am fairly certain that the four added notes are mine, I cannot be 100% certain of the definitions; except that, if original, why did I not retain these in their original far neater printed form, instead of handwriting them in? *
I have looked up Henry George's "Progress & Poverty" (condensed ed.), but cannot find them there. If anyone can provide another origin for them, I shall be delighted to acknowledge it – but for my part, since it is now well over half-a-century since this powerful diagram came into my hands, I fear that its further details are lost in the mists of time!]

*

---

* For this printing, the two definitions have been set out (in type) ahead of the diagram, for exigencies of space re the diagram itself; and the four notes are on the page following it, (typed, as the handwriting on the diagram may not be so easily read).

Chapter 2

*

The Iron Law of Rent and Wages

Original diagram from Land & Liberty – or from the erstwhile Henry George School of Social Science, both sprung from the movement now called The Henry George Foundation (UK).

*

THE IRON LAW OF RENT

All that is returned to labour beyond what the most marginal land will produce, no matter how great the effort put into the labour, will be taken by rent.

THE IRON LAW OF WAGES

The return to labour, however great the potential of the land that is worked, and however great the individual effort put into the work, will never be greater than the return obtainable from the most marginal land in use.

*

(Note: 'Labour' here includes capital, since true capital – that not entangled, with land rental capture – is the product of labour, and its distinction from labour is in reality but as a subdivision of it. See Chapter on Capital in Henry George's "Progress and Poverty", (condensed edition). SAH)

The Iron Law of Rent becomes

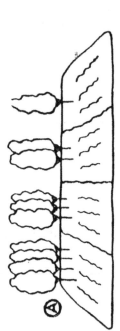

A — Different Grades of Land

Here are four sections of a piece of land, with fruit trees. For simplicity, let us assume you can get one bushel of fruit from each tree. On the best section, where four trees are growing (at left) you can get four bushels in one day. On the next section, with the same day's labor, you can get only three bushels. On the next land two, and on the worst (at right), only one.

B — First Comer — All Wages

So far, all this land is free. When the first man comes to pick fruit, which land will he appropriate? Naturally, the best. The best land is then the margin of production (indicated by the dotted line). With one day's labor he gathers four bushels. They are all his wages - the reward for his exertion.

C — Second Comer — Rent Begins

The next comer has to be content with the three-tree section. (This now becomes the margin of production). With one day's labor he can get only three bushels - they are his wages.

These two men work the same- still one gets four bushels, and the other only three. Why? Because of the difference of the land. The four-bushel land has a rent. Since it is one bushel superior, its rent is one (above the black line). Wages are three on both lands.

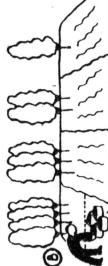

Ⓒ No I can now begin to make a small income for himself without producing anything at all - simply by leasing his land to another to work, in exchange for rent.

D — Third Corner — Further Rise of Rent

The third corner has to use the two-bushel land. (This land now becomes the margin.) The two bushels he gathers are his wages. The three-bushel land now has a rent of one, and the four-bushel land a rent of two. Wages on all lands are two. If this third corner wanted to work on the three-bushel land, its owner would give him only two wages and take one as rent. And if he were to work on the best land, that owner could demand a rent of two, leaving two as wages. That's all the third owner could get working for himself on his two-bushel land. The rent represents what the land-owners can get without working, but solely by virtue of their ownership.

E — Fourth Corner — All Land Used

The fourth corner arrives and the only land left is the worst land, on which he can get only one bushel. Now all the other lands have a rent in proportion to their superiority over this land (which is now the margin of production).

H — Effect of Industrial Growth

Industries grow up, new machines are invented and much more can be produced. The productivity of industrial lands has become seventy, which is greater than the town's productivity of forty. Since more is produced, new materials are needed, and this extends the margin of production to land that yields only one. Wages then become one, and rent is the excess on all superior lands.

Charts to F, G and H omitted

F — Other Natural Differences

The operation of rent applies with any factor that makes one piece of land superior to other lands. There are other besides agricultural differences. A good harbor makes land around it valuable. The land further away is less valuable.

G — Growth of Population

Here is a good piece of agricultural land that yields four. People settle in one section of it, and a town grows up there. Though land within the town is no more fertile than the land outside, a productiveness of a new kind has arisen. Through cooperation and specialization of labor, that section of the land is of much greater productivity. It now yields forty instead of four. If the four land were free, rent within the town would be thirty-six.

Ⓓ No, I can now make as much as No. 3 simply by leasing his land to another to work.

Ⓔ No, I can now make more than any of the others can make on their own labour, simply by leasing his land to another to work.

Arrows show law of the depression of wages

G The Iron Law of Wages

Notes from the diagram
of the LAW of RENT

*

(C)   No. 1 can now begin to make a small income for himself without producing anything at all – simply by leasing his land to another to work, in exchange for rent.

(D)   No. 1 can now make *as much as* No. 3, simply by leasing his land to another to work.

(E)   No. 1 can now make *more than any of the others can make by their own labour,* simply by leasing his land to another to work.

Small note to right of (E).   Arrows show law of the depression of wages.

*

The rain it raineth equally
Upon the just and unjust fella –
But more upon the just because
The unjust hath the just's umbrella.
(Source unknown)

Chapter 3

*

Revealing the Cat!

The **'cat'**

- that

got

the

'cream'!

On 'seeing the cat' – the *fat* cat – THE *fat cat* ... hiding in the natural Law of Rent!

*

For an explanation as to how the saying 'to see the cat' first arose amongst the ranks of those working for economic justice, I am indebted to an article by one, John Dun of Australia – from a publication of name and date unknown. From it I pluck, with grateful acknowledgement, the following introduction to this very particular cat:-

"For the benefit of those who are not aware of the reason why understanding Henry George's teaching is referred to as 'seeing the cat,' we [present here] the story of the concealed picture as told by James G. Maguire, at that time a judge of the Superior Court of San Francisco and afterward a Member of Congress from California, in a speech at the Academy of Music, New York City, in 1887. In substance he said:-

'I was one day walking along Kearney Street, San Francisco, when I noticed a crowd around the show window of a store, looking at something inside. I took a glance myself, and saw only a very poor picture of a very uninteresting landscape. But as I was turning away my eye caught the words underneath the picture, "Do you see the cat?" I looked again and more closely, but saw no cat in the picture. Then I spoke to the crowd:

' "Gentlemen," I said, "I can see no cat in that picture. Is there a cat there?

'Someone in the crowd replied:

' "Naw, there ain't no cat there. Here's a crank who says he sees the cat, but nobody else can see it."

'Then the crank spoke up:

' "I tell you there is a cat there too. It's all cat. What you fellows take for a landscape is just nothing more than the outlines of a cat. And you needn't call a man a crank either, because he can see more with his eyes than you can."

' "Well,!" the Judge continued, 'I looked very closely at the picture and then I said to the man they called a crank:

' "Really, sir, I cannot make out a cat. I can see nothing but a poor picture of a landscape."

' "Why, Judge," he exclaimed, "just look at that bird in the air. That's the cat's ear."

'I looked, but was obliged to say:

' "I am sorry to be so stupid, but I can't make a cat's ear of that bird. It is a poor bird, but not a cat's ear.

' "Well then," the crank urged, "look at that twig twirled around in a circle. That's the cat's eye."

'But I couldn't make an eye of it.

' "Oh, then," said the crank a little impatiently, "look at those sprouts at the foot of the tree, and the grass. They make the cat's claws."

'After a rather deliberate examination, I reported that they did look a little like a claw, but I couldn't connect them with a cat.

'Once more the crank came back at me. "Don't you see that limb off there? And that other limb under it? And that white space between? Well, that white space is the cat's tail."

'I looked again and was just on the point of replying that there was no cat there so far as I could see, when suddenly the whole cat burst upon me. There it was sure enough, just as the crank had said, and the only reason that the rest of us couldn't see it was that we hadn't got the right point of view. But now that I saw it, I could see nothing else in the picture. The landscape had disappeared and a cat had taken its place. And do you know, I was never afterward able, upon looking at that picture, to see anything in it but the cat.'"

[Reprinted from *Land Values*, June, 1915, 11 Tothill Street, London, S.W.]

How tantalising it is that someone – with whatever primitive photography of the time – did not manage to capture for us this most intriguing picture!

But yet – what need of it do we really have, when the matter is so plain? For this cat – which has seen fit to fatten itself by swallowing up a whole landscape – just what must be the effect of the exploits of so all-devouring a creature upon any population involved?

Oh I'm a saucy-savvy cat – for see
What saucerfuls of cream I've got!
Yes – I cream off the wealth
Of the people by stealth,
And the poor beggars wot it not!

The Cheshire Cat has nothing on me,
For my grin is invisible too!
Oh we're a merry band,
We who both hog the land –
And 'hog' it! – where the many serve the few

Oh the Cheshire Cat has nothing on us, on us,
This game of Monopoly is fun, fun, fun!
See – nobody objects,
Indeed they pay us their respects! –
While their *other* tribute's never, ever done, done, done –
Oh their RENTS are never, ever done!

*

*

Rent

You may tinker with the tariff and make some simple gains,
You may put on tolls or take 'em off, inducing party pains;
You may monkey with the money, but the lack of it remains,
For the Mother of monopoly is laughing as she reigns.

Rent! Rent! Who is it pays the rent?
A dozen days in every month the worker's back is bent;
Figure it in dollar bills or work it by percent,
But with his dozen days he pays just rent, rent, rent.

You may "minimum" the wages, you may let the women vote,
You may regulate the railroads with a legal antidote,
You may jail some Rockefeller, or may get a Morgan's goat,
But the Mother of Monopoly is laughing in her throat.

Rent! Rent! Who is it pays the rent?
A hundred days in every year a business profit's spent;
Figure it in "overhead", or state it by percent,
But all your hundred days are gone for rent, rent, rent.

You may institute Foundations, you may educate the dubs,
You may libralize the Bread Line, and establish Slummy Clubs;
You may ostracize the Demon Rum and eugenize the cubs,
But the Mother of Monopoly is smiling at your snubs.

Rent! rent! who is it pays the rent?
A score of years in life you spend to get one document;
From your cradle to your coffin you must bow to its assent,
And that's your little, old receipt for rent, rent, rent.

I look across the rented world and idle land I see,
Whose owner doesn't work it, for he's working you and me,
And on the first of every month all tenants bow the knee,
And pay the rent of vacant land, in great or small degree.

The worker's hands are busy and the business back is bent;
The idle lands advance in price and every single cent,
Of that advance is paid by us in rent, rent, rent.

by Edmund Vance Cooke
from The People's Advocate, *Adelaide, Australia, 1937*

*

"To see what is in front of one's nose requires a constant struggle." *George Orwell*

Ah, but the one in front of our nose here? – the cat in the RENTAL-scape?

CA – UGH! – T . . . !

*

And so it is with us, just as the Judge found – once he had seen the **cat** in the picture – that, whenever he looked at the picture again, he could never see anything in it but the **cat**.

Just so, as we look around today at our disoriented and crumbling society – here too, all becomes clear, as it finally dawns on us that it is the **cat**, equally, that fills the landscape!

Note: Where the landscape taken over by the **cat** is devoid of population, and there is no one paying any actual rent, but the landscape is desirable for one reason or another – (and how much of Scotland's land, indeed of land across the globe, is there owned in this way?) – the **cat** will be found lapping up the rental values *just the same*, in the masked, converted form into which these stolen goods are readily transformed. See on!

*

Chapter 4

*

Stolen Land – Stolen Lives

Stolen Land – Stolen Lives

*

S ince the pictorial Law of Rent makes so plain the robbery
at the root of our society – that is, the activity of its **cream-
besotted maurauder**, why is it not more generally recognised?

Firstly, it belongs to an economic structure that is now
centuries old, and hence so deeply embedded in society that we
are all born into a blind acceptance of it. (For this reason, let it be
repeated here: *responsibility for it today cannot be imputed to any
individual.*) Secondly, there is the matter of our education – or
rather, *mis*-education: that is, an equally centuries-long cover-up
of what is really at stake. (Indeed, what is *finally* at stake in the
great matter of today's *land title-deeds*, even the pictorial Law of
Rent does not quite disclose. But see on.)

What is the vague 'mystique' that has always surrounded the
ownership of land? – something I first became aware of at school
in Scotland, in my teenage years, having a classmate whose
family owned a castle – *with land!* – and who carried an
indefinable air of superiority about her because of that!

There is a peculiarly hidden-up factor involved in these land-
deeds – and one of which I am sure my classmate had no more
understanding that I did at that time! Pondering this today,
however, brings to mind the title of the musical "A Funny Thing
Happened on the Way to the Forum" – for a funny thing
certainly happened *on the way to the land market*!

This market required naturally a capital value for land, if land was to be bought and sold – transactions which, besides allowing the profitable hoarding and hence monopolising of land – would usefully establish land as something 'legitimately purchased', and so, like any other bit of capital goods, *owned*. (. . . Do I hear mutterings from Gaia here?) But how to acquire a capital value for land, when it has none? Costless bestowed on us, by a benevolent Creator – how to reckon a value for what is, in fact and forever, beyond value and beyond price?

The trick is revealed by certain legislation, which was passed in the 1980s, when crofters were to be allowed to buy out their crofts, whose chief value lay in the land. To invent a 'capital' sum, the government referred back to the *only* value which land does carry, that is, its *annual rental value* – and then multiplied this by X number of times to arrive at what would pass for a reasonable 'capital' sum. (Note the word "carry" above, for the value attaching to land is not inherent in land – it is *acquired* – acquired from the presence and activities of the community; the variation in the rents reflecting the comparative advantage or disadvantage, for occupation, of one site over another.)

It is no small matter that is here unearthed. In fact – it is the very heart of the land question. For how many people realise that what is being bought and sold on today's 'land market' is in fact our *stolen community-created rentals* – (yes, those same rents that were creamed off us by the **cat**!) – these rents being then bundled up for as many years ahead as it is found the market will bear. It is by this piece of bold and generally unrecognized trickery that our 'respected' (*totally corrupt*) 'land market' has come into existence.

Thus the 'mystique' surrounding these titles to land turns out to be, in the cold light of day, simply the *mystery* – stemming from widespread ignorance – as to the real origins of that bogus 'price' which attaches to land, when it changes hands in today's 'land market'; this so-called *capital price* being the final 'disclosure', or unmasking we were looking for, of those stolen – now cooked-up and re-presented – *rentals*!

For we now see why the cat finds still plentiful cream to lap, even should the landscape it roams be uninhabited. (See note at end of ch.3) For this new bogus 'capital price' of land, so cleverly conjured out of the stolen rentals, opens the door to the owner of this phoney 'capital' to the acquiring, from the bank, of a valuable *collateral* sum, upon deposition of the so-called 'title-deeds' as an equivalent of capital. Now, by the clever investing of this collateral sum in a further land deal, sufficient profit may be made, by means of it, also to redeem the deposited title-deeds. Thus whatever way the 'land price' card is played, (for rental takings or collateral), the holder of it holds a winning hand.

But the real 'price' in all this, of course, is the price paid by the community in having been tricked into surrendering their precious rental fund – created from the fruits of their labours and intended by a beautiful natural law for their own succouring; a fund able, as we shall see, to remove all social pain and distress from their lives, and in addition to provide a basic income for all. Tricked into surrendering it *for what*? To support a layer of so-called 'land ownership' which is not only unnatural and superfluous to society, but is wholly destructive to it.

Nor is this the end of the matter, since this layer becomes the begetter in turn of a further economic imposter and social outrage. For the wealth of *a whole community*, thus conjured into the hands of the few, becomes there *inordinate* wealth; and so we see the process by which, out of land monopoly, is begotten its equally ugly offspring – *monopoly capitalism*. Thus we live not in a capitalist society, but in a *monopoly* capitalist society.* When one considers further how this unnatural *monopoly capitalism* permeates and dominates today's stock-markets – with their huge trade in decidedly 'unholy' goods; and how it then proceeds to buy its way into the *political* process to determine the legislation of the land . . . one begins to see how the general ignorance and neglect, right at the start, of this matter of *the people's rents* – is a very big matter indeed.

It easily resolves various other 'mysteries' in our society also – such as the ever-widening divide between the rich and the poor, or the reason for the multitudes of 'deprived' and 'underprivileged' in our society . . . betaking themselves to drink and drugs. They are not 'underprivileged' or 'deprived', nor are they suffering from any 'poverty genes' (the latest disgraceful excuse). They are, quite simply, *robbed*!

---

* As AJ Nock points out in "Our Enemy the State", the term 'capitalist society' today is meaningless, since it applies equally to any society which exists beyond the hunter-gatherer stage. Thus the Soviet Union was a capitalist society, only there all capital was in the hand of the State – another form of monopoly capitalism.

Plain before us we now see not only the trick by which the LAND is taken from us, but how – from the vital matter of these *rents* that go with it –

**STOLEN LAND METAMORPHOSES
INTO STOLEN LIVES!**

Chapter 5

*

Hidden Gold:

Our Abundant Natural Social Fund

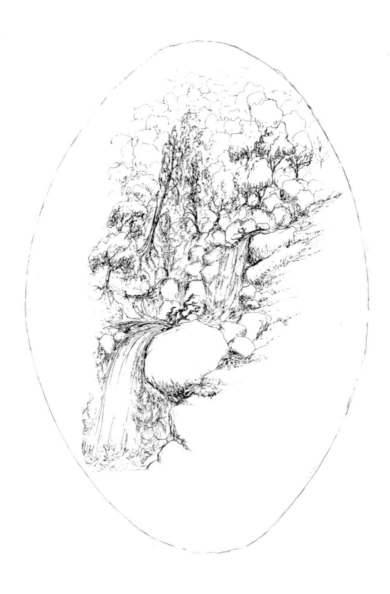

Hidden Gold:
Our Abundant Natural Social Fund

*

L et us pause at this point to examine more thoroughly the social fund we have lost in the stealing of our land's rental values. For in doing so we shall discover some remarkable and quite unsuspected features of it. Its loss to us is far more than just a monetary one. Going well beyond this, we find it to be an instrument truly fashioned for a community's cohesion and well-being.

The Law of Rent, made so clear in its pictorial presentation, is something we should all be growing up familiar with from earliest childhood, as part of our elementary *social literacy*. But as it has never been part of our school or college syllabuses – and as it is rarely come across in the great wide world outside of these – we cannot wait for slow changes there. Let us therefore make a start here in educating ourselves in that elementary 'social literacy' we so much need, and so begin to reckon what the loss to us of this, our true social fund, means for us every day of our lives.

Here, then, are certain remarkable features of our natural social fund, all of which, as the reader will see, are detectable, or deducible, from the pictorial Law of Rent. What knowledge I possess in this is of course owed to the great work of Henry

George, but I am much indebted also to Richard Giles of Australia, for his many helpful writings on 7) below.

1) The Rental Fund grows naturally with the growth of society.

2) The wealth that accrues to the Rental Fund from the presence and activities of the community, is greater than that which accrues to the labours of the individual members of it.

3) The earnings of Labour[*] under this Law, tending towards equality, there would follow a natural closing of today's 'mysterious' and 'unresolvable' gap between the rich and the poor.

4) As society grows, the socially derived wealth of the Rental Fund increases not only with society's growth, but also *in proportion to* the wealth earned by the individual members of society, thereby making the Rental Fund not only sufficient, but also ample, for all our social needs.

5) Following from 4) is the very evident sufficiency of the Rental Fund to supply, in addition to our social needs, a basic income for every member of the community.

---

[*] As pointed out in an earlier note, 'labour' here includes capital, since true capital – that not entangled with land rental capture – is the product of labour, and its distinction from labour is in reality but as a subdivision of it. See chapter on Capital in Henry George's "Progress and Poverty".

6) The honouring of the Rental Fund as society's true revenue would allow us to do away with its false substitute, Taxation – which robs Labour of its earnings, by allowing wealth from the Rental Fund to accumulate, instead, as unearthed wealth, in the pockets of its false appropriators.

7) The amplitude of the Rental Fund for our social needs is further highlighted by the fact that *all Taxation is paid out of Rent* – notwithstanding that, under Taxation, Rent also supports, as we have seen, a class of so-called 'land owners', by accumulating in the pockets of these errant appropriators of it, who also manage to evade much of Taxation; thus – a further injustice – throwing the main burden of supplying that false revenue on those least able to bear it.

8) Last but not least are the minimal costs that will be incurred in the administration – simplicity itself – of this <u>natural</u> systems of revenue. For land, highly visible, cannot move or run away, while no probing is required of the individual's personal circumstances. Compare this with the armies of employees required to operate a system of taxation – who themselves must devour a considerable proportion of the revenue raised. *

---

* **F**rom the torn off sleeve of the jacket cover of a book written some decades ago, "The Tax Gatherers", by James Coffield – (price given as "15s net") – I quote, with acknowledgements to its publishers: "James Coffield's startling exposé of our income tax system with all its anomalies, obscurities, inconsistencies and,

The final point – that all Taxation comes out of Rent – is the only one that at first there may be some difficulty in grasping. But it is an important point since (i) it refutes any argument that the Rental Fund would not of itself suffice for our social needs; and (ii) it renders superfluous any attempted complex computations as to what the Rental Fund would amount to.

Firstly – a quick scrutiny of the pictorial Law of Rent confronts us with the question: where else could taxes possibly be taken from? – a question finding a more amplified answer in the chapter in Henry George's "Protection or Free Trade" – "The Robber that Takes all that is Left"; land monopoly being the "robber" who takes from Labour all but its essential minimal living; while this "robber" is transformed, of course, into our great succourer and keeper of our precious Social Fund, by the society which lives in accordance with the natural Law of Rent.

As Richard Giles has helpfully put it: "Rent is natural, taxes are unnatural", and "before there were taxes, there was rent" – always there ready, i.e., to take up that "excess of production" which is windfall gain to the labourer. (See pictorial Law of Rent.)

This grasp of the connection between Taxation and Rent has been expressed in various ways by others, in the past, by whom the Law of Rent was well understood. It was this that the U.S.

---

above all, injustices, will be a revelation to even the most cynical taxpayer ... His argument is backed up throughout by concrete examples ... of actual cases that illustrate better than any amount of theorizing the evils of our present system of taxation ..." It is hardly surprising to hear rumour today, some decades on, that the system is in some danger of complete collapse.

Founding Father, Benjamin Franklin (1706-90) was speaking of, when he wrote (emphasis added): "Our legislators are all landholders, and they are not yet persuaded that *all taxes are finally paid by the land* . . . therefore we have been forced into the mode of indirect taxes". As Richard Giles comments: "the landholders believed they could escape with their rental takings intact, if they legislated to place taxes on production instead. But Franklin saw that they were mistaken in this".

Turgot, the highly respected and best known member of the Physiocratic school which flourished in France just prior to its revolution, was another who saw this clearly. As he wrote: "There is no revenue in a State" – (*note*: *in* a State, not *of* a State) – "which can truly be dispensed with, except the revenue from land." As Richard Giles expresses this, (*Good Government*, Oct 2005) – the rental value of the land was the only revenue that could be taken by the State without disturbing production. "Other taxes (on production) made their way into prices where they reduced the incomes 'sufficient' to keep labourers and entrepreneurs working".

Taxes on production can "make their way into prices", because all the goods of the kind being taxed can be up-priced together, so that the up-pricing is easily passed on to the consumer. But rent is of another kind altogether, being the payment of a *differential* – a differential in site values. Hence it does not fall on all sites equally, and therefore cannot be passed on. Nor can a higher rent be asked of Labour, the rent already set being the highest that can be extracted.

Thus, as Richard Giles sums up Turgot, increased taxes on production inevitably "generated a movement to increase wages and profits sufficient to restore 'equilibrium' in the economy. The only place these increases could come from was Rent. All taxation was, finally, a tax on Rent!"

More recently I have come across interesting mention, in the writings of Francis Neilson, of certain large landowners in our own Parliament who, in an earlier century, saw as plainly as did Benjamin Franklin that all taxes are paid in the end out of *rent*.

*

Andrew Carnegie, the Scottish businessman from Fife who made his fortune in America, once said:-

"The most comfortable, but also the most unproductive, way for a capitalist to increase his fortune, is to put all his monies in sites and await that point in time when a society, hungering for land, has to pay his price."

A society that looks on while the fruits of its labouring force are hijacked by the workings of a corrupt economic system, may be pitied for its ignorance.

But what is to be said of a society which, while knowing of a better way, continues to permit such hijacking – but that it fully deserves that doom which will inevitably be its lot.

*

Chapter 6

*

The Great Con Trick

of DEBT!

The Great Con Trick
of Debt

*

Conjured-up 'land price', we now see plainly, is the great *con trick* by which debt arises. Indeed, as Bill Pitt of Australia once put it succinctly: *debt* is the other face of *land price*. Quite simply – so! This readily explains the phenomenon of *slumps*. For when Rent which holds the whip-hand – gorging on the bogus booster ingredient of monopolistic 'land price' (and forgetful of the tale of the peasant wife who over-asked of the magical Fish, and lost all) – refuses to 'give' towards the restoring of the necessary 'equilibrium', (see previous chapter), and Labour can no longer make a living at the rent demanded, then of a certainty comes *slump* – the less comfortable part of the boom-and-slump ride guaranteed to any society which harbours land monopoly.

How much more must it be, then – how much steeper the ride – when this unwillingness to 'give' belongs to a scenario of out-and-out gambler rentiers who, while dicing with the already phoney 'capital' values conjured out of stolen land rentals are heavily dealing, besides, in extra risky (or sub-prime) mortgages – so to trade on packages of these hopelessly phoney combinations into ever more reckless hands? *Slump* then follows with a peculiar vengeance and ferocity: the rotten inevitable fruit of out-and-out reckless dealing in *fabricated debts*.

Today's trading in mortgages may have brought the banking world to collapse. But for those of us wised up to the antics of the **cat** in the picture – (who now parades the gobbled-up people's rents in their new guise of a trumped-up dazzling 'price' for land) – it is not hard to see that the whole banking mortgage business today is simply a fiasco: a trick played out upon entries *in wrong columns by the wrong institutions* – and got away with so far only because the *trick has not yet been seen!*

For that trumped-up component, in a mortgage, of 'land price', set down by a bank as a debit against its customer, should rightly – (translated back into its original reality of *community-created rental value)* – be appearing, instead, in the *credit columns of the local community treasurer's books!* – and this credit made up not of phoney 'capital price' payments for land, that place members of the community in debt, but simply – of the annual rentals owed for land occupancy; amounts now forming a *growing sum of community capital!**

Further, these annual rental payments are likely to be of sums without difficulty *paid up*, leaving no debtors, (while under the natural Law of Rent there is always available of course marginal land, for which no rent is asked since it yields none). For these

---

* Re local communities assuming natural power over their own revenues – (federating upwards for more helpfully joint enterprises): see articles 'The Unsuspected Lynchpin' and 'Scotland and Bioregionalism' in Part III of this book, and 'Community and Re-empowerment' in 'Birthright in Land', Part II, ch.1.

annual rental payments would themselves be hugely deflated by the removal of that land monopoly within whose orbit – of artificial pricing – they had previously existed. On this point – the marked reduction in land rents that would follow land monopoly's removal – we are fortunate in having, in fact, a unique and fascinating piece of direct historical evidence. It is owed to the work of D.C. MacDonald, published in 1891* - who snatched for us, from the passing panorama of history, the following report, placed in his work as a footnote to the powerful "Resolutions of the Skye Crofters" of 1885:-

"... owing to the sickly condition of the children of Liberty in Lowland Caledonia, Scotland is still held under Landlord Thraldom, excepting that the *Crofter's Act*, 1886, has produced an effect something like the taking of the *Bastille*. Rents in the Lowlands came tumbling down without any Land Court."

The rents came tumbling! What a beacon of light flashed briefly upon the dark scene of today's debt! – from that brief significant moment in our history when the landed power believed itself to be under threat! (Perhaps this might usefully alert us to just how much that landed power sees is at stake – when the horizon reveals the determination of a people to take back their full land rights!)

---

* "Birthright in Land, by Wm. Ogilvie, with Biographical Notes by D.C. MacDonald." (Kegan Paul, etc., 1891) O.o.p. For simpler reference, see my own "Birthright in Land – and the State of Scotland Today", (Peregrine Press, 1999), p. 167.

Yet even this is not all – even this does not reveal to the full the workings of land monopoly in laying wicked *debt* upon today's dispossessed. For also to be considered are its effects upon what are called the *improvements*, that is – any construction built by human labour upon land.

I have read assessments that the land component today of a *property* (the term used for land and buildings combined) is probably about 40-50% of the price of the whole in the market – which, taking the average price of a house (from a December 2010 report) to be £160,000-odd, would appear to leave a very hefty sum for the bricks-and-mortar part – thus placing firmly still in hostage to the banks anyone wishing to provide themselves with that basic human need of a place of one's own.

Such a computation by no means, however, gives the full picture of land monopoly's involvement in the scene. For as the bricks-and-mortar component of the property cannot, except upon land, come into being,* so every improvement to land, following from human labour, is contaminated by the existing land monopoly.

Furthermore: must not the cost of the bricks-and-mortar used include the (ever relentlessly increasing under land monopoly) cost of the *monopoly price setting* of the rent, for the right of access to the land required for the raw materials? – just as, must it not also take into

---

* As already stated, the term 'land' in economics embraces the whole of the natural universe, thus including such scenarios as the placing of a houseboat on a canal – for someone will own the water rights.

account the (equally relentlessly increasing under land monopoly) cost of the housing needs involved, of the workforce that must prepare the bricks and mortar? And what about the monopoly element as it further affects such things as the food and clothing required by the work-force? – and the transport that must bring them to their work? Thus on, and on ... Access to land underlies every single human activity, every human need, so that its monopoly while not readily seen, holds all in its trap.

Thus when any human scenario is considered in its entirety today, it becomes quite impossible to isolate the cost of the land component, in its full compass, in the purchase price of a house, or of practically any item that is marketed. Suffice it to say that the land monopoly element, which permeates every aspect of our lives, when pondered more deeply, begins gradually to reveal itself to us – (just as it did to the Judge in the story) – as the face and form of a certain lurking **be-whiskered creature**, who has eagerly gobbled the landscape up. That is, in economic terms: who has been driving up the cost of living (for all but itself), so to trample ever more of the population into a scenario of ever increasing impoverishment – in a process which has been going on for a very long span of time.

I well remember the words of Vic Blundell – (director and inspiring head teacher at the Henry George School of Social Science, near Victoria in London, which I so fortunately discovered in the 1950s) – who told us once that, after World War I, a working man could purchase a modest home for the equivalent of a year's wages. The sum he mentioned was, as I recollect, £300. But it is not that low figure which should strike us, but its rough equivalence to a working man's yearly wage.* For government's periodical resorts to inflation (whose original and strict meaning is simply the government's increase, via the printing-press, of the money in circulation, today called 'quantitative easing') – by automatically decreasing the value of each unit of money, works naturally to raise the price of things from time to time.

Quite a different matter is the ever increasing disparity, over long spans of time, between the yearly wage of a working man and the cost to him of acquiring a home. Here we recognise an unmistakable part of the repertoire of our indefatigable **cat**, being one of the many unseen effects of land monopoly upon a society ignorant of the working of the Law of Rent. For since there is no economic power superior to that of land-holding, no brake can be exercised upon it (beyond the temporary and intermittent cycle of boom-and-slump). Hence the greater the wealth that is produced by society under the dominance of such a monopoly, the greater the *proportion* of the wealth created, (*which is society's portion* – see Law of Rent), which must fall into those waiting claws. And this – *regardless of whatever increase in wages may be won* – (see arrowed line on Law of Rent diagram).

---

* It seems just as amazing that my weekly pay, in the late 1940s as a secretary in my first job, in London – of £4.19.6d, was considered a fully honourable sum. While tough, one managed – but I remember to this day the blow it was when my landlady increased the weekly rent by 2/6d to pay for the electricity – saying that I "read all through the night"!

Such is the dance between Rent and Wages – ever onwards and upwards. To the wage-earner – it makes no odds. Wages, ever outwitted by Rent, cannot win. Let the £300 yearly wage of nigh a century ago be increased even to £30,000 today – its actual purchasing power does not compare. Hence, perversely; for the great mass of actual producers of society's actual wealth, the human dream of owning a place of one's own must ever recede – a fact the more galling in that it is clearly a dream *already* paid for, in bogus (i.e. 'land-price'-based) *rents, many times over*.

How long are we going to allow this farcical situation to continue?

Only when we grasp the full compass of the **be-whiskered one's** reach into today's mangled economy, only when we have understood to the full its *predations upon the people's wealth* – shall we finally recognise, behind the facade of the bankers, the carefully screened identity of the *real* **fat cat** in our midst – *and continual destroyer*.

> The vital underpinning of the bankers' power is a society dependent upon *borrowing*; and a land-monopoly-based society is robbed so ruinously that it *must* borrow, being *bonded to debt*.
>
> That is to say, the underpinning of the bankers' power is, in the very first place, a *society bonded to trumped-up 'land price'*.
>
> *Of course*, the bankers operate a rotten system – creating loans out of nought, upon the legalised trick of 'fractional reserve banking'. But this is precisely why the politicians never more than pussyfoot (apt word!) around them: because the political layer of society *depends upon* that debt-based economy (kept going by loans), since its own vital

48

underpinning is a *society composed of indebted serfs* IN WHICH FREEMEN HAVE NO PLACE. (... The political layer does not recognise that the final stretch of this road – having sucked the serfs dry – is its own bankruptcy, and demise.)

Reform the banks as you will – we will still live trapped in a society of masters and serfs. By contrast: bringing the Law of Rent to bear on the *real* **'fat cat'** in our midst, THE LANDED INTEREST, will rid us of both *debt* and *masters* at one blow.

What are we waiting for?

*

Let us look deeper into this situation of masters and serfs, endemic in a society ruled by land monopoly. Those born into such a society with no birthright in land, are in debt before life's journey starts. For how can you work, in order to produce, in order to pay rent for land (or pay for anything at all) – if you have no land to begin with? Such are born to a birthright in *debt*, and it is only the few who will ever manage to break free from this debt-ridden situation, no matter how hard they work – if indeed they are lucky enough to find work at all.

For the opportunity to work is increasingly refused under such a system of land tenure, which – (the monopoly of land proceeding apace as it must) – brings the locking-up of ever great acreages under so-called 'title-deeds'. As Tom Paine famously said, "I never heard that the Creator opened an estate-office to issue title-deeds to land" – and that such deeds are nought but a trumped-up human legislative device, even a child in the kindergarten would be capable of seeing – and would doubtless enjoy Henry George's expostulation upon!

> "What more preposterous than that one tenant for a day of this rolling sphere should collect rent for it from his co-tenants, or sell to them for a price what was here ages before him and will be here ages after him."

(Do we say that the opportunity to work asks for some capital also? Well, we know where our well-earned *community capital sum* has disappeared to – and where to look for it!)

In viewing this glaringly obvious root cause of mass 'unemployment', (about which much plaint is made – but uselessly, for it is as much an artificial and trumped-up phenomenon as is today's monstrous 'debt') – as I say, in this scenario of the glaringly obvious, where on earth are the Trades Unions? – those 'trusty' bodies and 'friend of the working man'! What can possibly be said of these venerated institutions, who collect fees from their members in the face of the obvious, but that they are ignorant, witless, or fast asleep? – or possibly indeed all three! ... while of course being heavily dependent upon *the public's* remaining so!

Meanwhile we bow down and worship these invented title-deeds – for are not their holders elevated in our midst? Little do we realise – and ironically for a supposedly 'Christian' nation – that in doing so we are worshipping at the altar of one of the greatest of heathen gods! "Baal – god of the landlords", as the late Rev. Archer Torrey, in his "Biblical Economics", trumpets this situation of wonderful farce! – (while he gives a fascinating account also of the fuller reach of Jesus' mission – Jesus, who "drew after him too great a following of the landless poor". See Part II, ch.2 "Dispossession through the Centuries".)

But nor is this yet the full reach of the persecution of today's disinherited. For the pitiful dearth of the opportunity to work – something which the artificially unemployed must now *compete* for – carries naturally its own prime in-built mechanism for *beating wages down*. (How amazing that, after all this time, neither the Trades Unions nor the workers have apparently ever suspected the presence of a certain **cat** lurking in their landscape!) Add to this the further burden of taxation – (the artificial revenue needed to replace the natural one, now diverted to the pockets of its usurpers); while further to "grind the faces of the poor" are the exorbitant interest charges upon borrowings – borrowings they have no option but to resort to, to support their now ruined lives. There is a saying in Proverbs ch. 10, "the destruction of the poor is their poverty" – but we merely shake our heads over this statement, quite overlooking its *wit*! (Similarly with Jesus' solemn poke-in-the-ribs reminder, "the poor ye have always with you" – Jesus who knew well that poverty was the outcome of *errant human law*! See again Part II, ch.2.)

How outrageous it is that within this unspeakably corrupt system we have contingents of good people hard at work 'rescuing' legions of the unfortunate – those driven to the despairs of drink, drugs, violence and crime, and most terrible of all – the suicides, ultimate stamp of a ruined society. Meanwhile the glaringly corrupt framework of the whole passes unquestioned!

Such is the success of the landed interest in covering its tracks, such the ability of the **cat** to blind us to the clues as to its part in this dreadful scene – while let us be aware of, and ponder well, the essential background to it all: that is, the deliberate dumbing-down of generation after generation of school-children, by a State-sponsored system of education held fast in the clutches of *the landed interest.* (As what department of State activity indeed is not?)

Meanwhile the crowning achievement in all this is naturally – to get the people to believe that they themselves are to blame; that *they* are the ones responsible for their debt-ridden state, from not having worked hard enough, or for having mismanaged their lives. Further – that *they* are the ones responsible if they are out of work; and of course – (the final trick) – since they have made such a mess of things as to get into debt, and must now live a life of borrowing, that it is up to *them*, via their tax-monies, to bail out the banks upon which those borrowings depend!

Could brazenness go further? – or cruelty indeed? Meanwhile the people detect trickery, but are unable to raise coherent complaint – because they have not yet 'seen the **cat**' that has run off with their rents and their land. (I could not help a chuckle, naturally, when reading in the press one day last year of the exploits of a certain *Mr Madoff*, in our great global 'debt' crisis!)

Finally - to add to injury the ultimate insult: should things reach the stage where *dole* must be forthcoming, its recipients, in speaking of it, must use the term 'benefit'. *This* - for the mean and grudging hand-out from a State that has carefully first *dis*-benefitted the people of both their rental funds and their land! Yet who is speaking out today at the outrageousness of this term?

As for the stated aim of *rooting the fraudsters out of the social system,* why not begin with the *real* fraudsters and the only logical starting-point? For, in upholding the legislation and the structure of a society that has defrauded the people of both their land and its rents, the 'powers-that-be' that govern us are themselves operating and running the *biggest fraudsters' scheme that could be!*

Small wonder, then, if that 'power of governance' is itself wallowing in debt. For a power nexus which presumes to run a country on robbery – (filching from the people, via taxes ad lib., ever greater proportions of the fruits of their labours, while letting the real social revenue bleed into the pockets of its partners-in-robbery, the landed interest) – creates social havoc on a scale so vast as is beyond mending, no matter how much cash were thrown at it; and is on the royal road to bankruptcy from the start. Its stated aim of one day 'balancing the books' is a joke.

How is it we are so blind as to what is really going on? How is it we have not been able to delve below the surface of things and understand the *pantomime* that is taking place? It is as though we have lost some vital deeper dimension of understanding, and remain blinded to our situation because of this. Perhaps a clue is offered us by that third Horseman of the Apocalypse? – the one who rode forth on a black steed carrying a pair of scales in his hand. (Rev. Ch.6) For are not these scales the symbol of a people who view everything primarily in terms of merchandise? And have we not been happy to toss into these merchant-scales even the sacred Earth? This Earth which – a phenomenon beyond any power of man's creating – we should surely have cherished with our whole being, as the unfathomable gift of an unfathomable Creator, forever beyond value and beyond price.*

But where is it possible to start, in this day and age, when any concept of such a Creator has been lost sight of by so many?. . . (the same mysterious source of that marvellous 'music of the spheres' which resounds through our very frames. See elsewhere in this book.) Fortunately there is still one concept, one idea, to which all can relate: Gaia, our Earthly Mother – from whom we are made, bone of her bone and flesh of her flesh. And was it not of her, and our abuse of her, that the North American Indian Chief Seattle spoke, in his profound statement on the environment, which in recent times has been quoted round the globe? "(Man) treats his mother, the earth, and his brother, the sky, as things to be bought, plundered, sold like sheep or bright beads . . . How can you sell the sky, the warmth of the land? The idea is strange to us." But that "strange" idea is not strange to us at all. On the contrary – we have set the *merchandising of Gaia* at the very foundation of our economic structure.

It is as if the same wicked 'magician' who, with a wave of his magic wand, has carried off our land along with its rents, had, by

---

* I believe the third Horseman – with the reference to measures of grain – is generally taken to represent famine. Perhaps that is the significance of the warning from the "voice in the midst" that accompanies his appearing: "See thou hurt not the oil and the wine". Certainly, if we fail to honour in our lives the 'oil of thanksgiving' for that mysterious Creator's gifts to us, and the 'wine of inspiration' as to how to conduct ourselves rightly in that great Giver's sight – then famine is very likely what we shall reap!

the same stroke, carried off some essential and fundamental power of our understanding. We simply do not *see* the depth of the degradation in which we are sunk.

The awakening of these deeper spiritual energies – which alone can reclaim for us our land – is a task which awaits our undertaking. But for the present and right *now*, as we have at least our intellectual faculty – (which has disclosed to us a certain savvy **cat**) – let us at any rate see we make full use of *it* in addressing today's corrupt scenario!

"CUTS – CUTS – CUTS!" – they bully us. But who needs *cuts*? We have an unfailing, abundant and overflowing, natural social RENTAL FUND!

The devastating DEBT that it is solemnly declared we must confront? Simply – a huge invention of the LANDED INTEREST! – and we don't need *it*, either!

As for those BANKS, with their merry-go-rounds of gamblings with stolen goods: since we no longer need their loans, let them be left to *pay their own debts*, so reaping exactly what they have sown! No bonuses in *that* scenario!

And that pyramid of POLITICIANS hard at work promoting all these inventions of folly? Now that we have the natural Law of Rent to govern us – what place is there for any *politicians* in our lives at all?

And so – as a fitting and celebratory way of disposing of them – let us invite them all onto the 'pons asinorum'! We shall soon find out how many manage to keep their footing on it – and how many tumble over the edge!

*

Chapter 7

*

Conclusion

Conclusion

*

To conclude Part I, I would like to share a remarkable and prophetic letter, written to me in May 2005 by the late Dr George J. Miller, an eminent physician who also fully understood the land question. For it not only affords us special insights into our situation today, but plays its own part in pointing us to the pathway out of it we must take.

Eager to share the contents of this remarkable letter with others, I wrote to Dr Miller early on requesting permission to do so – which was at once granted; and I am doubly glad of that now, seeing that in the interval he has passed away.

The prophetic part of the letter is in its second paragraph – but I give it in full since the first paragraph provides the context and sets the scene, I share it in the exact form in which I have been sharing it from the start.

Shared with Author's permission
(since passed away)

24th May 2005

Dear Shirley-Anne,

I have had such a back-log of reading to complete recently, medical and political, that only now have I taken up Albert Jay

Nock.* Having only reached chapter 6, it is too soon to pass verdict, but already I am impressed with the mind of the man and his erudition, I am taking it slowly and making notes as I go along, for he casts a distinctly unusual and intriguing light on American history, the Confederation and the Constitution. He refers to a book by Professor Sakolski, The Great American Land Bubble, published in 1932 by Harpers, that sounds fascinating. I must try to get hold of it.

Nock speaks of two divisions of his Merchant State; the speculators, industrialists and public creditors who exploit rent, and the exploited debtor class. The first division of leading citizens, who control the executive and legislature though wealth, he believes will never relinquish their grasp on rent. Nor will they permit the debtor class the needed enlightenment regarding land without an almighty struggle. Calls upon reason, equity and justice will not prevail, though none can deny the underlying truths without resorting to flippancy. He speaks of the 'inveterate habit'. These leading citizens are unthinkingly given 'respect', with all its connotations of deference, simply because they have acquired wealth by means that are veiled. I remain more optimistic than Nock, though he does not overestimate the obstacles. I cannot help but believe that the great fault line in

---

* H is book, "Our Enemy the State". (ISBN 0 914156 01 2) "Our enemy", because it is the State which has legalized, and upholds, the fundamentally flawed land tenure structure, that allows the exploitation of the mass of the people by the privileged few. *S-A.H.*

the political economy will eventually bring us close to calamity on a global scale, and its imminence will force the realities to be accepted.

With best wishes,

George Miller

Dr George J. Miller, M.D., author of various works, including the 70-odd page "Dying for Justice", £7.95 – which should be in the hands of every sixth-former.

(Published by the Centre for Land Policy Studies, 2003
ISBN 1 901202 04 6)

The closing sentence of this letter is remarkable for its prophecy of the global economic collapse. However, it is Dr Miller's masterly summing-up of the perceptions of A. J. Nock – (whose work I would acknowledge as one of my great educators over many decades) – which is of particular value at this time.

Nock speaks of the determination of the ruling class to maintain their grasp on rent, and equally to forbid "the debtor class" the enlightenment that would set them free. But most significantly of all, (since the global collapse shows indeed no sign of forcing the acceptance of any underlying "realities"), Dr Miller reminds us of A.J. Nock's warning that, in this great struggle, "calls upon reason, equity and justice will not prevail".

And have there not been calls enough upon "reason, equity and justice", by his followers, since Henry George's time, in the on-going struggle to advance this great question? Nock's warning, given us seventy years ago – (1935 saw the first publication of "Our Enemy the State") – and given us by one who saw so deeply into the whole matter, seems therefore as significant for us today as it is timely. *Something else is needed – something more.*

The third Horseman of the Apocalypse has already issued us with a powerful warning – one which Chief Seattle's statement reinforces. The truth of Seattle's words is undeniable. None attempts to refute them. Yet we have built a society which directly flouts their wisdom. Somewhere, at a deep level of our being, we are living *out of touch with ourselves* – and that is a frightening situation.

Another saying by another North American Indian gives a salient warning: if you once divorce a people from the soil, they will presently become capable of any insanity.

Such as betaking themselves to the buying and selling of their Earthly Mother, and delivering thereby a direct slap in the face of the Creator?

There are obviously deep paths opening to us here, that we are being invited to travel. For considering the pivotal role played in the present debt crisis by our conjuring up of a phoney 'capital price' for Gaia, it is surely obvious that our present situation, in its origins, stems from our *betrayal of our Earthly Mother* - which has now justly rewarded us with *the great con trick of debt.*

*

The time has come for us to find our way back home.

Part II

*

Return Journey

"If you bring forth what is within you, what you bring forth will save you. If you do not bring forth what is within you, what you do not bring forth will destroy you."

(Words of Jesus from a recently discovered papyrus)

Part II

Chapter 1

*

Child of Gaia – the Terrene Man

"No man should be for too long separated from contact with the soil. Uprooted from there, he is easily uprooted from sanity in every direction."

(T.C. McLuhan, in "Touch the Earth")

Child of Gaia – the Terrene Man

*

W hile sorting through, last year, some old papers, with the thought of this book in mind, I came unexpectedly upon a small hand-written note whose existence I had wholly forgotten. Dated twenty-eight years ago, it read as follows:-

"In the snowy days of January 1982 I reached for a book that had long stood on my shelves – as yet unread – and began to read it through.

In its pages, the path by which the multinationals have arrived to take their present hold upon the social and economic life of the world – and particularly upon that of the Third World – is painstakingly examined. In 'The Restoration of the Peasantries', Dr G. T. Wrench traces how our capital-intensive, as opposed to people-intensive, economy, has come to take its rise from the *conversion of land to a capital asset."* (The key precisely, to that privatizing of land which, as we shall see in Ch.2, destroyed one after another the ancient civilizations.)"

Deeply impressed by my reading of this book, it seems I wasted no time in acting upon it, for the summary of its findings – which I produced in a sheet headed "Goliaths Unmasked" with extracts from Dr Wrench attached, a sheet that has had a prominent place on my shelves ever since – is dated February of that same year.*

---

* I am happy to think of the hundreds of copies of it that I must have shared over the intervening time. I well recall its first

"The Restoration of the Peasantries", published in 1939 – (my own precious copy of which was acquired second-hand from the book section of Wholefoods in Baker Street, in my London days) – has long been out of print, but copies are happily still obtainable through booksearch companies. My especial eagerness in bringing Dr Wrench's work before the public again sprang from the fact that, uniquely among the giants of the organic school which flourished in the early part of the last century – (Albert Howard, Robert McCarrison, Eve Balfour and others) – Dr Wrench was fully acquainted with *the land question*

---

big distribution at the Scottish Organic Gardeners conference in the Spring of 1982, at which lasting and valued friendships were formed; while one copy travelled eventually as far as the Philippines where it reached a movement for the Rehabilitation of Agricultural Lands, eliciting a request from them in April 1984 for permission to include it in a book being produced to help forward their work.

Another copy made its way to the Hawaiian Islands, where one of the indigenous islanders wrote me: "Thank you so much for the very helpful material" – (items he had requested from my 1981 booklet "The Land Question" which he had got from America, to which dispatch I had added "Goliaths Unmasked"). "I have never been able to get material like this. I sure would like to read Dr Wrench's books. Now I *see* where it all comes from ..."

It still delights me to think that so modest an effort sent Dr Wrench's work spinning across the globe to sow yet further seeds in other lands – alerting their peoples, in turn, to the full scope and reach of *the land question*.

and with the work of Henry George.*   While only one brief reference in his book reveals this directly, it explains why he was able so clearly to discern how the peasant peoples of the world have come to suffer such oppression under the system of *land capitalization* – a falsity leading inevitably, as we have seen, to the monopoly of land (now global) and thence to *debt*.

Dr Wrench was an agronomist, and his essential interest lay in the preservation of the earth's soils. It is well to remind ourselves why he should have been drawn to this particular sphere of earth husbandry, since it is one which most decidedly invites the interest of us all. As he writes of it:-

> "Historical periods of culture and civilization come and go, but the soil, the producer of life, is lasting. It continues, while they wax and wane. And if a civilization is such that it degrades the soil, then it is the civilization, and not the soil, that comes to an end."

Dr Wrench's interest in the soil embraced understandably a deep interest in its natural guardians – the peasant peoples of the earth. Of these, he wrote:-

> "The peasants are terrene producers, that is partners in the recreative power of the earth ... In contrast to this close

---

* Dr Wrench was possibly not entirely unique, in fact, among those giants, in grasping the land question. For I once read an article by Newman Turner – some musings written while 'leaning on the farm gate' – from which it seemed that, as a farmer, he had pretty well worked out the matter for himself.

familiarity is the urban ... 'the true urban is *not* a producer in the prime terrene sense. He has not the inward linkage with the soil ...'" **

These last words bring us an immediate reminder, from the quotation at the beginning of this chapter, as to how man first starts down that fateful pathway to "insanity in every direction". The primary "insanity", as it warned, from which all else follows, is our *severance from the soil*, since this brings a fatal estrangement from Gaia, our Earthly Mother – soon leading to our terrible further insanity of *commoditising* Her, and thence rapidly to the commoditising, and trashing, of all that clothes and graces this Planet. Such an accomplishment, (as we were well warned by the Third Horseman of the Apocalypse), will surely crown us with the title "anthropus mercantilis" – when the archaeologists of the future come to dig up our scattered remains.

As for the hunter-gatherers, (for whom Chief Seattle spoke), and the peasant peoples of the earth – any taking of such a path by them is impossible to imagine. The deep linkage of both with the soils of their land, upon which they knew their existence wholly to depend, assured that that land, which nurtured them, was for them forever beyond value and beyond price. Knowing themselves as belonging to the land, they could not be infected with the profane – absurd – notion that the land belonged to them.

The life of the hunter-gatherers is too far removed from our own to provide us with the necessary clues as to how this deep

---

** These last words were quoted from "The Decline of the West" by Dr Oswald Spengler, a book which Dr Wrench much admired.

linkage with the earth came to be so thoroughly destroyed – (for we were all terrene beings once), while the brutal treatment by the white man of the indigenous peoples, placing them in artificial reservations, has brought, for most of them, too sudden a collapse of their entire morale.

The peasant peoples of the earth however suffered no such sudden demise. As the essential providers of food for the new order, they could not be so disposed of; and it is in the clash between these two cultures, the terrene and the 'urban' – so vividly recounted in Dr Wrench's book – that we unexpectedly gain valuable insights into the painful process of the destruction of our own original terrene nature – and hence insights into the ineffectiveness, which so perplexes and disturbs us, of our struggle today against corrupt politicians and robber banks which seem able to do with us as they please. It also, crucially, points the way *back* for us, by which power over our own lives may be regained.

But first – for a term more helpful for our journey than the somewhat vague 'urban', (from the Latin, 'urbs' – 'town'). Such a term is readily available to us from the Greek, for their equivalent word, meaning 'city', is 'polis', and from this at once spills out to us the whole peculiar cacophony of the *political layer of society*; that layer which plays so large a part in our lives today, and whose area of operation is so far removed from the terrene. As to the essential nature of this world of politics, it is nowhere stated more precisely than by A.J. Nock in his book "Our Enemy the State", where he writes that the 'raison d'être' of the realm of politics, and – (whether or not understood by those engaged in it)

– its real purpose, is to enable, and perpetuate, *the economic exploitation of one class by another*; the essential basis of this exploitation being of course – what else? – the dispossession of the mass of the people from their land. For since man cannot live without access to land, land is forever the vital key to his economic independence – the ability to stand on his own feet.

It is from this *political* layer of society that has developed the highly centralised State so familiar to us today, which, growing like a cancer, siphons off ever more power to itself from the people, whilst ever protesting that it is doing the opposite. The whole of the State's apparatus exists, in short, to serve the charade – (rich in inventions like 'the Welfare State') – of sorting out the position between society's haves and have-nots, but *without* imperilling its own essential power to exploit; without, that is, going to the root of the matter and sorting out the fundamental question of the *right to land*.

Meanwhile the State moves, naturally, to take the sphere of education under its wing – with the tragedy following that the understanding of their real situation, by the uprooted populace, becomes in the course of time so blunted via the State's programme of *mis*education, that the great mass become believers in State power – unable to imagine a life without the State; and so become themselves another, but sadder, form of the corrupted *political man*, far estranged from the original terrene.

It was precisely this highly centralized form of the political State which – at the time of Dr Wrench's sojourn in India, where he spent a considerable number of years – the peasantry of that country was now involved with. For India was at that time held under British colonial rule, and British rule was of course precisely that *political creation* which A.J. Nock describes, powerful and highly centralized. Thus it was here that Dr Wrench became acquainted, at first hand, with a truly terrene people, suddenly confronted with the threat of the overturning of their entire terrene way of existence. For the British Raj, with its unshakable faith in centralised political control, was intent upon pushing the peasants of that country into the acceptance of a new directing of their lives. This – by an overhead authority, and one long uprooted from the soil, whose workings ran completely counter to their own accustomed and natural way of doing things.

For the peasant's way was always to look to his own community – linked as its members were through a common allegiance to their soil – to organise all necessary life-support systems, which were accomplished naturally via that linkage. Thus were the tasks of sanitation, poor relief, watch and ward, education and justice, etc., all dealt with simply, without the overseeing by any overhead body of what the peasants regarded as their own affairs. Similarly, all necessary "public works, such as the erection of public buildings, the making and protection of water reservoirs and tanks, the making and care of canals ... being for the common weal were carried out by the common will, that is by free labour". (No unemployment in *that* community!)

The way of the British Raj was instead – to place a tax upon the villagers, and then to pay bought-in labourers to do the work. To this 'insanity', typical of the uprooted man, the Indian peasants naturally raised strong, albeit fruitless, objection. Of course, this is the way *we* do things – only we don't see the 'insanity' of it any more! (Less simple, of course, in a centrally structured society. But then – isn't that insanity itself?) Further, the peasants found themselves persecuted by an endless stream of "wallahs", or overseers, sent on their rounds by the central administration, who, besides being charged to oversee matters the peasants had always overseen with full competence for themselves, burdened the villagers with the expense of their bed and board, which they were required to provide. Nor, naturally, had colonial rule overlooked its very first task – that of dispossessing the Indian peasant of his fields. For the precise – (round-about and treacherous) – way in which this was accomplished under British rule, see the extracts from Dr Wrench's writings in Part III ch.3 under "Dispossession ...".

With his deep feelings for the peasants, and understanding of their "traditional passion to manage their own affairs", Dr Wrench realized that the profound "detestation" which possessed them on being treated thus, like children, was no ordinary thing; but that so powerful a feeling, issuing as it did from man's deepest nature, arose from *a genuine injury to the inner being*.

We would do well to hold up a mirror to ourselves here, since it is ourselves no less we are looking at. For no matter how far we may feel we are removed from those Indian peasants, we are, at our deepest level, that same person ourselves – the *terrene* man. We no less, and no matter how many layers of superficial covering would obscure it from us, are ourselves children of Gaia, bone of her bone and flesh of her flesh – beyond any matter of choice by us and whether we know it or not. Therefore in us is the same passion buried - to "manage our own affairs", in our own communities.

In this matter we, in our society, find ourselves in particularly dangerous territory – for here we enter the realm of *mental health*. Carrying deep within us the same "injury to the inner being" as did those Indian peasants – the same experience of its ravagement and abuse – we however, being so long estranged from the source of this injury through too long an acclimatization to political rule, can no longer decipher the signals of its distress. Hence these can manifest only as a vague enveloping sense of depression and anxiety. Is it any wonder, then, if our society suffers from widespread mental illness? For we too, as children of Gaia, in our deepest being, know no less than did those Indian peasants confronted with a bullying colonial power, that – with our fundamental Gaian linkage – it is *to each other* we must look for succour; in short, that "it is in the shelter of each other that the people live", (to quote a Celtic saying) – and *not* in the shelter of the State.

But the State knows nothing of that. It only knows that the bottom layers of the pyramid – the layers that hold it all up and upon which its own existence wholly depends – are beginning to crack, and to crack dangerously.

Thus – ignoring entirely the savage cruelty of its dispossessing of us, but ever sanctifying and upholding it – *the State*, unwitting of the irony of its situation – sallies forth to offer us its aid! So, a column I chanced upon from the Stirling Observer in September 2005, issuing from the Scottish Executive (as it was then) under the logo "Healthier Scotland", proffers the reader its advice on mental ill-health! – while confirming just how prevalent it is in our society, with "depression and anxiety", precisely, high on the list.

Just how many of these problems, one wonders, could not be traced back to that original *dispossession and robbery* – (for it involves also the people's rents), or to the huge fall-out from it? ... destructions now bringing its victims back full circle once more into the embrace of the very same political destroyer – in that branch of its activities we carefully button up under the name of 'social work'.

The heart of the terrene man beats in us as strongly as ever – however far below the surface in most of us for most of the time: the terrene man, in ever-increasing multitudes across the globe today, uprooted – *dispossessed*!

And *the State* thinks it can help us back to sanity!!

Is it any wonder if the oblivion of alcoholism has now bred addiction among the Scots, a people always peculiarly hefted to their land? For the sense of anguish from the memory of an unnamed something lost – something buried in our psyche too long and too deep – finally becomes a memory too painful to endure.

And we think we have a problem with *alcohol*? And – that it can be solved by raising the price of the stuff!!

Zola knew better!

> "If you shut up the truth and bury it under the ground, it will but grow and gather to itself such explosive power that the day it bursts through it will blow up everything in its way."

And what if part of it *im*plodes before reaching the surface? Do we not have an epidemic of suicides also today? Or is it *still* not enough?

*

From another angle, Viktor Schauberger – extraordinary genius of the last century, known as the Austrian Water Wizard – extends the warning already given us by Dr Wrench against the degrading of our soil. For he shows the implications, in their fullness, for Gaia's lost children – those who have allowed a political personality to dominate the original terrene man. The following passage from Schauberger pierces to the heart of this 'anthropus mercantilis', for that speculation in land he speaks of which Dr Wrench's writings show leads to the soil's degradation, follows directly from the *commoditising of the land.* (Who will say that Viktor Schauberger did not understand the land question?)

"A free people must grow out of a free earth. Any people that violates Mother-Earth has no right to a homeland, because in soils destroyed by speculation, high-quality races can find no abode, i.e., they are physical masses divorced from all connection with the Earth. Masses without roots perish. They have to travel the terrible road of decay until, like unsuitable fertilizers, they lose their stubborn wills and only when they have reached this condition, and starting again from the very beginning, will they be allowed to enter the mighty course of evolution."

(Quoted in "Living Energies" by Callum Coats. Gateway Books, 1996.)

From these stark words of warning, let us turn to a more hopeful look towards the future – one captured for us in a certain Sufi saying: "The earth has sworn unto the day of Paradise that all truths will come to the light sooner or later". "Unto the day of Paradise": indicating that our painful overturning will come to its end when the human race has finally awakened to its true destiny and consented, *contented*, to become – as Edmund Bordeaux Szekely foresaw it must be - "the gardeners of the earth".*

> "The world is not subject to random accident but is governed according to inner law ... Left to herself Nature would have supplanted the earlier vegetation with newer forms, and not only would have transformed the world into a blossoming garden of immense fertility and stable temperature, but in addition would have renewed herself in cycles."
>
> (Viktor Schauberger in "The Water Wizard" translated and edited by Callum Coats.)

What a partnership awaits us with that glad awakening!

But where stand we at this exact moment in time? What freedom is open to us at this precise point in our history, to start on that stern journey back to our roots and to sanity? Merely *locally* –

> "In his book 'Stone Voices', Neal Ascherson writes: 'Scottish local government is preoccupied with control, and a condition of silent, divorced dependence is what it prefers

---

* A nother extraordinary soul, and co-founder of the International Biogenic Society. He died in 1975 leaving us, besides his splendid translations of the Essene Gospels, a whole library of profound and inspiring writings.

from its tenantry – an archipelago of undemocracies, run by power cliques who want as few people as possible to participate in running their own lives."*

Going rather deeper – and revealing how deep the rot goes:-

"How It Really Works

"... There is no doubt that a powerful ... establishment exists, which employs a disarming rhetoric of public service – the words partnership, consultation and consensus feature regularly – but which often seems to act in ways that protect the interest of the most influential stakeholders ...

In the 1980s, in a brilliant book entitled 'Governing Education', Andrew McPherson and Charles Raab of Edinburgh University delineated the 'assumptive world' of the educational leadership class in Scotland. They showed that, in order to be admitted to the inner circles of the policy community, potential members had to demonstrate both deference and trustworthiness ...

... The socialisation process was subtle, encouraging a form of 'groupthink' and enabling any potential dissidents to be identified and marginalised.

... what emerges is a very unhealthy picture of a nation which values conformity more than critical thinking or creativity, and which rewards those who are prepared to play by the rules of a rather discreditable game ..." **

---

* Quoted from a speech by Laurence Demarco, Jan 07. (Acks. to Comment, Feb 07.)

** From Walter Humes' "Self-deception at the top", from the Scottish Review, No. 215, 03.03.10. The above extracts taken, with acknowledgements, from the column published in Comment, April 2010.

Ah – the "educational leadership class" in Scotland – fine-groomed, fine-*tuned* by, and to, the *political sphere*! GOTCHA! But – hardly the picture of a *nation*! Of a *political culture*, methinks!

And the fruitage for our children of the work of this vaunted "leadership class" – sitting at the top of the educational chain? 20% of the population of Scotland is reckoned to be functionally illiterate! Can we not grasp it once and for all: *whatever the State touches* – WITHERS!

In the face of the 'achievements' of this vaunted educational leadership – busily replicating in the land its intellectual degeneracy and moral bankruptcy – happily there comes, from another quarter, a cheering shout of a very different order: one focussed on a practical and powerful step we can begin to take, right now, at the start of that journey which beckons us back to our roots and to the arms of our Earthly Mother.

"Warning Bells to Politicians

Ring in 2010

At the beginning of 2010 a movement known as the 'Parallel Community' launched its intent to start taking action from the grassroots. It is 'dedicated to creating a return to common sense and honesty in all aspects of living' and it is encouraging action to be taken at the local level ...

...'We are NOT looking for civil unrest ... or even civil disobedience ... but ... are firmly in favour of civil 'non-compliance'. This means that we question the qualifications of those who seek to control us for control's sake, and if we find them wanting, we take appropriate steps to refuse to accept their judgment ...'

The movement has its base in Cornwall and more information can be found at: www.parallelcommunity.com"*

There is a saying – perhaps a line from a poem? – about the rapid change from day to night at the equator: that in two strides comes the dark. So, it seems to me, in the search from out of our own dark present, for a return to the light of sanity again and our Earthly Mother's embrace – two strides may well be required for the accomplishment of such a journey. For ere we can make the full return to *Her* – of more veiled face – we must first surely awaken to the full purpose of which the chiming bells, above, bring us potent reminder: *it is in the shelter of each other that the people live.*

So, by giving ourselves first to the re-establishing of that original kinship we were born into – and born to enjoy (that kinship which the State has done its best to shatter); by so *uniting our strengths,* we can fit ourselves for the taking up of our vital, essential task: that is, the public unmasking of that not-so-savvy **cat**! For here is placed in our hands the key that cannot be taken from us – the key to a *public confrontation at last* with the political establishment; so to reclaim finally our stolen lives and stolen land – *our birthright in Gaia,* along with the cancelling of *falsely conjured debt.*

In tackling our task in two stages, in this way, we shall in fact be on firm ground. For it accords with a basic principle of homeopathy: first in – last out; and conversely, *last in – first out*! That is – the *last* symptoms of an underlying disease to appear are the *first* to go.

Thus our *first* step in the journey back to retrieve our painful loss must be the reversal of our *second* suffering: the traumatic exchange of our original terrene family for an unnatural dependence upon the political State. It is here that begins our journey of full return to our Earthly Mother – whose first and most painful loss to us will find *its* reversal, in turn, if together we summon strength to accomplish the initial one.

And what a glad reversal it promises to be!

> So when the world is asleep, and there
>> seems no hope of her waking
> Out of some long bad dream that makes her
>> mutter and moan,
> Suddenly, all men rise to the noise
>> of fetters breaking
> And every one smiles at his neighbour
>> and tells him his soul is his own.

From "The Dawn Wind", (Rudyard Kipling, 1865-1936)*

*

---

* With acknowledgements to Peter Mackay, in whose remarkable book, "We Have Tomorrow: Stirrings in Africa, 1959-67", (Michael Russell Publ. Ltd., 2008) – I came upon it.

Simple and fresh and fair from winter's
    close emerging,
As if no artifice of fashion, business,
    politics, had ever been,
Forth from its sunny nook of shelter'd grass –
    innocent, golden, calm as the dawn,
The spring's first dandelion shows its trustful face.

(Walt Whitman)

Part II

Chapter 2

Dispossession through the Centuries: The Tripping-point of Civilizations

*

The Relevance today of the Essene Teachings

84

The buying up, by rich countries and international corporations, to ensure their own food security, of farmland in the world's poor countries, is the new form of land-grabbing, or 'neo-colonialism' – now taking place across the globe.

Thus are the peasant peoples of the poor countries dispossessed of the land they need to grow their own food.

(Summary of a report in
The Guardian of 4th July 2009)

The hideous end-fruitage of our hideous and prolonged love-affair with *silence on the land question: the commoditising of the Earth.*

*

Edmond Bordeaux Székely:
Discoverer and translator of
The Essene Gospels

O n my shelves stands a book of unassuming title, "A Philosophy for a Fair Society"* – but its opening chapters are of riveting content. For they trace the destruction of those civilizations of the past which have indulged in the privatization of their land, and so brought ruin upon themselves. For the privatization of land is the royal road to *land monopoly* – a force carrying an inbuilt time-bomb of destruction for whatever society tolerates its deadly embrace.

The story that unfolds starts from Bronze Age Mesopotamia, at around 3,500 BC, and runs on through Biblical, and classical Greek and Roman times. Following it we find – hardly a surprise – that the question of the just sharing of land, and of the revenues arising from land settlement, has been with us for a very long time – in fact, for as long as the history of civilization, or settled societies; and that the way it was dealt with, or *not* dealt with, settled the fate of those civilizations of the past.

This story has vital lessons for us today as we, in our own land-monopoly-strangled society, come to see, from this vast tapestry, how those earlier civilizations came to grief – and so can recognize ourselves as the latest, about to be added to their number.

The land question – the question of the *right to land* – running as the chief thread through all of this past history, is a question we should have studied in depth at school – but for very obvious

---

* B y Michael Hudson, Fred Harrison, G J Miller & Kris Feder, publd. By Shepheard-Walwyn (Publrs.) Ltd., 1994.

reasons, did not. It is a history full of fascinating further glimpses along the way. For instance, who would have thought that our familiar saying, to 'wipe the slate clean', originated all that time ago in ancient Mesopotamia? We discover, too, what Jesus *really* meant when he said, pointing to the image on the coin, "Give to Caesar the things that are Caesar's" – not quite the 'excuse for every tyrant' that these words have since been ignorantly construed to mean!

But how could the way nations dealt with their land *not* be the centrepiece of history? We have but to remind ourselves of that fundamental axiom of economics, so clearly recognized by Henry George, to see why this is so: *man seeks to satisfy his desires with the lease possible exertion.* For if everything – but *everything* – that we need for life on this earth involves, as it does in the first place, access to land, then the holding of land is clearly the economic trump-card in our efforts to satisfy those desires. However, with man's inbuilt tendency towards the "least possibly exertion", that trump-card stands in danger of being converted to a whip-hand – if the trump-card of your fellow can be wrested from him, so that you can command the exertion of *his* energies in place of your own. Such a temptation drove man in ancient Mesopotamia, just as it has driven him in every age – and overwhelmingly now, in ours, of boasted 'global' reach. However, the stern truth remains that we all arrive on this earth with a mouth to feed, and a pair of hands with which to set to work and feed it, so that *self-support* was clearly intended as the rule of life on this earth –

and not that one human body should be bent under a double load in service to another.

In ancient Mesopotamia, where the royal rulers needed a fit people to serve them both in their armies and in the fields, they naturally looked, to meet their needs, to a *fit and sturdy* citizenry – that is, to a *free, landholding* body of people, not one exhausted from doing that double service. Thus it was that there arose, in those early times, the practice called 'wiping the slate clean', when "for century after century the acquisition of land by public officials or merchants was reversed repeatedly and indeed, almost regularly, by royal Clean Slates. These cancelled personal debts (including back taxes) and returned the land to its traditional holders".*

How fortunate we would have been to have discovered such a history at school, where bright young minds would readily have got the idea of resuscitating those Clean Slates today! And how wise this would have been, for it was precisely those Clean Slate *reversals* of overweening land privatization which, from time to time, undid the damage of that privatization, for those earlier societies.

---

* Quoted from the article in Land & Liberty's Double Issue of 1995, "The Privatization of Land – how it all began", by Michael Hudson – an article reporting on an International Colloquium on Privatization, held in New York shortly before.

As this article explains, early peoples did not leave us written statements of these things. The evidence was painstakingly pieced together by archaeologists and scholars from what written records there were: "mainly abbreviated notes (largely receipts and internal accounts from the public temples and palaces) that took for granted the economic context".

It is all set out for us in "A Philosophy for a Fair Society", where the contributions by Michael Hudson and Fred Harrison trace the history of those earlier civilizations as being essentially an on-going struggle over this question of *land privatization*. As to the ruin which ancient Rome ultimately suffered by that route, the Roman writer Pliny leaves us in no doubt. With the economy of words peculiar to the Latin language, he sums it up in just three: "Latifundia perdiderat Italiam". Since the verb "perdiderat" is linked with our "perdition", there is no problem there! "Latifundia"? * We can turn simply to the words of Isaiah who, viewing a similar scenario as it confronted the Children of Israel half a millennium earlier, had roundly declaimed against those who "add house to house and join field to field, till no space is left and you are alone in the land". (Isaiah 5:8) And how is that, indeed, for a description of Scotland today – more than two thousand years on?

From another fascinating book, "Biblical Economics" by the Rev. Archer Torrey,** we make the discovery that it was, in fact, this very evil of *land monopoly* which Jesus was referring to, in the dramatic scene when he stood up in the temple at the start of his mission, and stated that he had come to fulfil "the law and the

---

* Latefundia: from the Latin 'latus' – 'broad, wide'; and 'fundus' – 'bottom, lowest part', also 'a piece of land, farm, estate'. Well – land is always their *foundation*!

** His series of articles under this title, published in Land & Liberty in 1979, was later extended to a book of the same title; published in its 5th edition, in 2005, by the Robert Schalkenbach Foundation (USA).

prophets". In these words of Jesus we stumble, in fact, upon a unique chapter in the history of the Clean Slates. For when Moses, the great law-giver, led the Children of Israel out of Egyptian bondage into the promised land, and gave them his famous Ten Commandments, he added to these another, sometimes referred to as the *Eleventh*.*

This Eleventh Commandment was the *law of the Jubilee Year*. Under this law, on the Jubilee Year – which fell at every fiftieth – the land originally allocated to the different tribes, (and by the tribes to their clans and thence families), should it have been alienated in the interval, *went back to its original holders;* and where debt had been involved in its alienation, it went back *unencumbered by those debts* – the 'slate wiped clean'!

This was a simple matter under the law of the Jubilee Year, for in fact land was never actually sold, only leased, and the lease could not exceed forty-nine years. As we learn, "the concept of selling land . . . does not exist in the Bible except as a crime". Let us ponder that! Where we read that land was "sold", with rare exceptions it simply means that it was leased, or rented. (Archer Torrey.) What a give-away! And what ruse of mis-translation by those translators of the Bible – who were evidently determined to incorporate into the Scriptures approval for our immoral buying and selling of land, to invest our corrupt ways with Biblical authority! (*Or*, felt politically impelled to do so.)

---

* See "The Eleventh Commandment", by Francis Neilson, (Robert Schalkenbach Foundation USA), and "My Neighbour's Landmark", by Frederick Verinder, (Land & Liberty Press Ltd, 1950).

A full account of this great Law is given in Archer Torrey's book, and what it achieved for the Children of Israel was something exceptional; for it made it finally impossible that either land alienation or debt *should ever become a permanent part of their economy.* And let us ponder *that too!* For the 'Clean Slate' was now removed from the arbitrary jurisdiction of a ruler, to become a permanent and inbuilt part of the people's law – a law which fell to be enacted every fiftieth year by the people themselves.

Another interesting feature of this society during the reign of the law of the Jubilee Year – a period called 'the time of the Judges' – is that, throughout it, "there was no central government. The Law applied, but if a dispute occurred, judges, who were acknowledged wise men and women from various tribes, decided these cases and set precedents. It was a unique set-up among advanced countries of that day." John Kelly, in his article "The Bible and Henry George".*

---

* See Nov-Dec 06 issue of Groundswell, (published by Common, Ground, USA). One is struck by the similarity of this description to that of the society, also established on the Law of Rent, which grew up on Gosaba, an island in the Ganges Delta, in the first part of the twentieth century. (See "Birthright in Land ...", Part II, ch.3).

This would seem fully to bear out a conviction I have long held, that where the natural Law of Rent is allowed to operate, there is no need for a centralised governing power, since the Law of Rent in operation is a fully sufficient governing power in itself. (See further "Birthright in Land . . .", Part II, ch.1, "Community and Re-Empowerment).

This same article by John Kelly reveals further that, re debt – without waiting for a Jubilee Year, every seven years all ordinary debts (those not pertaining to land) were wiped out. What a piece of simple wisdom, to place the ultimate responsibility for sound judgment, in such transactions, upon the lender – who must use careful judgement, as he stood to lose what, after those seven years, was not repaid! No bailing out of defaulting banks in that society! What leagues ahead of us they were in the application of simple common sense to the ministration of public affairs!

A further revelation from John Kelly's article is that the "tithe", as it is referred to in the Bible – the payment made annually by each landholder to the community for its communal purposes – was quite simply a *land rent*! Another instance of the art used by these official translators of the Bible, to hide from us the true and contemporary significance, for us, of this law of the Jubilee Year. However, as we shall presently see, by an immortal piece of poetic justice the sleights-of-hand of these translators finally boomeranged, achieving for them an 'own goal' which they had not anticipated!

How interesting – and how significant for us – that Moses, in establishing the primitive form of land justice (suitable for that society) of the Jubilee Year, should have ensured the placing at its foundation of the natural Law of Rent – as these tithes, now unmasked, reveal!

Moses had clearly seen that unless the land question was dealt with by a just and specific law – incorporating also a just form of social revenue for society's support – he might as well have left the Children of Israel in Egypt; for they would only otherwise, in the course of time have fallen victim to a similar bondage amidst their own people; as is precisely our situation of course today. What huge lessons await our discovery in Moses' Eleventh Commandment!

Just such a bondage it was, of course, that Isaiah came to lament at that later date. For the Children of Israel had so far fallen away from this unique and beneficient Law given them by Moses that, by Jesus' time, the Roman historian Josephus could describe Galilee as "an astonishingly fruitful country where, except for a very small minority, the people lived in abject poverty, ground into the dust".* What a reflection upon ourselves! – the only difference being that the poverty of our own 'ground-down' ones exists within the ardent embraces of a 'Welfare State', a term concocted to fool us – (and the more fools, us, if we thus refer to it).

How did the Children of Israel come to desert this fundamental economic law, which had kept the whole nation in so prosperous a state during obedience to it of more than three hundred years? – a state beautifully described as: every man sitting under his own vine and his own fig tree, with none to make him afraid (I Kings 4:25 and Micah 4:4).

The law of "the least possible exertion" operates also, unfortunately, with great subtlety in the mental realm. Thus the day came when the Children of Israel began to hanker after a 'father figure', someone whom they wanted to 'take care of

---

* John Kelly, ibid.

them'. (In *that* flourishing state! 'Who so blind as those that cannot see?' -!) Despite Samuel's stern and repeated warnings to them that such a ruler would bring them to ruin, forsaking the Land Law, taking their best fields, etc., and that he would turn them all into serfs – (sounds familiar?) – they were not to be dissuaded. And so indeed it all came about, successive kings making alliances with, and intermarrying into, other nations where their own great Land Law had no place. Finally they became entangled with Phoenicia, whose king typically had complete sovereignty over all the land, granting portions to whom he pleased, with the ordinary people living as serfs just as Samuel had predicted.

Now it was the custom of those times that a nation's chief god blessed its laws. Hence the law of unrestricted land privatization, ruling in Phoenicia, was blessed by the Phoenicians' god – and this god was none other than the famous (or infamous) Baal! Thus 'God's people', having exchanged their true Land Law for the immoral one of the Phoenicians, found themselves, to boot, worshippers at the altar of the Phoenicians' heathen god!

"BAAL – God of the Landlords!" – Archer Torrey's ringing proclamation of this achievement! And so it became that – not the land law of justice and freedom which had so prospered the nation, but the usurpive one of a heathen and alien god's oppressive rule, came gradually to extend its cruel domain – and not just geographically, but on through history. For Baal's land law spread in due course from Phoenicia (or Carthage) to Rome – the Roman soldiers triumphing in the Punic Wars against Carthage having been given estates in North Africa. Thus the old Roman system of a free peasantry was finally replaced by that of Baal; and when in due course Constantine, at the head of the Roman Empire, was obliged to recognize Christianity on account of its popularity, the question of these *Baalistic* land laws, which then ruled via the official Christian church, came under no review.

So we come to have the 'Christian' church of today, in its many denominations – arrant betrayers, all, of Him whom they claim to be their founder!

Archer Torrey, in his book's first appendix, "The Church and the Land", gives an absorbing overview of the progressive ruin of the peoples of the world from this beginning, wherever the so-called Christian nations then spread. This chapter, as a final updating of our real history – with the successful staining by the Christian nations of every foreign land where they came to hold power – should be in every school syllabus. Particularly and startingly, Archer Torrey's chapter uncovers for us our own responsibility for the 'terrorism' of today. "The rise of Islam was in protest against the Christian landlords' exploitation of the indigenous peoples of North Africa and the Middle East . . . the church became dominated by the landlords to the extent that all of North Africa rebelled against Christianity and became Mohammedan under the slogan, taken from the Bible – "The land belongs to God", (Lev. Ch. 25), and so – "the land belongs to Allah". So who were the original and real terrorists?* Meanwhile the church remains one of Britain's biggest landowners, bowing down to its very own chosen god, *Baal* – unchanged! *

Meanwhile – (I interpolate these words in early 2011) - that earlier cry from "the indigenous peoples of North Africa and the Middle East", that "the land belongs to Allah", echoes strangely in our ears indeed, as news bulletins from that part of the globe report its various people erupting in equally fierce opposition to today's non-Christian rulerships, which – (just as the earlier Christian ones had done) – have brought crushing poverty to their peoples by ignoring that "the land belongs to Allah", and instead treating the land with all its resources as their personal perquisites. I have not read the Koran, but I cannot help wondering if its pages may not, upon close study, reveal likewise some definite teaching on land justice, even if not arriving at so clear a resolution of it as the Jubilee Year.

The law of land tenure is, as we have seen, the make-or-break law of any society. The Israelites, under Moses, got it right by recognizing that the root of this matter lay in moral and spiritual territory. "The land shall not be sold in perpetuity", (i.e. leased in perpetuity), "for the land is mine" – as the God of Moses and Isaiah spake it to them. (Lev. 25.) That is, we human beings

---

* See "The Predator Culture", by Fred Harrison, (Shepheard-Walwyn, 2009), for its brilliant research, likewise, on the West's responsibility for today's terrorism; and for its extensive further research – including how Britain's colonial policy, in deliberately interfering between the Tutsi and Hutu tribes, was directly responsible for the terrible Rwandan massacre.

respect that the land, which has been freely gifted to us by a great and mysterious Creative Power, is not something that any of us can ever rightly claim to *own* – or therefore, buy or sell; a recognition that surely resonates with those of any religion, or of none.

We today, however, lie under an opposite conviction: that is, that the land is anyone's who can grab it – while we remain oblivious of the image of that false god so indelibly now stamped upon it!

Perhaps we do not notice, either, the words "fid. def." stamped on those coins that bear the royal image. But somewhere above the gods are laughing at us! "'Defender' of what 'faith' indeed?"

'Own goal' for those assiduous mis-translators of the Bible hardly describes it!

Finally – just to clinch the anathema to Christ that was the betrayal of Moses' great law of land justice – a law he proclaimed at the start of his mission he had come "to fulfil" – here is John Kelly's explanation of the apparently enigmatic tribute-money story, when the high priests sent their agents to Jesus to try to trip him up, by asking him in public if it was permissible to pay taxes to Caesar. (For to *deny* it was permissible would be counted as seditious and reported to the Roman authorities.) Jesus, pointing to Caesar's image on the coin, by his response – "Pay to Caesar what belongs to Caesar, and to God what belongs to God" – trips *them* up instead!

As John Kelly explains, although the Land Law had now lapsed, it was by no means forgotten. It was something fully familiar to the Jewish people, and indeed studied as part of their law. Now what did this law teach them? Firstly, that under the Law of Moses, it was forbidden them to pay tribute to any other country or king. So what did those people owe to Caesar under their law? Nothing! And what did they owe to God? Why, the *rent on His land*, the 'tithe'! The agents, unable to answer a word to this, departed "marvelling" – but the high priests must have fumed when they were told of it!

John Kelly's analysis of this matter further gives the lie to the church's teaching that Jesus was concerned entirely with the kingdom-of-heaven-to-come, and had nothing practical to offer to the poor of today. Clearly, to Jesus, the kingdom of heaven was intended to overflow onto *this* earth *now*! This is borne out also by his Beatitude, proclaiming that *the dispossessed shall have the land restored to them*. For the words we are more accustomed to hearing from the Bible, that "the meek shall inherit the earth", is apparently yet another politic 'smoothing-out' by those Bible translators – who, Archer Torrey reveals, were also "careful to avoid the word 'justice' as much as possible, and to substitute the vague 'righteousness' ... 250 out of 278 times"!

Commenting on the customary explanation of Jesus teaching, "Heaven is where the kingdom is, but it will come later", John Kelly sums up the matter finely:-

> "I am not sure how we have managed to turn Jesus so upside down ... It is not what he said. His message was that the Law is still relevant (and) that it will provide for the needs of society."

> As he continues: "The Biblical Law of Moses was not a fluke. It was not meant just for the ancient world of Canaan. It will still work today. The Bible is a map.

(Henry) George's ideas will work today. 'Progress and Poverty' is a map. They will work because they are based on the same basic truths: no grants of privilege, equal access to the land, and payment of the land rent but no taxes on labour or capital."

Just imagine the electrifying effect it would have on our emptying churches, were their pulpits to proclaim the full message of Jesus in all its blazing clarity today!

*

I laid down my pen on this article where it concludes, as above, in September 2008 –when I fully expected this book to be completed and published in 2009. But life took a different turn.

Taking the article up again towards three years on, I am aware however that it is incomplete. For another and broader panorama unfolds out of this matter of dispossession – and it is one in which a significant role, once more is played by Jesus. Thus, while many are the great souls who, since ancient times, have trod this earth, seeking to awaken mankind with their message of an existence beyond time and space, Jesus holds among them a unique place.

As we have seen, the kingdom of heaven he taught was not one confined simply to a realm *beyond*. It was a kingdom waiting to overflow, in full measure, into our lives *here and now*, this patterning on earth being accomplished through the return to the community, every year, by every landholder, of their holding's full rental; the significance of this being the impossibility, which follows from it, of there ever arising a market in land. Thus the law of the rental return becomes man's acknowledgment, due, that this Earth, with all its wonders, the gift to His children of an invisible Creator, is not open to sordid squabbles amongst them as to *ownership* of it. It is available to us, strictly and only, for the purpose of its humble inhabiting, for our nurturing and use of it – as its shadowy passing tenants, which is all that we are here.

It was not just, however, the cruelty of the dispossession of the great mass of humanity from the land that Jesus was concerned with, in man's misappropriation of the Creator's great gift. His cosmic gaze with equal ease took in a further and yet greater horror: the coming of the environmental destruction which, at a later age, that misappropriation would inevitably bring to pass. An age that has now caught up with us.

It is hardly surprising, therefore, to discover that – in equally unswerving manner – Jesus issued to mankind a chilling warning as to the fatal consequences which, in this further sphere, he would reap, should he persist in his chosen pathway. Equally – nor should it surprise us that 'the powers of darkness' or 'the princes of this world', have since done their best to see that the record of Jesus' warning on this matter never came to light. For it is not one contained in the Bible, belonging as it did to ancient teachings of a different lineage.

However, very wonderfully, in the last century, through the dedicated searchings of a remarkable man, these ancient teachings have emerged once more to the light of day. The unearthing, through a long travail, of these long-lost records, was the work of one already mentioned in a footnote in Part II: Edmond Bordeaux Székely. *

Székely's adult career had an extraordinary start when, fresh from university, and as the result of a remarkable essay he had written on St Francis – ('the last of the Essenes') – he was given a special introduction to the Prefect, or keeper, of the Vatican Library, and in particular to its Secret Archives. In particular –

---

* With Transylvanian forebears eminent in philology and literature, Székely grew up in France and received his Ph.D. from the University of Paris. Besides holding various other degrees and professorships, he became well-known as a philologist in Sanskrit, Aramaic, Greek and Latin, while also a Hebrew scholar, and proficient in ten modern languages.

Co-founder – along with Nobel prize-winning author, Romain Rolland – of the International Biogenic Society, his most important translations, in addition to selected texts from the Dead Sea Scrolls and the Essene Gospel of Peace (millions of copies in 26 languages), are selected texts from the Zend Avesta and pre-Colombian codices of ancient Mexico, besides later works on the Essene Way of Biogenic Living.

He was author of more than 80 books in a wide range of subjects, amongst them Ancient Cultures, Psychology, Ecology, Metaphysics, the Dead Sea Scrolls, the Essenes, Jesus, Buddha, Yoga, Zarathustra, Science, Art, Music, Literature, Health, Nutrition and Biogenics.

(For the above information, I am indebted to the International Biogenic Society. For a complete catalogue of Dr Székely's writings, apply to his successor, Norma Nilsson Bordeaux Székely, IBS International, P.O. Box 849, Nelson, B.C., Canada V1L 6A5.)

because these latter held a wealth of ancient manuscripts that had successfully been preserved from destruction through long centuries of a war-ravaged Europe. It was from these manuscripts, in their ancient languages, that Székely was finally able to decode and unravel the history of the *Essene Brotherhood*, which had existed in ancient times – and to which, in his time, Jesus had belonged.

The teachings of this Brotherhood have a special relevance for us today, in as much as, to the Essenes, man's relationship to his Earthly Mother – to Gaia – was *as sacred as that to his Heavenly Father*. But this originally sacred relationship to our Earthly Mother on this planet has, of course, long been severed by the Baalistic land tenure which has now spread across the globe; and it was his presaging of the hideous outcome, for the Earth itself, of man's ill-chosen path, which – as we shall see – evoked from Jesus the terrible warning that points to our day.

From Székely's fascinating record of his discoveries in these Secret Archives, recounted in a slim volume entitled "My Discovery of the Essene Gospel of Peace", I quote the following extract as an introduction to the long-lost history of this ancient and unique Brotherhood:-

> "They lived in the desert, on the shore of an ocean of sand. They came to this burning wasteland because it was less cruel than the persecution they suffered from their fellowman. And in the burning desert they planted a garden which grew and flourished for many hundreds of years. They guarded among them the most ancient knowledge and the greatest treasure of holiness the world had ever known. They were the Brotherhood of the Essenes.

Even they were not sure of their origins, so lost in time was the memory of their beginnings. Moses had been one of them, and the prophets of old. The Children of Light of ancient Sumeria were of their blood, and healers and teachers from the ancient time, before the Pleistocene Cataclysm, which we call the Great Flood. The Brotherhood has always been with us.

When they planted their garden in the desert, they watered it with loving care. They rose at dawn to commune with the Angels of the Earthly Mother, and to contemplate her manifold gifts ... They read from the book of the Earthly Mother, and used their understanding to achieve total harmony with their environment. They communed with the Angels of the Heavenly Father at dusk ... They taught the holy law ... They wrote songs of praise, of gladness, of sorrow ...

They sent out healers. And one of them was Jesus, the Essene. He walked among the sick and troubled, and he brought them the knowledge they needed to cure themselves. Some who followed him wrote down what passed between him and those who suffered and were heavy-laden. The Elders of the Brotherhood made poetry of the words, and made unforgettable the story of the Healer of Men, the Good Shepherd. And when the time came at last for the Brothers to leave the desert and go to another place, the scrolls stayed behind as buried sentinels, as forgotten guardians of eternal and living truth ... beneath the shifting shadows of the desert."

But not forever! Not ultimately lost! For as Székely relates, in the last pages of his riveting account, his long search in the labyrinthine Library of the Vatican was finally rewarded:-

"The original manuscript of St Jerome, believed lost in the fifth century, fortunately survived in the Benedictine

Monastery of Monte Cassino and in the Secret Archives of the Vatican. Among these manuscripts was the complete text of the Essene Gospel of Peace."

As placing Székely's great discoveries in their more historical context, I quote the following extracts from the Introduction to his book. They point us to a very different kind of world – but it is a world we may be forced to our knees in acceptance of, if we are not indeed to perish from an Earth we are rapidly making uninhabitable:-

"Many words are devoted to St Francis in this book, and with reason. In addition to all his other attributes, he was also the last personification of the Essene spirit. Since the gentle troubadour of God brought his message of love, purity and simplicity, no one has appeared who has represented so totally the Essene spirit.

With the coming of the industrial age, things of the spirit have assumed less and less reality in our lives, and now we have almost completely forgotten that we are born of the Earthly Mother and the Heavenly Father. The god of the twentieth century is technology – whose vast machines are wholly dependent on limited fuel sources – a computerized god we have programmed to produce material things, most of which we do not need and much of which is even harmful.

A good example of how our priorities have shifted in the last few hundred years is the reaction of the world to the discovery in 1945 of the Dead Sea Scrolls. True, there was great excitement. But it was the excitement of a major archaeological find, not the celebration of a spiritual rebirth. The mass of books and articles that followed the discovery almost all dealt exclusively with dry technical details and confusing theological arguments ...

What has happened to us? There was a time in our past when the very air crackled with wonder, when birds sang songs of mystery, and it was possible to meet a saint in bare feet on the dusty road, and soar with his spirit into unknown realms of holiness ...

That state of wonder and awe before the miracle of life, which burned so brilliantly in the Essene Brotherhood at the Dead Sea, and which faded out with the passing of the last Essene, St Francis, was mine to kindle once more with the discovery of the Essene Gospel. It is a book of wonders, not only for the wisdom and guidance contained in its pages, but because it shines and glows with the lost spirit of ages past, when the distance between man and God was not so great, and when all of nature sang with the voice of angels ...

Before Dr Székely passed away in 1975, he had completed translation of all four books of the Essene Gospels. I shall leave readers to make, from these, their own further discovery of the Essenes – but concerning Book One, "The Gospel of Peace of Jesus Christ, by the beloved disciple John", Dr Székely recounts in his Preface:-

"The Essene Gospel of Peace is one of the most extraordinary books in history. Since its first edition more than fifty years ago, it has been translated into seventeen languages and has had countless editions and reprints ... Yet none of its publishers – and there have been many, in various countries – have ever made financial profit from its tremendous popularity. They have, without exception, made the book available at cost, motivated by some unseen altruism to place the contents of the Essene Gospel within reach of everyone ..."

Nor, apparently, has it ever been advertised commercially, its message, in truest tradition, being passed directly from one discoverer to another.

Plunging further into the Essene Gospels, it was in Book Four* that I came upon the warning referred to earlier, the warning given by Jesus of the grim destruction of the environment that was to come – his heart-chilling indictment of human folly from which, as from a thunder-clap, rolls forth his prophecy of the doom that threatens us now.

Just eight words suffice to declare it: *Man shall sell his Earthly mother into slavery!*

*

What is this blindness which afflicts us? – and more especially those who, bent on rescuing Gaia's children, furred, feathered or finned – or her own skin and sap, Earth's forests and sacred waters – yet cannot lift their gaze to *Pacha Mama herself?*

---

* An extract from Book Four, containing this passage, is included in "Birthright in Land", in the chapter "Three Fundamentals" towards the end. This same chapter contains Chief Seattle's well-loved speech, "This Earth Is Precious". I have read somewhere that this was probably not actually written by an Indian chief, but is rather of authorship anonymous. If this be the case, it must surely have been written by one acquainted with the Essene Gospels, for some of the phraseology used in both, in describing the destruction of the environment we are now bringing upon ourselves, is quite remarkably similar.

106

Further – what is to be said of that fast declining institution calling itself the 'Christian' church, which not only bows down to our Baalistic land tenure, but has ignored the brightest jewel of all Christ's teaching for our very own predicament at this time?

Then let Earth rather be our temple! For only then shall we worship the Creator aright, great Giver to us of our sacred Gaia – as She herself brings us once more to our senses and we *cease from buying and selling our Earthly Mother!*

*

The loving friend to all who bowed
    Beneath life's weary load,
From lips baptized in humble prayer,
    His consolations flowed.

The faithful witness to the truth,
    His just rebuke was hurled
Out from a heart that burned to break
    The fetters of the world.

No hollow rite, no lifeless creed,
    His piercing glance could bear;
But longing hearts which sought him found
    That God and heaven were there.

                        Samuel Longfellow

*

Part II

Chapter 3

*

"In Quest of Justice"
and Other Writings:
the Legacy of Frances Neilson

Towards an Awakening –

the sound of "fetters breaking"

(Kipling)

*

"In Quest of Justice" and Other Writings: the Legacy of Frances Neilson

*

I do not recollect when I first read Francis Neilson's book "In Quest of Justice" ... only that it was many years ago and that I found it rivetting. With this lasting impression of it, I some years later sent a copy to a friend – one equally inspired by the concept of radical economic justice (so clearly set out by Henry George); and in sorting through some old files in preparation for this book, I came again upon his letter, dated 2nd August 2003 – a letter I now vividly remember receiving. I can think of no better introduction to Francis Neilson's truly fascinating work, and so reproduce this extract from it below:-

> "... The one most important thing to say in this letter is that I received "In Quest of Justice" by Francis Neilson on Saturday, having been awake since before daybreak. The book arrived with the early post and I could not stop reading until late that evening, leaving the last few pages – intentionally.
>
> Absolutely, totally, completely glued me to the spot. Nothing I have read to date has had such an impact on me ... John."

What is it that makes "In Quest of Justice" so compelling a read?

As material which I knew would be an essential ingredient of this book, I re-read "In Quest of Justice" in November 2009 – and to my surprise found it to be a new experience. Earlier, it had been the economic question which had held my attention; now it was – the political! The political question constructed always, of course, upon the economic – but *the political*. That is – the power we know today as more and more spreading its blight of creeping centralization in practically every department of our life; a power which we refer to as *the State*. It was Neilson's findings concerning this political power – findings which turn so much of the history we are taught upside-down – which held me so powerfully this time.

This new experience of Neilson's book reflects, of course, my own journey in the interval. For in more recent decades I have come to see that the radical decentralization of political power is as essential for a free society as is its radical economic decentralization (accomplished via the natural Law of Rent). The political power – which is the robber of our *social power* (the underlying and real 'big society' that has always existed) – is well summed up by A.J. Nock, in his own remarkable writings, in the title of his book – "Our Enemy the State".

The publishers of Neilson's book - (see Acknowledgements) – have kindly allowed me to use freely quotations from his actual words, to present my findings of 2009 in the only way I felt I could: that is, as running notes made from his lectures – (for as such his book originated) – as by a keen young student actually present at them ... which, then, is exactly what I became! (Note: The underlinings in these notes are my own addition, as are any bracketed insertions – points I felt I wanted to highlight – as any student would – as I went along.)

I precede my notes with these brief extracts from the book's covers, which give an idea of the scope of this work – contained in just 120-odd pages.

"In Quest of Justice" is the record of a search for the fundamentals of man's spiritual and physical existence. Francis Neilson defines justice as "the law of Providence inherent in nature", and traces this concept through all the earliest communities – in China, Persia, Egypt, Babylonia, India, Greece and Rome ...

The law is as ancient as justice itself and can be traced through the Old Testament, in Vedic literature, ancient Chinese history, in the Code of Hammurabi ... The landmark was the symbol of economic justice ... "Thou shalt not remove thy neighbour's landmark, (Deuteronomy 19:14) ... (T)he earliest record of the use of the boundary stone has been found in China (2112 B.C.)

The seekers after justice in every age had an identical message ... Economic justice was the tradition of the people ..."

A Student's Notes from "In Quest of Justice"

Lecture I: The Natural Law of Justice.

"... the problems which (Henry) George* set out to solve ... are so ancient that there is scarcely a chronicle of a people's growth and development that does not show how injustices arose, and what evils befell the people <u>under the aegis of the State</u>."

"... the wretches of Rome who fell victim to the curse <u>symbolized by the debt pillar</u>" – which came to take the place where more anciently the sacred landmark had stood. (Inevitable outcome! – and just think of our 'debt pillars' today!) The acknowledgement in earlier times that a <u>just sharing of the earth</u> was the essential basis of a <u>just society</u>.

"... for a long period forms of economic justice were upheld by statutes devised both in pagan States and in Christian realms." How the memory of these primary laws endured in the people themselves, and the roots of Christianity were "embedded deep in pagan soil". (But what would today's 'Christian' churches know about <u>that?</u> - !)

Of how, in India, "the most beneficent systems of government have always been those which have recognised <u>the Village Community</u> as the basis of administration". Sir Henry Maine, a 19th century British Indian magistrate, in his "Ancient Laws".

The "primitive sense of economic justice, which precludes the possibility of their arising in the community one who would <u>batten upon the labour of others by owning the land</u>, is, however, not peculiarly Indian; it is worldwide". From "History of India" by Mountstuart Elphinstone. (Sound observation!)

---

* The great expounder of the natural Law of Rent for our time, his seminal work being "Progress and Poverty", (1879).

"... the records given to us by the investigators of the nineteenth century show that all communities began their economic existence in this way, and <u>only the coming of the political State</u> violated the principles upon which the community established itself. Here is the distinct different between a people governed only by economic law, <u>and one dominated by political law</u>" – (!)

It is made clear by Letourneau, in "Property: Its Origin and Development", that in our ancient past "a system existed not only in India but wherever a village community was established, that was without statute law and the political machinery for enforcing it".

"... there is no greater fallacy in the minds of the people than ... (to believe) that mankind is incapable of looking after itself and that a police force is necessary for keeping it in order. One has only to ... (reflect) upon what exists today under government by force to realize that our modern States are divided into two entirely separate sets of people: the one economic – the producers of wealth; the other political, parasitic – the non-producers who batten upon the produce of labour. As Franz Oppenheimer showed conclusively in his remarkable studies on "The State": <u>the function of the political means is to exploit the economic means.</u> ** (And what more simple illustration of this than the MPs' expenses scandal of 2009? - !)

"Once our minds are free of the fogs of ... lawyers' law, and we are receptive to ideas that our systems of education do not countenance ..." – (!)

** I note that AJ Nock, whose brilliant book "Our Enemy the state" appeared in 1935, was familiar with Oppemheimer's work, which was published two decades earlier.

Socrates' definition of justice: "Justice is the institution of a natural order in which a man can produce food, buildings, and clothing for himself, removing not a neighbour's landmark ... doing his own business, not being a busybody, not taking what is another's, nor being deprived of what is his own ... so that he may ... be his own master, his own law, and at peace with himself."

Further quotations, from Hesiod to Lord Acton (Regius Professor of Modern History at Cambridge), all bear similar witness. "We should now gather from these various sayings and definitions ... that justice is from the beginning and is not a mere legal term as it is understood by men today. Justice is indeed so closely interlinked with the conception of natural law that it is impossible to dissociate the two." Neilson's definition: "Justice is the law of Providence inherent in nature."

How it is a <u>change in our thinking</u> that is required. As H.G. knew – "the kingdom will never be taken by force". Neilson warns against "the danger of over-emphasising the material gain to be achieved by untaxing wealth and taking rent for the use of the community, of which too much has been made in the past". (Neilson was writing in 1944, but is this not still an apt warning? – part of the reason the movement has languished for so long?) How H.G. urged, all through his writings, the need to aspire to "a higher plane of culture". (Cf. Viktor Schauberger's similar warning that "man thinks an octave too low". "Henry George was a social reformer, not a fiscal reformer" – Richard Giles of Australia.)

Maine reminds us: "Of the Statute Law – (i.e. our human legislative devices, as opposed to natural law that is "from the beginning") – it is only necessary to say that it was scanty during the republic, but became very voluminous under the (Roman) empire"– (!) Interesting that, writing of the British empire in India, Dr Wrench noted exactly the same thing. Similarly, in

"The Essene Gospel of Peace", Book 4 – how when man "stepped from the Holy Stream of Life where his body, his thoughts, and his feelings were one with the Law" ... he "began to use only his own deeds, making hundreds of laws, where before there was only One". It is surely a solemnizing thought that, under the 'beneficent' overseership of the E.U., we are now blessed with a labyrinth of these human legislative devices that run into the thousands – or maybe by now it's thousands upon thousands? – that reach out even to the curve of a banana skin! A little pondering upon natural law will surely raise certain doubts as to the 'beneficence' of this overseer!)

"(A)ll ancient communities were <u>economic and not political</u>" – i.e. "private ownership of land was unknown". But equally, every man held and worked his separate piece to produce what he required. No Socialism. It must be kept in mind that "for long, long centuries, both in the ancient empires and in the countries of Christendom, this system was carried on until the land was taken by force from the people and they were reduced to peonage".

"No one has attempted with any degree of success to controvert the axiom that the value of land is created by the community." (Because it is a <u>rental</u> value – not a capital value.)

On this great question of justice, the ancient records show that "the world's deepest thinkers in all the countries gave their ripest days to the study of it and have left us a precious literature which contains in the clearest terms warnings of the disasters that will overtake us if we transgress the laws of nature". Therefore, "while there is time, let us reflect and learn from history the fate that is in store for us".

Lecture II: The Landmark.

In ch. 1 "we found that the settlement of all people who have given us early records was on the communal basis of land for the use of producers ... (and) that <u>absolute private ownership of land for the purpose of exploiting labour was unknown</u>". Here we shall look deeper into "the system ... by which the early communities determined the boundaries of each landuser's plot" – i.e., the landmark.

... How the first attempt to assemble the wide evidence of the adoption of the boundary stone as the landmark is in Fred Verinder's admirable "My neighbour's Landmark" * "Perhaps the earliest record we have of a just economic land settlement is that of China." In a much later period, we have "the Code of Manu", the law book of India – the king advising the planting of trees to mark the boundary limits. "<u>Before the advent of Europeans into India,</u> the soil had never become personal property like ordinary goods. Moreover, the user of the piece of land had no right to sell it. We find the same basic ideas whether we turn to the east or to the west. In lands as far apart as India and Ireland early records show similarities of economic settlement that are amazing." Ireland's Brehon Laws. Similarly with Egypt and Babylonia, as well as Greece and Rome. The god Terminus. These similar laws concerning the landmark are found in the ancient books of peoples "living far apart and with no means of communicating with one another". The landmark was "the basis of existence <u>before the State came into being</u>", while the irreversible decline of civilizations that deserted the landmark writes upon them <u>"like a monstrous epitaph ... the vanity of political action"</u> – (!)

---

* $L$and & Liberty Press Ltd., 1950.

"... men left to themselves to work out their own way of life" did so perfectly intelligently and successfully <u>"without the State and its mercenaries"</u>. This sets a big question-mark beside our conception today "of the necessity of the political State ... for the maintenance of order". How "the prejudice of many of the British commentators on law of the nineteenth century must be held responsible for a great deal of nonsense that has been written by legalists on the importance of the State" – (!)

There was also <u>the Mark</u>, which differed from the landmark. It took in the wasteland around the village community – marked by natural features. Again, it was a custom that was general. How much of the confusion of thought about the Mark in some books of modern authors "may be attributed to the advent of the State and its laws made in defiance of custom" – (!) for a thoroughly reliable work, see "The Saxons of England", by John Mitchell Kemble: "... the Mark is a community of families or households ... and must be assumed (to have met) the demand of society in ... an early stage of development: for example ... for ... supplying ... peace, security and freedom for the inhabitants of the district."

Re slavery in early times, "in nearly every case ... it appears in the record of a people who have migrated and who in their movements to other lands have been engaged in conquest ... war is the mother of slavery (which) is an imperial institution. Tribute is the object for which nations war and ... rent is the essential of all tribute systems ... the means by which free men are put under the yoke." "The Nemesis of Nations" by Romaine Paterson deals with slavery as it arose in Hindustan, Babylon, Greece and Rome, all of which empires crumbled. (And grim reading the book makes, some of the worst conditions being in Greece's silver mines – but I doubt if such things form part of our educational system's 'classical studies' syllabuses!)

The great motto of the Greeks – "Know thyself". If we would rid ourselves of our present woes, we must learn how they came about.

*

[Note: I am omitting my notes on Lecture III "Justice in the Bible", and Lecture IV "Jesus and Justice", having already, I believe, sufficiently explored these two aspects of justice since those notes were made. See my previous chapter.

I would mention however that, interestingly, Neilson – like John Kelly (see previous chapter) – understood exactly what Jesus' reply meant, when the Herodians attempted to trip him up with their question about the tribute money; his reply making fully plain to all present that "if the things that were Caesar's were rendered unto him, Caesar would have nothing and would be obliged to work." Neilson also mentions Ibsen's "Emperor and Galilean" as being the only written work he had come across which perfectly understood Jesus' words.]

Lecture V: The Medievalists and Justice.

The dominant idea of the early Christian Fathers gave us the same gospel as Henry George:-

"No man shall come into our commune who sayeth that the land may be sold. God's footstool is not property." St Cyprian.

God gave the same earth to be cultivated by all. Since, therefore, His bounty is common, how comes it that you have so many fields and your neighbour not even a clod of earth?" St Chrysostom.

"The soil was given to the rich and poor in common. The pagans hold earth as property. They do blaspheme God." St Ambrose.

"They wrongfully think they are innocent who claim for themselves the common gift of God." St Gregory the Great.

("The pagans hold land as property". Where does that place us? - !) These sayings of the Early Fathers make the clearest distinction between land and property – between what the Creator has gifted to man, and what man produces, showing "an economic wisdom" far ahead both of the lawyers of the State and of our popular ideas today. Hence Voltaire's statement – on such a foundation "man should be self-governing". Compare the "utter confusion" of the books of modern economists and sociologists – their false teachings aided, of course, by the "drug of forgetfulness administered to us daily by the State" – (!)

Other remarkable thinkers of these earlier times (spanning 2nd to 13th centuries): Clement of Alexandria, with his "Exhortations to the Greeks"; Boethius – "The Consolation of Philosophy"; Erigena – "De Divisione Naturae". The foregoing, who all looked to the same tradition of justice as that sought by Henry George, lived in what are called the 'Dark' Ages – (by a perversity that could only stem from the political State!)

Coming into the Middle Ages: Bernard of Clairvaux – "The Steps of Humility"; St Thomas Aquinas – "Disputed Questions"; and the great 13th century mystic, Meister Eckhart – "if God were not just, man would not care in the least for God". See his "Book of Divine Confidence". Unlike today's political view of justice as belonging to statute (i.e., mammade) law, all of the foregoing saw justice as "that which was from the beginning". The "amazing labours" of these thinkers of the so-called 'Dark' and Middle Ages.

"While all this essential work of knowledge was pursued in the cloister, the political powers were at work undermining God's constitution. What a story have we here – the civil wars that went on for centuries, the object of which was to take the land – God's footstool, as Bernard of Clairvaux called it – from the people and reduce them to the wages of slavery."

In "Anglo-Saxon England" by F.M. Stenton, ch. XIV, "The Peasants and Their Lords" – "is to be found the clearest statement I have read of the changes that took place from free communities of land users to the degradation of serfdom".

The insurrectionists who, under Wat Tyler and John Bull, marched on London, responded to the King's 'What will ye?' with – 'We will that you free us forever, us and our lands; and that we be never named nor held for serfs'" – (words whose piteousness could hardly be exceeded. They knew what they were going towards – those "satanic mills" that could never have been manned but for the slave labour acquired from <u>land dispossession</u>.) Bernard Gilpin and Hugh Latimer, among others, wrote vividly of the dreadful sufferings of the peasants, now dispossessed; as also did Thomas More.

Difficult to fix a date "when the awful process of denuding the peasant of his land began in Europe ... when the first Peasant Wars were waged against the land-greed of the nobles" – but in England, roughly the time of Richard II. "From the peak of favourable conditions for the English labourer, which was reached in the reign of Henry VII, there comes a swift decline which reduced the peasantry to beggary and starvation. Such was the result of taking the land from the people."

With Henry VIII came the dissolution of the monasteries, and increased power of the nobles via land seizures – the monastic lands too falling into their hands. The iniquitous Statute of Labourers of 1351 – to stop the rise in wages following the Black Death. "The assumption of political power (by the land-grabbers) was complete".

Edward VI's parliament passed laws of the utmost cruelty, including beating, branding and chaining of the "slave", (as he was now openly called) – and execution if he twice ran away.

These terrible times succeeded the <u>enlightened</u> ages – (which we have been deliberately brainwashed into calling 'Dark').

Now the guiding principles of the great early philosophers were completely lost in "the rationalistic orgy of what has been called the Renaissance". Thomas Cromwell's reign completed the destruction of the economic system which had endured in large part up to the end of the Wars of the Roses. "Liberty took flight", and none dared protest.

This was no mere quarrel between two factions of the church, as we have been led to believe. The real issue went far deeper. JR Green's "A Short History of the English People" (published late 19th century) gives an incomparable account of what was really taking place, which began with the economic change in the condition of the people via forced enclosures. Meanwhile the political power, becoming concentrated in the hands of the great landlords, rose to its greatest height, and everything that was worth the name of honest dealing was swept away ... A palsy fell upon many of the monasteries which had been the centres of communal life. In looking more deeply into these changes, that came so rapidly, we shall find that the terms Renaissance and Reformation "have been used to cover a multitude of the grossest evils".

Out of the 'Dark' Ages there arose the glory of the Gothic. When men were free they built the cathedrals of Europe. Visiting these cathedrals, we can contemplate the kinds of men who created such marvels.

Green's "Short History of the English People" tells the true tale both of the fatal destruction of real learning (as the monasteries were swept away), and equally of the degradation of the people, which were the underlying reality of the times vaunted as the great Renaissance and Reformation periods; and, in summary, of how "the peasants of Europe were reduced to a slave status" – which the four hundred years since have done nothing to reverse.

Lecture VI: The Political Economists and Justice.

This period of the Renaissance and Reformation lasted c. 250 years, from early 14th to mid 16th century. See especially ch. IX of vol. 2 of Spengler's "Decline of the West" – for "all the awful consequences of the liberation of what he calls the ego".

"The emancipation of the self, abandoning the rules and disciplines which gave to the Middle Ages its distinctive character of equity and orderliness, turned man amock in nearly every activity of life, and led to orgies of devil worship and witchcraft that made bedlam of every country in Europe for many generations." How the changes that had now taken place "caused bewildered man to cast off the spiritual chains of the church" and instead "shackle himself to the war-chariot of the State".

If the Renaissance was a mark of "the rebellion of the ego", Neilson sees in it something more: that, even if indirectly, it was connected with "the desire of the ego to batten upon the labour of others".

The end of the 14th century marked the beginning of the period "when the political power realized it could entrench itself securely by exploiting the economic power". Increased wealth went with increased poverty and vagrancy. The stronger the State became under the Tudors, the "more widespread the economic woe for the victims of the conspiracy ... The supremacy of the ego was the aggrandisement of the landlord, and it is on landlordism in Europe that we must squarely place the blame for our present woe.

Remarkably, however, towards the close of the reign of Elizabeth, men's minds began to turn back to an examination of the principles upon which the liberties of the people were originally founded, and a school of what is known as political economists arose. In 1594 appeared Richard Hooker's "Ecclesiastical Polity" – which in turn inspired John Locke's "Of Civil Government". Unfortunate that Hooker's great work – which dealt with the whole realm of economics, religion and politics – has been so neglected by Georgists. It influenced other such writers right to the time of Henry George's "Progress and Poverty".

Locke's work, in turn, even influenced big landholders in the House of Lords to <u>support</u> a land rental value tax as against a salt tax, in Walpole's government in 1732 – (!)

It is remarkable that with Hooker, Locke, Adam Smith and Kant, the greatest minds in Europe turned again to the same inquiries as had attracted the leading thinkers of earlier times – and Henry George's writings reveal his own deep study of them all.

*

BUT WHAT HAS HAPPENED TO THIS GREAT LEGACY SINCE – SO BRILLIANTLY SET BEFORE US BY NEILSON?

THE POLITICAL POWER – WHICH STRUCTURES AND OVERSEES OUR EDUCATION – HAS A GREAT DEAL MORE TO ANSWER FOR THAN JUST THE PERVERSION OF OUR ECONOMICS.

*

"Systematic, universal brain-washing is the crime, tendentious mental conditioning calculated to mislead students, to impoverish their ability, to bend their minds to the service of a system that funnels power and wealth to a parasitic minority!"

Thus Professor Mason Gaffney well sums up the achievement of our educational institutions today. (See "The Corruption of Economics", Shepheard-Walwyn, 1994.)

Fortunately, to re-educate ourselves, we now have the legacy of Francis Neilson to build upon that of Henry George – George, who so vividly foresaw the corruption at every level which would ultimately destroy any society that failed to root out land monopoly. (See his chapter "How Modern Civilization May Decline", in "Progress and Poverty").

Francis Neilson, with his scholarly researches added to the deeply perceptive gaze which (like Henry George) he brings to bear on the scene, now reveals to us that that entire political realm, which has so persecuted man ever since it arose from its land monopoly origins, is in fact an imposter in the scene, and an entirely unnatural growth upon the body social. Moreover – that in the long history of man's settlement on this earth, it is a comparatively late-comer on the scene as well; and that man, through long ages in earlier times, managed his social affairs far better without it. For so long as the landmark, or boundary stone, was respected, an entirely different morality ruled – it was well understood that if you did not work you did not eat.

In his book, "A Short History of Progress", Ronald Wright – pointing out how states "arrogate to themselves the power of coercive violence" – refers to this "venomous bloom" of the state in the brilliantly descriptive phrase he quotes from J.M. Coetzee (in the latter's book "Waiting for the Barbarians") – as "the black flower of civilization".

From the work of both A.J. Nock and Francis Neilson, we now know that such "coercive violence", being the innate character of the State, the political State is "the black flower of civilization" itself!

As we have seen, the demise of this treacherous bloom will come about when man finally wakens from that "long bad dream" which "makes him mutter and moan". It is a flower in whose withering away we shall doubly rejoice – as it takes with it the shadow of a certain black cat that has long been hiding under its parasol.

*

What, finally of the "other writings" of Francis Neilson mentioned in the heading to this chapter? Times, alas, is running out – but I was determined at least to speak of his masterly dealing with Plato's "Republic", which presents to us Socrates' famous colloquium on this subject with his student friends.

Now, on reaching back to that tray of Neilson's other books laid aside last autumn, to my delight I have re-discovered a copy of a letter I now recall writing at the time to a friend, describing my huge enjoyment of this chapter in Neilson's book "The Eleventh Commandment".

Here, then, is what I wrote, on 16th November 2010:-

One thing I have done in the past couple of weeks is indulge in reading more of Francis Neilson: "Modern Man and the Liberal Arts", The Eleventh Commandment" and "The Cultural Tradition". He is just the most brilliant writer, because of the vast erudition and scholarly intellect that he can bring to bear on what he reads, *along with* his incisive Geoist perspective.

His taking apart of what the normal run of critics have made of Plato's "Republic" puts you in stitches ...! Socrates was brilliant – he saw the essential *economic* foundation of life on earth* - while today's generally-read-by-students critics of this dialogue, (just like the contemporary people who held the dialogue with him) – are all swimming in the rarified upper atmosphere of the *political* scenario, feet well off the ground. Socrates makes mince-meat of his contemporaries, but *gently,* and they are so blind they do not even see what he has done with them! Neilson's critique of "The Republic" must be a *unique* piece of writing – and if I were a teacher, how I would love to take it with my class! And what they would *learn* from it – as Socrates makes fools

---

*See where quoted on p. 118.

of his questioners and they don't see it! One's pupils would learn from it in the *best* way – from sheer enjoyment!

All that I will add to this is, firstly, my note that in "Modern Man and the Liberal Arts", Neilson's two chapters on the dispossession of the English peasantry – along with Dr Wrench's fine work on this – does for England what Andy Wightman has now done so splendidly for Scotland, with greater thoroughness, in his recently published book "The Poor Had No Lawyers!, (Birlinn Ltd, 2010).

Finally, from "The Cultural Tradition", as my closing piece, a passage to make us pause indeed – with the preamble leading up to it. (From my notes made as for "In Quest of Justice"):-

> England has never recovered from the economic changes brought about by the Acts of Enclosure, which deprived the common people of their birthright in land, and scattered them abroad. In The Winter's Tale and other plays, Shakespeare gives us a hint of the terrible conditions of the time ...
>
> Most of the great civilizations of the past fell into decay and their vaunted empires to ruins, the last of their survivors being reduced to the status of the fellaheen. (Exactly as it is with us today – only our fellaheen are the inhabitants of our terrible inner city ghettos.)
>
> As Lord Russell says, it is stupidity and ignorance that have brought us to this pass. The saying that "Salus populi suprema est lex" – the welfare of the people is the supreme law – is today an empty figure of speech, so far has a civilization of megalomaniacs carried us on the road to destruction. In the old days men had a far, far higher sense of their rights than they have now. Yet here and there people are beginning to understand that the human basis of today's political democracies (so-called) is a landless proletariat.

We may well ask ourselves, as we slide towards the same collapse as those civilizations of the past:–

"... (W)hat man today, who must compete for a job in the labour market, join a union, and be under the dictatorship of a labour czar, would not change places as a politically free man with the serf of the Middle Ages, who had twelve acres, a hut, privileges in the lord's forest, and could earn sufficient in thirteen weeks to keep himself and family for a year?"

*

Part III

*

Kaleidoscope

including...

Author's Writings ...

Reclaiming our Language – Imposter Terms

Scenes from a Tapestry

Other Scenarios

Amazing Grace and the Music of the Spheres

Of The Spirit

In Farewell

The intuitive mind is a sacred gift and the rational mind is a faithful servant. We have created a society that honours the servant and has forgotten the gift.

(Albert Einstein)

Chapter 1

*

Author's Writings

– Subsequent to publication of
"Birthright in Land ...", 1999

Articles

Letters

Reviews

The Wizard of Planning Law
– and of much else besides ... DEBT!*

I n the ongoing saga of the plans for the Curling Rink we may well deplore the lack of amenity space, but this is only part of the picture of which we need to see the whole.

I remember vividly a visit I made some years ago to Perth & Kinross's Planning Department, when a map was brought out and it was shown me that the great difficulty lay in obtaining land. Against what we are taught to believe, that 'land is scarce' – here is the truer picture given us by Jason Cowley of the New Statesman:

'The UK's top five landowners (excluding the Crown Estates, the Ministry of Defence and the Forestry Commission), are: 1) The Duke of Buccleugh: Acreage 270,900 (with value £598m and Subsidy Entitlement £20.4m) and 2) Estate of Atholl Dukedom: Acreage 147,000 (with value £200m and Subsidy Entitlement £11.0m) ...'

So, land is not scarce, it is simply locked-up – with the two top landowners sitting right here in Scotland. Presumably, we are not meant to notice such things! – (not to mention the subsidies).

What next in the economic scenario – which translates into the political order of course? The engrossed monopoly of land then further engrosses itself by a huge suctioning of capital – (including those subsidies) – to the sphere of monopoly. Hence *monopoly capitalism* – (we should call our system by its right name).

Thus, society grows its million-and-billionaires ... whose next wish is to take over Rannoch. Is it possible that such a power could have overlooked the political sphere of Planning? Indeed not, as we know from the Scottish Government's piece of 2008 legislation, which skewed Public Inquiries firmly in favour of the developers. No wonder, then, if smaller fry, struggling with this Wizard to achieve their own vision for their communities, too

---

* O riginally published in Comment, Sept. 2009. New title here. See Acknowledgements.

often feel that, somewhere behind the scenes, a hidden power is busy turning Burns's words upside-down on us, as it *'looks and laughs at a' that'*.

But the ingenuity of this Wizard ever finds fullest play in his original hunting-ground, the land, for here the takeover is a three-pronged business. *Firstly* there is the land itself (which it is obvious we all have equal birthright to). *Secondly,* via corrupt human legislation, the people are got to pay rent to one who gives them nought in return – for not even a wizard made the land. But *thirdly* – whence originate these capital sums that change hands in the land market, when land was a free gift and costless? We don't pause to see that these are, in fact, the rent under another guise – now set up to win large collateral at the bank; or bundled up, in advance, for sale in expectation of years of 'safe' pillaging ahead (in a society under his spell), and most of it representing the purely paper value of its monopoly content.

We can now see the huge power exerted over us by a false educational system, which denies us knowledge of the salvation awaiting us all in the Law of Rent. For this natural law reveals that the rental values of the land, being created by the community and not by the individual, belong to no person, but to the community itself where they arise. Thus, they are, logically, society's original true social revenue – (and as such indeed, they served for some 250 years following the Norman Conquest)*.

Further, the fact that the land is local, and that its values are best known locally, indicates that these rents are best collected and disbursed locally too – which surely signifies that society is predestined to be decentralist in form – with all its developments evolving organically as the local inhabitants wish, and falling within the competence of the community itself.**

---

* See Richard Colden's speech to the House of Commons on 14th March 1842.

** See especially following article, "The Unsuspected Lynchpin".

Meanwhile in transgression of this natural law (and of sheer common sense) we are taught – we believe – and we award degrees in economics – according to the myth that land is capital – as if by some magic issuing from the industrial efforts of man! But how could it be otherwise, with Watchful Wiz overseeing our curriculums?

How long until we see that the whole political set-up which oversees and endorses such a system is hollow? How long till we recognise that the colossal 'debt' we are wrestling with is itself a Whiz-wiz conjuration? For by our grasping of the fact that the rental values of the land, community-created, are owed back to the community, the spell of this hideous 'debt' is broken – by the natural magic of the natural Law of Rent.

We now see how this colossal 'debt' is in reality an upside-down people's credit – bar its invented content, (the monopoly element in the rentals, and the 'legerdemain' entries in the banks' ledgers in expectation of those monopoly reapings, all of which are but paper representing no actual wealth, nor then debt either).

We see further, how this people's credit has been deliberately turned upside-down, to maintain a regime of land lordship that has taken from us both our land and its rents, with every sphere of society suffering its grim repercussions; a regime now setting its sights on the last of the community assets that we thought were ours, its 'slow stain' spreading, even it seems, to such places as Pitlochry's Kingfisher Bar.

No wonder, then, if we are squeezed dry and cannot pay our mortgages. No wonder if the banks are laughing up their sleeves at us – and that the State, hand-in-glove with them behind the scenes, appears incapable of exercising any real control! They've all got us just where they wanted, and they know we'll never work it out ... until we have worked out The Land Question!

Note:

The above article casts no aspersions upon any individual, no matter what may be their position within the present system. It is the structure of our society that is at fault, and no individual is to blame for that. It is a responsibility in which we all share, and the united efforts of us all are needed to restructure it aright.

*

See further chapter "Community and Re-Empowerment' in "Birthright in Land ..." ISBN 0 9535426 0 2.

Community Empowerment
The Unsuspected Lynchpin!*

Centralisation

The American Ralph Borsodi interestingly worked out how it was that his wife provided for them more cheaply by canning and preserving home-grown produce, than by buying in from factories with all their advantages of mass production. He stumbled on a natural law overlooked by economists – namely, that whatever the economies achieved by centralising production, these were always overtaken by the attendant *dis*economies of the distribution that must follow.[1]

The same concealed falsity today roams the political sphere, in the supposed economies of ever-increasing centralisation of political power – now increasingly trampling our communities. (Holyrood – Westminster – Brussels ... where next?) Here the 'distribution' is in the form of rivers of communication that exhaust everything in their wake from forests to frayed tempers. Anyone arriving from another planet where life was lived more sanely, would think we were crazy to carry on as we do!

How much longer are we going to endure this madness? – or how many more battles, up and down Scotland, ere we weary of it? For a surprisingly simple way, in fact, exists for communities to take back – in a way that cannot be refused – power over their own lives; a way to realise that "political self-sufficiency" raised by Comment.

The Power of Local Revenue Creation

There has been some discussion in Comment's pages, in recent years, about the locally-created revenue that flows from the

* M ain body of an article published in Comment, Dec. 2009. New title here. See Acknowledgements.

land's rental values via the natural Law of Rent, and about how this should be collected and disbursed locally. But what about the power of *assessing* those rental values? Has anyone yet paused to consider the implications of *that*? Certainly one such pause, made recently by one inhabitant of Highland Perthshire, on this very matter, proved of quite extraordinary outcome!

One day early in September, while sitting in the porch and pondering the threat to Rannoch of which I had just been reading in the latest Comment, I found the words unexpectedly forming themselves in my mind. *"Open Thou mine eyes that I may behold wondrous things out of Thy law"* (Psalm 119). I thought – that's strange! – because it's the Law of Rent I'm thinking about! I was considering its application to the Rannoch situation. Nothing further came, and so presently I got up and fetched the issue of Comment with the Rannoch article in it, wondering if it could afford me any further clues. And suddenly – I saw it!

For years it had been obvious to me that, in the operating of this Law of Rent, land being local, the rents must be locally collected and disbursed – thus beautifully opening the way for the economic empowerment of local communities. But this would not be enough, of course, were a centralised political power still to claim authority over the use to which the land was put. (Windfarms and Donald Trumps and the Beauly-Denny Line, "for the greater good" ...) Now, suddenly, here in our hands, as yet unrecognised, was the very lynchpin that had been missing from our situation – the point where the political power intersected with the economic – and the *economic* carried the political with it!

Land Beyond Price

It was an electrifying moment! It had always seemed obvious that the power to assess these rentals must lie with the local community, as those best knowing these values at first hand. But now I suddenly saw that the power to assess these rentals need not limit itself to placing an actual rental value on all land. Land could be assessed just as truly – and far more truthfully – as being *beyond* any rental value, as being to that community precisely *'beyond value and beyond price'*. I saw that the community now had the freedom to declare that there was land which should be placed beyond the reach of any development at all – whether vulgar or industrial; land that was to be treasured in itself, for its value to the community for *what it was* – an especially precious part of our homeground.

I saw, moreover, that the same power would operate in our towns, to preserve vital areas of green space and to rule against developments considered out-of-place, while in our larger towns and cities (whose unnatural growth is wholly due to dispossessed populations) the politico-economic power will rest with the various village-sized areas which make up such towns, and whose plight is frequently as desperate.[2]

Thus the Law of Rent places in our hands this supreme gift: to write upon our environment itself what it means to us.

Does this seem too utopian a prospect? I said earlier that the way for communities to take back power into their own hands was one that cannot be refused. This is because it is an introvertible fact – which the illustrated Law of Rent makes fully visible for all to see[3] – that, under the present structure of society, the people are robbed of both their land and its rents. No political body confronted with the illustrated Law of Rent will be able to deny this, and the present ignoring by the Establishment of this twofold robbery depends entirely upon the knowledge of this natural law being kept suppressed.

Galvanising Threats

Perhaps these burgeoning development threats are just what we needed to galvanise us. For it is communities at present embroiled in battles over planning, and distraught at what threatens them, which by working together can finally break the silence on this fundamental, incontrovertible economic law – by acquainting themselves thoroughly with it, sharing their knowledge of it, and encouraging others to do likewise.

Certainly nothing fundamental is going to change – there will continue these incessant battles with a bullying Establishment – until the people themselves arise, unite their forces, speak with one voice, *and make that voice heard*. Nobody else is going to do it for us – (and certainly no political body). The vista of a free, empowered and happy life opens before us – but we have to make the effort ourselves to enter that 'promised land'.

This recognition of the political potential of the Law of Rent leads to a deeper understanding of the uniqueness of this system of public revenue. For it is one that achieves the wedding of a system of revenue which is a blessing to the people, with a system of land governance which blesses the land, as stemming from those whose home ground it is. No other system of public revenue does this. Of no other system can it be said that it truly blesses land and people alike, (while of course entirely dispensing with the curse of taxation).

It will surprise many to learn that this is how life was once lived, for long stretches of time, by people across the globe. For as long as the vital *landmark*, which delineated the boundaries of land, ensuring a continuing birthright in land for all, was held sacred, no political layer of society existed at all, for there was nothing to bring it into existence.[4] Thus there is nothing utopian about the concept of living free from the shackles of political power.

For local communities to federate together for certain joint ventures, (while ever retaining the essential economic purse-strings), a helpful patterning towards such a structure is provided by the Bioregional movement – active so far mainly in North America and Canada. Indeed the Bioregional movement and the Land Rent movement need to get together, for they are made for one another! - (albeit the former has yet to discover the natural Law of Rent).

Here is a brief but apt quotation from a founder of the Bioregional movement which catches the fuller vision, above, of a society governed by that natural law: *"Imagine a society divided into territories and communities where love of place is an inevitable by-product of a life lived mindful of natural systems and of patterns experienced daily – however far removed this may seem just now from the gigantic, destructive society around us."* (Kirkpatrick Sale, in The Ecologist, 22 Feb 02).

It is *political self-sufficiency*, bestowed by the natural Law of Rent, which opens the path to that new society.

*

References

(1) Acknowledgements to John-Paul Flintoff's *Through the Eye of a Needle*, a treasure of a book with some hilarious passages. (Green Books, 2009).

(2) One need only mention officialdom's shameful closing of the Ark cafe near Waverly Station in Edinburgh – or its attempts to build a giant incinerator right in the town of Perth.

(3) See *The Land Question* – this is available as a free download at http://www.commentonline.co.uk/supplement/index.htm

(4) See *In Quest of Justice*, by Francis Neilson, also the works of Dr G T Wrench.

The Beauly-Denny Folly*

**Proposal passed by the Scottish Government in 2009
to erect some 600 super-giant pylons right down the spine of
Scotland, through some of the most picturesque scenery
- in the face of much expert testimony against.**

*

The repercussions of the Scottish government's recent decision on the Beauly-Denny Line rumble on, but to understand that decision we must look far deeper than present controversy has reached.

It is not government but behind-the-scenes big business that makes the decisions today – whether it be for wars against foreign lands or warfare against the people at home. Hence public inquiries are followed later by the bluffing – or dithering – of ministers under questioning.

The reason our landscape – as our society – is in the hands of big business is because our land is in the hands of big business. For land monopoly – which dispossesses a people of their land, and so renders them powerless over both rural and urban scenarios – is the biggest business of all, along with its natural offspring, monopoly capitalism.

Moreover, this all-underlying landed interest has, through the ages, used every possible legislative device to secure the ongoing disempowering of the people, in unseen ways. Thus in 1965 an Act was passed which, by subtly changing the goal-posts, re-patterned our agriculture – and so, vast stretches of our countryside as well, with huge loss of wildlife habitats. Agricultural productivity was no longer measured as *per acre*, its only true measure, but *per man unit* – as though labour were scarce! This allowed the useful 'logic' of a new land clearance, and in place of labour the exhaltation of big machinery, crude

---

* First published in Commentonline, January, 2010.
See Acknowledgements.

artificial fertilizers and batteries of poison sprays – which have naturally taken their toll on our health and brought big profits to big business. By the same 'logic' further legislation has served to turn our own tax-money against us, in ways of which we have little idea.

Since this system of run-away greed controls both our legislature and our executive, we must understand clearly that no human legislation will now protect our environment – as the Beauly-Denny business makes plain. For this decision was given in the face of a quite extraordinary opposition of both organizations and individuals – and with experts in energy contributing their support.

But if no human legislation can save our landscape, where then can we look for help? Right to hand! For we have neglected – that is, the people have been held in long ignorance of – a certain natural law, whose operations have power over unnatural land monopoly. This law is the great natural social Law of Rent. As already seen in past articles in Comment (most recent Sept and Dec 09), this natural law demolishes at a stroke the false land market (key to land hoarding and monopolising) by revealing land's phoney capital price to be in origin its annual rental value – a value created entirely by the presence and activities in the community and hence owed back to it. Thus the cancelling of land monopoly restores to the community its revenues along with its land.

Hopefully those concerned about our environment will now – from the Beauly-Denny fiasco – finally grasp that if they would save our landscape they must at last control our fundamental situation of land monopoly; a force which, having largely destroyed our society, reeling under its social ills, is now fixated upon our environment. By doing so – by adding their voice to the cry for essential fundamental reform – they will also save themselves from being duped in future by this all-underlying monster of consuming greed.

We must now examine briefly, in the interests of us all, the true identity of today's cry for these huge sustainable energy schemes; for curiously it shares, certain features of cunning with our old 'friend', land monopoly.

If we are really serious about renewable energy – then first and foremost what about that most elementary and 'green' energy of all – renewable after only a good night's sleep! – the energies of the human body? Pushed off the land, running waste in our cities from enforced unemployment – (land monopoly's great tool for keeping wages down) – hordes of these wasted lives now roam our society, whether sunk in obesity, or – finding no fit outlet for the fiery energies of youth – in orgies of violence, abuse or escapism, wreak their vengeance on a society which has no place for their energies – or for them.

Is social havoc on the one hand destroying us? – and 'affordable housing' escaping us on the other? Young people's primary need is to fly the next and build a shelter for themselves. With disabling land monopoly once removed from the scene – (with its peculiarly disabling effect upon our thinking!) – we might then see that what we are looking at is not two different intractable problems, but one grand solution to them both! Exactly as Permaculture teaches – to turn our problems around and find we have solutions instead! And simple bender dwellings are within the scope of anyone.

In the new scenario of freedom, with a flow of land from former large estates – (Scotland at present is more feudal than Brazil) – hence with a people standing at last on their own feet, on their own soil: is it really possible to imagine that the inventive Scots – combining their engineering skills and innovative genius – could fail to produce all the energy they need in mini-scale, leaving unmarred the land that is their home?

Of course other matters come into the equation too. Scotland is to become "the green supplier of Europe", we hear. But what is that Chinese proverb about the best way to feed a hungry man being – not to give him a fish but to teach him how to fish himself? Just so, by far our best export in the sustainable energy field would be the example of what we have done for ourselves – especially as we would be 'exporting' just land tenure at the same time!

Can we not imagine the derisory words that would flow from Burns's pen at his proposed 'homecoming' to such a 'home' as is now planned! – while the idea that a Scotland so prostituted to big business should be the land that Wallace suffered and died for, is something too hideous to contemplate.

But what of the factories we so depend on at present? It is so difficult to unwind our paralysed thinking! In the new scenario of freedom, big conglomerates lose their hold, and craftwork flourishes. Meanwhile, I wonder if our economic students are ever referred to the passage in the works of Scotland's famous Adam Smith, where he acknowledges that factory work causes "mental mutilation"?* Plenty of others have said the same – most notably Gandhi. To mutilate one's landscape for the mental mutilation of one's people – or any people – seems a poor sort of bargain!

Moreover, what of the part these factories play in today's mammoth carbon footprint from our gas-guzzling commuterdom? – the daily droves departing for those 'all-worshipful' companies of job-bestowers – factory jobs being a huge part of the scene? Another huge plus for those screaming for sustainable energy, surely – for gone would be that crazy commuterdom, and its huge carbon footprint with it.

Having touched on commuterdom – what of computerdom in this new society? It should hardly surprise us that the whole pathway of modern IT, having developed under the 'vampire' of monopoly capitalism that cares for neither land nor people, is the source of

---

* A powerful statement from him, as he had to hold his pen in check, from the misfortune of having as his patron one of Scotland's foremost dukes!

huge pollution, both in its manufacturing and in its running – a pollution in which inevitably we are ourselves caught up.* Hopefully the rediscovering of the real environment in our new freedom – the wonder of earth, water, mountains, sky, stars – will presently woo us to more interesting occupations. And who knows, Gaia may well be about to nudge us in that direction anyway!

Nor must we forget the host of energy-drainers that we shall be rid of: the emptying of our prisons, and timely demise of the armies of rescue services a sick society requires. Plus – as communities take back power over themselves – quangos galore ... For all these, and more, must be put in balancing 'contra' scales.

Can Scotland do it? – can she resurrect herself? Read ch. 7 of Tom Johnson's "History of the Working Classes in Scotland" – and weep for what has been lost ... or rather, take heart from it! And need it be said that such a people as the opening of that chapter describes, would never have allowed their landscape to be vandalised.

All cultures are rooted in the spiritual, and the cry *"I will lift up mine eyes unto the hills ..."* is a cry from the soul in all ages. Those who understand the land question will not be tricked. Today's fevered cry for sustainable energy on a grand scale has a familiar ring to it, for it comes not from energy-need but from energy-greed – and boomerangs in the face of its utterer, the one great Unsustainable for any society: that old devil, Land Monopoly itself – intent upon keeping us enserfed.

There is a brilliant saying by Thomas Jefferson, American president and radical decentralist: that the idea that one man, or

---

* See "Environment & Health News" 2000; 4:3 (15) p.23, (from Muir of Logie, Forres IV36); The Kompetenzinitiative at www.kompetenzinitiative.de; Numerous articles in WDDTY *(What Doctors Don't Tell You)*, including recent Dec. 09.

one body of men, can rightly oversee the affairs of a nation, is "the acme of absurdity". We see again that small clique at St Andrews House, seat of the Scottish government, who have given the go-ahead for the Beauly-Denny Line – and suddenly we recognise the scene for what it is: the latest performance in that pantomime of "the acme of absurdity" which Jefferson so brilliantly spells out.

For those who would take a stand for our land of Scotland, there is but one way forward: a demand for the instituting of the natural Law of Rent, for an end to land monopoly.

Can we do it? I think of that line from G K Chesterton (as uttered north of the Border): *We are the people of Scotland who have not spoken yet!*

*

Postscript*: Campaigners have learned that the hidden but real agenda of the government in holding all these purportedly "public consultations", is to draw all the organisations opposing a development into their net, so as to have, in writing from them, their strongest points of opposition.

From this exercise, the government is then able to discover, from the Reporter's final written submission on the matter, whether in going forward with their plan (fully decided upon ere the consultation was begun), they would be completely in the clear, or whether, in deciding 'subsequently' in favour of the proposed development, there was any point on which they could be caught out legally.

A useful exercise is thus made of the "consultation", by the government – while a trusting public is most thoroughly "duped", indeed, by these repeated stage-shows of "consultations", which indeed are meaningless. And it explains too why the government can so lightly ignore, at the conclusion, even certain points of advice from the Reporter – (as has happened with the Beauly-Denny Line). Thus are the people quietly made a laughing-stock of. Simone Weil, the French philosopher and activist, wrote that she knew of nothing more painful than watching simple but honest folk being made fools of by the legal process in France. I feel we know it now at first hand.

---

* The above – published usefully in the printed Comment of February 2010, as a pointer to my article in Commentonline – was rushed off to Comment subsequently, on its deadline, following a certain 'fascinating encounter'!

The Rise of Globalization!*

The article, "Fermented Stimulants and the Rise of Globalization" (PCA #51), contains much of interest, but I would like to fill in a gap in its description of how globalization arose. The article states that "sugar and its associated fermented stimulant commodities ... gave birth to colonial rule on a global scale", but in the following paragraph admits that "if the people who work the fields had any measure of control over the land they worked, they would be growing food to eat, not luxury stimulants for [others]." That is, at the base of the whole ugly edifice of globalization lie the strictures placed upon the mass of people in their relationship to the land: they may work it, but only at the behest, and the direction, of the landed overlord (literally, the "Superior", as our legal terminology here in Scotland put it! – only recently annulled).

Therefore, in the writer's next paragraph, where he states that today "the primary mode of domination has shifted to subtler instruments of global capital, such as the International Monetary Fund, and World Bank," I must place a question mark by the word "primary". It may appear so, but in reality, not one whit has it shifted. Domination's foundation is, and forever remains, the original dispossession of the people from their land. We are so used to turning a blind eye upon this foundational scenario, so trained not to notice it, that we just do not see it any more. This does not alter the fact. For it is upon this foundation that the whole gamut of these "subtler instruments of global capital" took – and take – their rise.

The historical process is clearly traced for us by the early 20th-century American, Gustavus Myers, in a fascinating volume

* First published in The Permaculture Activist, USA.
Issue 54 – November 2004.

Entitled *History of the Great American Fortunes* (The Modern Library, 1907, republished 1936). Although he was a contemporary of Henry George, it seems that Myers was innocent of any knowledge of his fellow-countryman's work, and knew nothing of the Law of Rent. He simply records what he saw unfolding before his eyes, as these American fortunes built themselves up from their first foundations – the incomparable fortune-building foundation of the monopolizing of land! His book needs digging out from libraries again, since it shows us so exactly whence arose these industrial giants, whose masked faces it is we find greeting us once more in the global commerce and banking scenarios of today.

Forced Labour

Underpinning this whole global business there is, naturally, a distinctive political philosophy. Let us examine this as we get it straight from the horse's mouth: the evidence given before the Native Labour Commission, Kenya (under British rule), 1912-13, "Settler after settler came before the Commission and demanded in the most precise terms that the natives should be forced out of 'Reserves' to work for wages, by clearing their land so that they should have less than they could live on. Lord Delamere, himself owner of 150,000 acres, said: 'If this policy is to be continued that every native is to be a landholder of a sufficient area on which to establish himself, then the question of obtaining a satisfactory labour supply will never be settled'." (From "A Lesson from History", by W.R. Lester, *Progress,* Australia, July 1992). Those who desire a "satisfactory labour supply" are, of course, those who possess big reserves of land and capital with which to employ it, on their terms.

Let us not be naive enough to believe that this political philosophy was born of colonialism. Good heavens, no! Britain was simply transferring to her colonies that practical political philosophy by which she (her ruling elite that is) had already successfully dispossessed her own people of their land well before, through such measures as the enclosure of the commons and the more recent Highland Clearances. Even that arch-enemy of capitalism, Karl Marx, ultimately came to see that "the root of all capitalist exploitation is the expropriation of the peasant from the soil" (though this later conclusion of his is naturally not to be found in the generally circulating editions of Das Kapital). Here is how another brilliant 20th-century American writer, A J Nock, sums it up: "Expropriation must precede exploitation. There is no other way to make the political means effective." (From *Our Enemy the State*, a slim but terrific volume, and just another that needs rescuing from a long oblivion.)

No other way! What other way, indeed, could there be? For although crude shackle slavery was outlawed in America in the late 19th century, just as in Russia there was a much trumpeted freeing of the serfs, there was nought for either these ex-slaves, or ex-serfs to do, since they were landless, but virtually to sell themselves back to their former masters for a job at any price. And just to increase their woes, these former masters now wielded major power over capital as well as land. The following illuminating passage is from Gustavus Myers: "The inevitable rule ... has been to utilize the surplus revenues in the form of rents [i.e., what was not required to allow these landowners to live in idleness and luxury] "in investments in a great number and variety of corporations. Thus ... [they] finally became not only great landlords, but sharers in the centralized ownership of the country's transportation systems and industries". Note the word "centralized". What, then, are the global reaches of industry, commerce and banking today, but merely the inevitable and logical extension of these same avidly centralizing, land-robbery-based powers?

The forces of globalization will never be defeated until we cease our fixation with what appear to us as the World Bank, transnational corporations, and so on, and recognize these

21st-century disguises for what they are: simply the more sophisticated masks of that same savage force of land-grabbing and dispossession which has been operating on this planet for centuries, and for centuries making the children of Gaia its slaves. It is time we ended our fascination with what are merely the outward trappings of the one unchanging, all-underlying power; time that we discerned the essential nature of these cunning overlords who are now operating a global economy. For then only will their power be dismantled, when its false basis is understood.

The Roots of Power

Even Leopold Kohr, in his otherwise splendid *Breakdown of Nations*, does not see where it all springs from, as he ponders Hitler's rise to power. It is left to the Austrian Bruno Heilig, a leading journalist of his time, to tell us. Heilig, as foreign editor and correspondent of newspapers in Austria, Germany, Hungary and the Balkans, saw and recorded Hitler's drive to the top, and subsequently survived Dachau and Buckenwald to write his grim account, *Men Crucified*.

Heilig wrote, "The Nazi regime is not Hitler's, the man's, achievement. Nazidom has grown organically out of a rotten democracy, and the rottenness of that democracy is the natural consequence of unequal economic conditions; and unequal economic conditions obtain all over the world owing to the instituted private appropriation of the rent of land. Therefore every country is potentially a Fascist country ... The private appropriation of the rent of land is the deadly enemy of mankind." (*From Why the German Republic Fell.*)

Do we see Fascism on the rise again today? Then let us note. We have been warned.

Later in the article about the sugar economy, (from which I learned so much of interest), is the statement: "Resistance takes place on many planes ... The cumulative choices we make about food have profound implications". While giving that statement its full due, and honouring the writer's clearly remarkable journey in restoring his health through fermented foods, it must be said that, to the dispossessed of Scotland, this ground for resistance would appear too restrictive by far. We want our land back! (And perhaps, in view of Heilig's warning, this is just as well.) As our own forebears taught us (as did Heilig and Henry George), this means doing away with that "deadly enemy of mankind ... the private appropriation of the rent of land." For it is from this, the false privatization of the land rents, allowing in turn their phoney capitalisation, that power over land first originates, with all the subsequent phoney global empires constructed upon that original, phoney basis.

We need a general awakening to the absurdity of today's scene, this scene wherein a limited clique of human beings buy and sell to one another outright, once-for-all titles to the earth, this earth which none of us made, and which is a mystery beyond the knowing of any of us. How can any one of us possibly have a title to the earth above that of the poorest peon surviving in a Third World shanty town, or the most wretched slaver-in-the-fields for some pretended overlord?

Such grabbers of a dismembered Gaia we have for too long deified, through laws of land tenure which set them above moral law. Now, amidst today's planetary destruction, we can no longer afford not to recognise the infantile state of our development which such laws reflect. Nor can we continue to "pass by on the other side" our desecrated Mother.

We may protest for all we are worth about the commoditizing of the Earth and its resources, but until we achieve the quantum mental leap that will bring us to examining and questioning the foundation of today's titles to land, we must remain ourselves – permaculturists though we be, and for all our permaculture achievements – partakers in that on-going, relentless destruction of Gaia which continues throughout every moment of every day.

*

Shirley-Anne Hardy was born in Africa of Scottish parents and received an honors degree in Russian in 1968. She is the author of "Birthright in Land (by William Ogilvie) and the State of Scotland Today," published 1999. Her Essay, "Where Stands Permaculture? Where Stand We all?" appeared in PCA #49.

Scotland's 'rural idyll'
– a Carnegie UK Trust view!*

An examination of an interim look, by Alan MacDermid,
at the Report of the Carnegie UK Trust's Rural Commission
– (scheduled for publication in January 2007)
– Published in The Herald on 6 June, 2006

*

The Review Article of the Carnegie Trust's Rural Commission Report, "Paying for the Rural Idyll", is of considerable interest – but, it must be said, rather for what is missing from it, than for what it contains. There is certainly a sincerely expressed and very commendable concern, over both the present condition of rural communities and their yet grimmer future prospects. The Report highlights the concentration of land ownership as a key reason for this. Naturally, since where land monopoly rules there is only one way its screw on the community twists, and that is – tighter.

What appears to be missing in this Report, however, despite all its concern, is any hint of an understanding that the concentration of land in so few hands is an entirely unnatural phenomenon, and one which persists solely on account of a fundamental and entrenched error in our thinking: that is, that land has a capital value – when it has none.

It is this phoney structure of land capitalization which, allowing the outright buying and selling of land, thus opens the way for its buying up and hoarding – for no purposes of use by the buyer at all, but simply to exploit the other side of the picture: that is, the increasing numbers of those who, finding themselves

*Published by Comment, July 2006.

bereft of any foothold in the land, are placed in the absurd position of having to pay to some human overlord for the right to stand on their own soil.

> *"What more preposterous than that one tenant for a day of this rolling sphere should collect rent for it from his co-tenants, or sell to them for a price, what was here ages before him and will be here ages after him."*

(Henry George)

Since land had no cost of production, it has no capital value, for the cost of its production is all that gives monetary value to capital. Hence our society's boast of being "smart" – "successful" – "twenty-first century" Scotland, is extremely hollow. We in fact exist in a state of infantilism, for – trapped in the false belief that land is capital – we are unable to meet the very first requirement of any society pretending to adult status: that is, the requirement to honour the obvious *birthright to land* of every one of its people.

We boast of our recognition of human rights, of which the very foremost is the right to life. But persisting in the above infantilism, we fail to see the obvious corollary: that the right to life must include the right to land, since without land life cannot be sustained.

The fact that land is not capital, and has no actual capital value, received useful incidental corroboration towards the end of the last century from the government itself, when it became necessary to settle the exact figure at which the crofters should be allowed to buy out their crofts. How was this sum fixed? Why, *at X times the land's annual rental value*, of course, since this is the only real (monetary) value that land has!

It is but a step from here to the recognition that the rental value of land has, on the one hand, nothing whatever to do with the holder of the land's title-deed and, on the other, everything to do with a community's need for the use of its land; the rental value measuring, within that general need, the specific locational advantage afforded to its occupant by one piece of ground over another – this making for the variations in the land's rental values. Without the presence of a community desiring access to land, land might be of *use* to its holder, but rental value would not arise.

Hence the only conclusion to be reached is that these community-created rental values, which are at present paid over by the mass of the people to the "owners" of their land, are in fact owed *back*, by every landholder, to that community; and that – in a community giving the requisite attention to its affairs – these rental values would be a required payment to the community, from every landholder, annually.

Redistribution by Use

The question so long vexing us, of the concentration of land in so few hands, will thus be resolved; for the land will then naturally re-distribute itself. This will come about because – its holding having now become a liability (for the annual rental payments), instead of an asset (having the power to extract rents from others) – none will wish to keep more than he can himself well make use of. With this step comes the great discovery which awaits rural and urban communities alike: that the land itself, and the rental values it generates, are a community's prime resource, and more-over – right to hand!

A grasping of this somewhat more realistic view of the matter stands entirely on its head the findings of the Report with which the Herald article opens – that: *"Rural communities must give up the subsidy culture which has sustained them for decades ..."*

It is not, of course, the rural communities that have lived off subsidies all this time, it is the landowners – and not just for decades, but centuries! It is they who have, all along, been subsidised by the ever-more-hard-pressed-and-drastically-drained rural communities ... who, for their part, have all this time been pouring their well-earned wealth (the land's rental values) into the landowners' coffers, while in addition having to endure the taking from them, by these latter, of their land!

Truly, the ones that are living off "hand-outs" are not the rural communities – as is imputed in this Rural Commission's Report – but the landowners. No wonder, then, if these rural communities are forced to look, in turn, to the government, to make up their losses ... while ever the government turns a blind eye to the original stripping of these communities by the landed power.

When we consider that the same game goes on, under land monopoly, in our urban areas, we surely see why they, likewise, are continually strapped for cash, and that – in terms of sheer common sense – our economic arrangements haven't got a leg to stand on.

Thus the whole of present concern about our rural communities – as indeed about our urban (including all too many ghetto-like) ones – is in reality but the reflection back to us of our own mental infantilism which fails to see the obvious: namely, the illegitimacy (no matter how humanly legislated) of the dispossession of a people from their soil, in face of the elementary and unarguable fact – that every individual of a nation has an inalienable birthright in their own land.

Infantilism

This infantilism of thought has of course long been carefully guarded and nurtured by a ruling Establishment which also arranges for our education, the result being that we are never invited – either at school, college or university – to give a single thought to the great land question. The reason is simple. The Establishment is itself hoisted upon the pillars of the power that land monopoly bestows. For rent robbery is not the end of it.

Dispossessing a people of their land ensures that the latter lose their bargaining power. For labour's power to bargain depends upon the alternative option of self-employment – which means, in the first place, equality of access to land. Muscle-power or skills which are landless can only set to work upon another's permission and on another's terms. Hence a docile, because disempowered populace is the hope! Meanwhile, as capital is more and more subsumed by the owners of the great original something-for-nothing (land rent), and as the refinements of machinery advance under monopoly capitalism, so people become more and more redundant – and hundreds, or thousands, suddenly find themselves out of work. Hence the ever-present, ever-to-be-desired pool of cheap (because dispossessed) labour. That idyll of our times (as they solemnly repeat the chant!) – "the creation of jobs", would be hilarious, were it not so loathsomely dishonest and the whole scene not fraught with such suffering. Meanwhile the Trades Unions, historically blind to the real enemy – (not capital but land monopoly) – pose no threat whatsoever to this apparently unassailable power!

Public Education

The only way out of the terrible blindness caused by our present habit of infantilism is by a huge drive in public education. But since practically the entire educational system is in the hands of the Establishment (along with its countless well-reined-in-subsidiaries and quangos), so the great question becomes: *how is this great drive in education to be accomplished?* Our deliverance can only follow as we begin to see through the long cover-up of our real situation. For so far as the title of the Herald article goes, "Paying for the rural idyll", the "idyll" is all the landowners', and the people are "paying for" it – in every sense!

Did we but know our own history – (the subject of a similar centuries-long cover-up) – we would know that Scotland produced in the past an exceptional number of thinkers who well fathomed this matter of the great Natural Law of Rent: namely, that the land's rental values, and not taxation, are a society's true revenue. But since it was a penal offence, until the Reform Act of 1832, even to question the land laws – (a good hint of their dynamic!) – the suppressed writings of such as William Ogilvie and Patrick Edward

Dove, which mightily questioned those land laws, have taken some time to uncover, and are only now really coming to light.*

With such a background, and in whatever way it comes about, how can one doubt that the people of Scotland will one day – and sooner now rather than later – find their own way to bringing forward this great matter. And when that day comes they will achieve not only the emancipation of their own serfdom – they will signal freedom also to millions of others, similarly enserfed, across the globe, who like ourselves have thirsted too long for justice and liberty.

Proposed revolution

Time is running out. For if any doubt that retribution will presently be exacted from a society which founds itself on economic madness, they need but turn to the brilliant article by Dr Gavin Putland, Cuckoo Economics, (www.grputland.com), for a severe awakening.

The Herald article quotes from the Carnegie Trust's Rural Commission; "Our final report will be going out in January, and it will address the concentration of land. It will be a revolution."

With all due courtesy, it must be pointed out that:

- *For so long as we continue to endorse, as does this Rural Commission, the Scottish Executive's feeble "get-out" of a land reform policy, which places upon the people of Scotland the burden and folly of buying back their own land;*

---

* *B irthright in Land: an essay on the Right of Property in Land.* Wm. Ogilvie 1782, Reprinted 1891 and 1970.
The Foundation of Social Justice. P E Dove, 1850. Republished New York 1895 and again in 20th Century.
Birthright in Land – and the State of Scotland Today. Peregrine Press, 1999. ISBN 0 9535426 0 2. Includes extracts for Ogilvie and Dove.

- *For so long as we seek solutions in such "buy-outs", (as the Rural Commission would have us do) – buy-outs which pour yet more taxpayers' money into the coffers of land-robbery because we will not challenge the legitimacy of land-monopoly-based power;*

- *For so long as we avoid recognising that land is not, never has been, and never can be capital, and therefore cannot be bought or sold, (no matter what title-deeds may claim to the contrary); in short,*

- *For so long as we continue to walk in giant circles around the great natural law of social living, the Law of Rent:*

for just so long will the state of Scotland remain essentially exactly as it is today, regardless of however many people may genuinely lament that state, or may aspire to bring about change, or even radical change.

It is high time that we came to our senses on this great matter, and "put away childish things".

Justice and freedom must at last be sovereign in Scotland, to resurrect her people.

Nothing else is needed – *nothing else will do.*

*

Andrew Carnegie, the son of a handloom weaver, was born in Dunfermline in 1835. The family emigrated to America, where Carnegie flourished in business before making his fortune in the steel industry, finishing up worth $225,000,000.
He set up a philanthropic trust fund which endowed various organisations aimed at bettering mankind. The Carnegie UK Trust spearheads the philanthropist's work in Britain.

I sent a copy of my July 2006 Comment article, above, to the Carnegie UK Trust's Rural Commission at their headquarters in Dunfermline, with courteous covering note – and awaited with interest the final appearance of their Report containing its proposed 'revolution'.

This was published a year later, on 20 June 07, my response to it, below, appearing in Comment's July 07 issue,* under the heading –

A Charter for Rural Communities
A Big Re-Think!

*

*

*

See over!

---

* Incorporated in this article is a small follow-on, which appeared in Comment's Aug 07 issue.

Note: A charter for rural communities naturally applies equally, in its fundaments, to urban communities as well.

W hat has emerged is a quite extraordinarily, toned-down affair, since Alan MacDermid's interim review of it in The Herald of 6 June last year, when our appetites were whetted with such statements as the following: *"The report points out that the UK's 40 million acres of countryside are owned by an estimated 189,900 families, while 17 million private homeowners (accounting for 55 million people) own only 10%, with a third of the land owned by the aristocracy and the monarchy"* – and, (quoting the very words of the Commission's director for rural programmes on the work of the Report) – *"it will address the concentration of land. It will be a revolution."*

Phew – the reader must have wondered! Whatever lay ahead? Certainly, the Report's further content, as gleaned from that interim review, gave us no great promise – but having just worked my way through the laborious hundred pages the Commission has finally produced, "damp squib" is hardly the word!

Can it be that someone, somewhere, in the interval has taken fright? At any rate, nowhere in this Report is there to be found any statement of real concern about the concentration of land ownership, - or any of those former statistics. And this, despite Kevin Cahill's book *"Who Owns Britain"*, (out fully eighteen months ago), with its successor *"Who Owns the World"* revealing the concentration of land ownership in Britain to outstrip even that in South America!

The Commission's failure to confront this matter in its Report is the more reprehensible, since the question of the ownership of land is the most fundamental question to confront any society. Let us be clear on this. More land cannot be made – while all of us, for our very survival, depend absolutely upon access to land. Hence, if some members of society are allowed to claim absolute ownership of it, the rest of society is then held to ransom by them. It is as simple as that – despite all attempts to divert us from thinking about the matter, by an Establishment terrified that this issue might ever seriously be raised. He who finds himself without access to land except upon payment to some human overlord has had his birthright stolen from him, and – no matter what pretended democracy he may inhabit or what its genteel trappings – he is fundamentally *enserfed*.

"Support the rural wealthy to transfer capital assets for sustainable community development" (p.26) – is the best the Commission's Report can come up with on this huge subject. "Support the rural wealthy" must surely ring rather quaintly in the ears of the dispossessed! (Meanwhile – who cares if, in the hand of the "rural wealthy", land has ever been used *sustainably*?) In another massive blunder, the Report makes clear (p.25) that the parties surrendering these "capital assets" are to be richly rewarded, a whole host of agencies being called upon to "enhance" the needed finance!

This brings us to the crunch of the matter. Right at the start – it is an error for the Report to refer to land as a "capital asset" – (and even when buildings are part of the "assets", land is the all-important underlying component). For land, being freely gifted to us, does not have a capital value. The buying and selling of chunks of the Planet which goes on – originating in theft – is an entirely phoney game; a game played out purely, and brazenly, for the *power over the dispossessed* it confers. Meanwhile, for our ignoring of this matter, a cheap pool of dispossessed labour and chronic unemployment, is the price society pays.

How does land come to register a monetary value, when intrinsically it has none?

The value it registers, for those holding land superfluous to their needs, is the value of the *rental reapings* that may be expected from it – for as many years ahead as the market will bear; or, alternatively, the unchallenged right to strip land of such things as, say, its timber, totally regardless of the well-being of people or of the Planet. For those purchasing land purely for their own work or home-base, it is if course the ransom they must pay to escape from the ranks of the dispossessed.

It is clearly a first priority for society to bring an end to this unnatural and sordid game. And there is a way to do it. Quite simply – land rent is at present paid the wrong way round! Since the rental values arise purely from the people's need for their land – registering also the preferential use of one site over another and not one pennyworth originates from the title-deed holder, so – every penny of these annual rental values must be repaid to the community every year (those living on what is called marginal land, carrying no rental value, being of course excepted).

Thus landholding is converted, at one stroke, from an asset to a liability, so bringing the surrender of acres superfluous to the holder's personal need. Thus the community receives back its land, and at the same time its original natural revenue – with no need for the addition of taxes at all. (Land rent was society's original revenue – which gradually became privatized, bringing us the plague of taxation. See Richard Cobden's speech to the House of Commons, 14th March 1842.) Thus society harmonizes itself with the natural *Law of Rent*. What a chance for the Carnegie Report, in calling (p.79) for "learning exchange", to have placed acquaintance with the *Law of Rent* at the top of its agenda!

Now that the situation of our rural communities is seen in a clearer light, what remains to be said of this Report?

Clearly a lot of research and effort has gone into the making of it. It is just unfortunate that, due to longstanding deception and cover-up, it has all been done without any questioning of today's false economic framework.

This false framework is the inevitable begetter of complexity in the solutions it presents, since the solutions must attune themselves to this falsity. This, in turn, weighs the reader down with much heavy verbiage, while another feature of the complexity created is the number of hoops that must be jumped through to negotiate this jungle.

The Report also (p.75) states clearly: *'Top down economic development will continue to play an important role in the economic revitalisation of rural communities.'* Thus rural communities are not envisaged in this Report as ever being truly empowered to manage their own affairs. The fact is that genuinely empowered communities are an idea that fills the Establishment with fright!

There is a slightly humorous side to the whole thing, in that most of the hierarchical bodies called on to support local communities are themselves – through taxation – *supported* by these communities in the first place! For where do government and other public bodies get the funds to keep them in business, but from tax-money. – and a good deal of it wrung precisely from the people at the very bottom of the pile!

In short, full of rhetoric as the Report is on the matter of "empowerment", local communities are clearly envisaged as tied on-going to Nanny's apron-strings! No place is anywhere given to the ideal of self-employment – enterprising individuals striking out on their own, unaided, to do their own thing. But then – how *could* it be, in a country of locked-up land? Freedom to do your own thing, unoppressed and un-'approved' by the system, is in general strictly the domain of those who have no ransom to pay – like the "rural wealthy", who, to develop their skills, have no need to be part of "community development" schemes.

The Report cannot of course escape a reference (p.62) to our "increasingly affluent" society! – a buzz term we are fed with to saturation point today. So let us enjoy, on this very theme, a splendid early version of "the emperor has no clothes", from the pen of Charles Dickens in his novel *"Hard Times"*. Little Sissy Jupe is recounting to Louisa the schoolmaster's explanation that morning of "national prosperity":

> *"In this nation there are fifty millions of money ... Girl number twenty-one, isn't this a prosperous nation, and ain't you a thriving state?"*

"Miss Louisa, I said ... I couldn't know whether it was a prosperous nation or not, and whether I was in a thriving state or not, unless I knew who had got the money, and whether any of it was mine."

(Dreadful precocious child!)

Finally, I wonder if the Carnegie Trust is aware of the following statement by their own founder? – a fabulous give-away on the rooking of communities!

> "The most comfortable, but also the most unproductive, way for a capitalist to increase his fortune, is to put all his monies in sites and await that point in time when a society, hungering for land, has to pay his price." (Andrew Carnegie)

Crack that nut, Carnegie Commission! – and rural communities, or rather – the whole lot of enterprising individuals we are, hungering for freedom – could well have been tucking into your promised 'revolution' by now!

*

Farmers & 'Farmers'
- The Great Hide-Up*

The Review of Kevin Cahill's book *'Who Owns the World'*, highlighted in the March issue, has prompted a response in the April issue from the local branch of the NFU. Understandably they take exception to the claim that "owning land makes you wealthy", when it is scarcely so for those farmers who need all their acres just to manage the family farm. Equally understandably, they baulk at the claim that subsidies prove farming to be inefficient, when *"eg. Milk – average cost of production is 19p and the payment to farmers is 17p"*, (the 17p price being dictated largely by the supermarkets, of course).

What is not recognised in the above is that the whole question of farm income and farm profits is bedevilled by a false system of land tenure which, in carefully concealed ways, manipulates both the farming and the business scenes.

"The profits to be made in agriculture today are due entirely to the rise in land values" – so said a London merchant banker, addressing a meeting of the Scottish Landowners Federation in 1979.

- *Where does this place the small family-owned farm?*
- *More pertinently – where does it place those who hold acres surplus to their needs?*
- *And most importantly – where does it place the tenant-farmer, who has no land to call his own at all?*

Little heed was paid at the time to the words of that London merchant banker – (save of course by the Scottish Landowners Federation). So no wonder if, some thirty years on, a quantity of unexpected chickens are coming home to roost!

---

* First published in Comment in May 2007.

Land Monopoly

The Scottish Landowners Federation has recently assumed the more 'modern' title of the Scottish Rural Property and Business Association (SRPBA) – a name of somewhat unblushing confession to a merchant banker's view of the scene! This view is, of course – for those with surplus acres to their name – that rural property is a *business in itself*. Therefore, as such, it gears itself – not to the laborious production and marketing of farm produce, but rather to the marketing of those *land rental* values, which are most *un*laboriously (indeed freely!) produced for the landowner, via land monopoly.

Those who have no land to lease, but need all their acres to farm themselves, are naturally rowing a very different boat; and, even more so, those with the misfortune to be landless – the tenant-farmers, liable to be ousted, should rising land rentals propose a better 'business' be made, than farming, of the land they occupy. Meanwhile the profits from such changes of use – (higher rental revenues, or a capital reaping from the sale of these rental prospects) – go entirely to the title-holder of the land: that is, to the passive (or idle) partner in this strange 'farming' business.

Are these the workings of an *honest* society? – where non-producers are allowed to appropriate huge slices of others' wealth-creation, (for the rental value of land is owned entirely to the presence and activities of the surrounding community) – while its productive members are held to ransom – or lightly discarded to the rubbish-heap of the unemployed?

The effects of such profound economic and social injustice are scarcely confined to the world of farming. The society which founds itself upon a concealed and sophisticated form of robbery need not look far for the source of the plethora of social ills that it breeds. *"If some people get something for nothing – then it follows that others get nothing for something"* – a sure recipe for social discontent on a rising scale. So, is this not a matter that concerns every one of us?

What is sorely needed are some clarion-calls to shake us awake to the truly rotten foundations of our society. But even when these do appear – how many of our local farmers have yet, I wonder, taken the trouble to read Duncan Pickard's masterly small volume of 2004? Just 68 pages long, of arresting title *'Lie of the Land: A study in the Culture of Deception'* – and written by a working farmer in Fife who is also a PhD – this book received some notice in an article in Comment in May 2005. Had our local farmers been familiar with its contents, they would undoubtedly have been able to put their finger on the real flaw in Kevin Cahill's book – for unfortunately this author seems to be entirely ignorant of all but the more obvious working of land monopoly.

Really, without understanding the mechanics of miscreant land tenure – and how to establish land tenure *aright* via the workings of the natural Law of Rent* - it is just not possible to make sense of today's farming scene. For instance, those holding land mainly as an investment, invest also in the stock market. Hence they will tend to favour the business world, (*including* the supermarkets which are so busily destroying the income of real farmers today**). For they are naturally more concerned with getting a good return for their investments, than with their tenant farmers getting a good return for their labours – e.g., the 19p/17p ratio.

If that really hurt *their* pockets, we would soon hear about it! – for we have it straight from the horse's mouth: the chairman of the new SRPBA addressing a recent meeting of that body in Perth, as reported in The Courier of 27 March. *"We have been excellent at influencing the Scottish Executive and those that know us ... and respect us ..."* Well! – we may be sure that if those ruling in the SRPBA – (and largely the same interests rule in the NFU) – did not like the present farm price situation, we would soon see some changes in the scene!

As for the subsidies which are so essential to today's real farmers: for those able to *rent out* land, what are they but a most welcome hand-out, raising yet further the rental value of their acres and sending them laughing all the way to the bank! – while making life no less harsh for those in the position of tenant-farmer, of course. And do we still, in our stupidity, wring our hands over the widening gap between the rich and the poor?

As we can see, so many of our controversies today, which appear to be about farming, or business, or whatever else – and rippling out to embrace the worlds of drugs, violence, even suicides – in reality root back to our society's hopeless entanglement with a *false system of land tenure.*

'Culture of Deception'

If today's real farmers are truly concerned about their situation, and if they wish to hand on the family farm to their children as a viable concern, then they must take some real responsibility in the matter. They must get to grips with the mechanics of land tenure, and raise the demand for an end to the treatment of land as an investment proposition. That is, they must raise the demand for the return of all land rentals, annually, from every landholder, to the community – from which alone they arise; these revenues to replace entirely the present false system of taxation. For this is the essential step that must be taken, if farming is to be freed from the huge *"culture of deception"* (Duncan Pickard) in which it is at present caught up.

With land no longer an asset to hold, but a liability on account of the annual rental demand, land will finally cease to be hoarded. *"Those who farm the land will own it, and those who own the land will farm it"* – to quote Duncan Pickard again. Then farming will become the wholly honest occupation it deserves to be.

174

As we have seen, it is not genuine farmers alone who are defrauded by our false land tenure. If, then, farmers will take up this challenge, and educate themselves in the land question, they will bless not only themselves, but in due course, the whole of society.

*

Footnotes:

* A more thorough study of this may be made from the classic work by Henry George, "Progress and Poverty", of which an abridged and recently modernized edition is with the A.K. Bell public library in Perth.

** Again, the supermarkets have built up their empires mainly upon the accumulation of assets in *land* – which is the root of their ability to undercut the small businesses that must bear the burden of the *rental* payments on their sites.

*

Having sent a copy of this article to the TGWU (Transport and General Workers Union), I was pleased to receive a note in reply: "Thanks very much for your article, which I will be happy to publish in Landworkers next (August) issue." It did duly appear in the August 07 Landworker – but greatly shortened, and not revealing, quite, its *radical* nature!

"Dwellers in the Land"

I n January 2002, an article appeared in Comment concerning a piece of hill land of 1,100 acres – for long neglected and over-grazed – called Dun Coillich, which was up for sale.

Open to the community of Highland Perthshire to purchase with the help of the Scottish Government's Scottish Land Trust Fund, the writer urged the community at large to register their interest in this venture, for its support in all practical ways.

My response to this article was published in the Feb 02 issue of Comment, under the heading "Dun Coillich". I have here given it a more all-embracing title - one acknowledged to the book of that title by Kirkpatrick Sale, a founder of the sane and beautiful Bioregional movement, re which, see my own article which follows this, "The Bioregional Movement and Scotland".

*

Before we all get carried away down a very false (however well intentioned) path I too have a dream. But there is this difference: that my dream – one that is embedded deep in the Scottish psyche – embraces, along with environmental, also social regeneration, seeing the two as one. For such, fundamentally, they are.

Furthermore, the realisation of this dream requires not the immoral setting up of any "Scottish Land Fund". Have we lost our wits? Or are we brought so low that we Scots really believe we have to *buy back our own land?!* What an innings, incidentally, for the modern incumbents of those originally stolen acres – quite enough to bring forward a discreet queue of offerings-for-sale, with the ever-ready public purse now being brought into play! And what, in any case, makes country-folk – just to fill **their** begging bowls to buy out **their** bit of dream-land – entitled to impose upon the tax-payers of our crowded, slum-ridden cities, in a far worse plight than they and sinking under every kind of social ill?

The essential need today – of both our collapsing society and our collapsing environment – is for Vision: the vision that sees the problems Scotland faces as one **Whole** – and sees how every part affects every other. If we then, in Highland Perthshire, in this very heartland of Scotland, fail – in our urgency to fulfil our own particular "dreams" – to take account of that whole picture, it will surely go very ill with us.

The author of the article writes that "the wilderness shrinks before a tide of humanity". Strange! I stand here in Highland Perthshire and look around me. Huge stretches of empty land lie open on every side, and I cannot but recall the plaint of an old trapper in this area: *"I have watched the highland clearances go on and on – the departure of people from this land, without end, through all my days".*

The fact is that the land of Scotland – as elsewhere – is suffering because it has lost its true guardians. For the true guardians of a landscape are the people who belong to it. The desolation of the landscape, described so vividly by the author, has not been brought about by a "tide of humanity", but has come about under a small oligarchy while the mass of the people have gone. It was when there were people on the land that the birds flourished too, as any ornithologist knows, and the same goes for the rest of the wildlife.

We need a new vision. *"I see a million hills green with ... trees and a million neat ... homes snuggled in the hills. These beautiful permaculture* plots hold the hills from ... to ...".* J Russell Smith's

---

* I have used today's term, not yet current in Russell Smith's time – for he was, in fact, an early and outstanding pioneer of the permaculture movement. His great classic, "Tree Crops – A Permanent Agriculture", first published in 1929, has been successfully re-printed and most recently with an introduction by the well-known environmentalist, Wendell Berry.

vision encompassed the hills of his homeland, which was America – but it fits, just as well, our own "hills of home". We see that JRS was wiser, in his envisioning, than to make an artificial divide between the regeneration of the land and the regeneration of its people. For the ruin of a people is always partnered by the ruin of the land – an invariable we cannot turn aside from, just as we cannot turn it aside. It is hardly surprising, then, that we find JRS's vision encompassing also *"a democracy of land ownership"* – for he recognised the regeneration of a landscape could **only** come about as the people themselves held a direct stake in their land.

We, in Scotland, are particularly fortuned, then. For, in the matter of just and democratic land tenure, we have excelled in thinkers and writers who are the very guides we so clearly need at this hour. William Ogilvie, Patrick Edward Dove, Morrison Davidson, D C MacDonald and others, have all furnished us with the key to democratic land-tenure – that essential key whereby we may accomplish the regeneration of land and people together; and do it all without contributing a penny to those dissolute "buy-out" funds such as we now see a degrading race to set up on all sides.

But why have we never heard of these Scottish thinkers and writers? Because our history has been stolen from us along with our land! How truly indeed we inherit the saying that *"a people which does not know its past has no future"*.

Time, methinks, to reverse that situation! Let us recover our vision along with our history – blaze an example for the rest of humanity to follow by setting a real regeneration of this Planet on foot at last!

*

The Bioregional Movement
and Scotland*

My introductory note to the above article, as follows, appeared in the printed Comment of February 07:

I read with interest of the Bioregional proposal put forward in Comment by the Upper Tay Development Group, since I feel that a Bioregional movement is something that Scotland could very much do with.

However, not finding in the UTDG's proposal anything reflecting the movement as I know of it, I have written a response inviting them to set such a movement on foot, and Comment has kindly agreed to put this on its website.

To this was appended by Comment the following information:-

The detailed critique and suggestions are contained in a 2,500 word article: http/www.commentonline.co.uk/general/Scotland and the Bioregional Movement.htm

*

---

* I have reversed here the original heading to my article ("Scotland and the Bioregional Movement") for this more logical setting – since it is the Bioregional movement that embraces Scotland, not vice versa.

U pon spotting in January's Comment an article on a Bioregional proposal for this area, I read on with interest. How indeed could my interest not be sparked, as one well acquainted with the splendid 1993 volume *Boundaries of Home: Mapping for Local Empowerment,* a collection of writings by bioregionalists in North America, where the movement began, contributed to and edited by Doug Aberley, a Scot and leading bioregionalist now residing in Canada, who – as I found to my delight – dedicates his book "to the future of Caledonia – old and new!"

Bioregionalism takes as its starting-point our need to re-discover the natural areas and boundaries of the place we live in, frequently delineated by watersheds and river systems, and very different from those imposed on us from above. But before looking at the Proposal for this area, let us gain an idea of what Bioregionalism means in its full scope, through a few quotations from Doug Aberley's book. For Bioregionalism has now been going in North America for several decades and Doug, working at the heart of it, is one of its most experienced practitioners.

It is important to note at the start the sub-heading of Doug's book – *Mapping for Local Empowerment,* since the mapping of their home terrain by the local people of an area – those who actually inhabit the land – lies at the very heart of the Bioregional movement. This is, firstly, because it is the local people who best know their home ground and the features in it important to them. Secondly, because – (as indicated in the last two words of Doug's subtitle) – local people, working together on this task, discover from it a hitherto unimagined source of power in their hands. For such knowledge of their home terrain is a powerful thing, since there are unlikely to be any people more expert in it. (I should add that many warnings are given, in the book, against allowing this mapping to be taken over by officialdom, or experts of any kind, although some good help may be sought from such.)

Doug speaks in his book of the role, in the bioregional vision, of this kind of map-making, as being "an absolutely critical validation" of a community's potential and purpose(p.16). And that purpose is, of course, for the community to take back power, both ecological and economic, over its own bioregion. For while the term Bioregionalism might suggest at first that its sphere of interest is limited to that of geography – water-flows, flora and fauna, etc. – this is by no means the case, humans being themselves an integral part of the "bio" scene. Here is a key contribution from Doug Aberley's book: "The bioregional alternative is as much concerned with achieving social justice as it is with stewarding life within ecological carrying capacities ... issues such as the elimination of poverty ... will have extremely high priority. (p.111). And action is called for: "by understanding how major parts of the existing economy are structured, you will be empowered to begin their transformation." (p.125). Worthy echoes, here, of utterances on economic justice from earlier children of Caledonia, mentioned in these columns by this writer – utterances to our disgrace still well suppressed. So it is especially interesting that Doug Aberley is a Scot.

Having been thus powerfully launched, a decade ago, into the world of bioregional thinking, I turned with interest to read of the Bioregional Proposal put forward by the UTDG (Upper Tay Development Group) in conjunction with the Centre for Mountain Studies at Perth College (University of the Highlands and Islands), and backed by the Highland Perthshire Communities Partnership (HPCP); a Proposal now lodged with the European Forum for Mountain Areas – with a view to liaising with a similar mountain locality from somewhere among its EU member states. Sad as it is to say it, and with the best will in the world – I found it extremely hard to recognise their Proposal as being a bioregional initiative at all – let alone a bioregional vision!

This Proposal – (for the "bioregion of the Ben Lawers massif", as it is identified, and for this interesting information on our bioregion I am grateful to them) – certainly gives us an accurate picture of our bioregion as it is today – i.e., in its present shameful state of decline. Pointed out are the familiar features of "lack of affordable housing ... limited employment opportunities ... loss of local retail and post office facilities", etc, etc, along with the "centralising tendency" which rules. What is *missing* from this description, however, - entirely missing – is an actual *bioregional view* of all this!

The various contributors to Doug Aberley's book – (six experienced bioregionalists besides himself) – would not dream of putting forward a bioregional proposal on such a basis! Setting to with the vital tool of *map-making* – (every step of the way described in Doug's book) – such men and women of vision, via tell-tale layers of maps going back in history, would waste no time in stripping away the various layers of alien imposition on their landscape, achieved precisely by today's unhealthy "centralising tendency" (which the UTDG's Proposal notes as being of "negative" impact – but apparently has nothing further to say about!) The maps drawn by the bioregionalists in Doug's book – retracing the picture step by step in time – would enable a tracking of the gradual process by which those earlier self-reliant communities were destroyed; and in doing so, their maps would reveal the real resources of their land – contained within it and fully utilised by those earlier settlements. Hence such maps speak volumes not only of our decline since, but of the consummate folly of it.

Re the UTDG's Proposal, I note that it goes calmly along, also, with the "50% rise in tourism ... targeted for 2015 by regional tourist interests". Interestingly, I do not recall a single mention of tourism figuring anywhere in Doug Aberley's pages, (which surely evokes the thought – "how cheap are we willing to sell Scotland?"). The UTDG's Proposal also notes, without comment, today's shift to a "service" economy. Do I hear a deep belly-laugh from Gaia at this? – who sees a more pressing form of "servicing" ahead for us: that of our own physical forms – with food! And where indeed will the tourists be in that day?

The great virtue of bioregionalist mapping is that it prevents us from simply skating along on the surface of things, as we are accustomed to doing, and *compels* us to think more deeply about our situation. One wonders if the UTDG and its partners have not heard of mapping as an essential bioregional tool? If not, one wonders what their background in bioregional studies is? – and that of their European counterparts? (I could not check their website references, being adversely affected by screen-gazing.)

It is a relief to turn to Doug Aberley's clear statement of the matter. He writes of bioregional mapping as "an ambitious assignment, but the type of challenge that must be met if we are to take our aspirations for social justice and ecosystem continuity ... into the terrain of empowerment and practice." He adds moreover that if we truly wish to reclaim our terrain, we "must clearly understand the forces that subjugate land and life". (pp.3-4). It must be said that the UTDG's Proposal on Bioregionalism does not express even the *wish* to understand these – in fact, it is hard to see what it has to do with real Bioregionalism at all!

That the Bioregional movement does not itself yet, for all its admirable searching, have quite the full picture re those "forces that subjugate land and life", is part of the huge interest for Scotland of the whole Bioregional scenario. For does it not draw us straight back to those earlier "children of Caledonia" whose air Doug Aberley seems naturally to breathe – and whom he would surely recognise upon the smallest hint. There is one point where he comes so close to stating it, it is almost as if he were giving us a secret clue! It appears as the last word in the following, where he refers to the necessity of "dismantling an existing economic system whose structure partially depends upon its mystery". How excellently put that is! But that this "mystery" should confront us still is entirely due to the suppressed wisdom of those earlier Scots, such as William Ogilvie, Patrick Edward Dove and D C MacDonald. It centres on a bizarre feature of our economy: its treatment of land as capital. Something we have come so to take for granted, that we are no longer aware of the "mystery" it shrouds"

The curious thing, from the point of view of the UTDG's Proposal, is that this long cover-up, and the distortion of the economy ensuing from it, has already been fairly dealt with in the pages of Comment, in no less than six articles over the past four years. For this reason I shall not tediously repeat the matter here. Suffice it to say that there was highlighted, in one of these articles, a book by Duncan Pickard (2005) of the title *Lie of the Land: A Study in the Culture of Deception* – a "culture" ruling Scotland today and exposed by the book as the real force behind our sharp rural decline. This book at least should surely have captured the UTDG's reading attention, and so – (even had they not heard of bioregional mapping) – have alerted them, in the setting up of their bioregional initiative, as to the real enemy of rural communities today. So what *are* we to make of the UTDG and its partners? Have they all been away on a long holiday? Or do they just not read their local paper?

I should like to say here that I am sure the members of the UTDG and its various partners are people of excellent intent – but their efforts are crippled by a failure to grasp the fundaments of the socio-economic scene confronting us. In their liaising with Europe they would focus upon a conflict between rural and urban communities – (highland areas being "subordinated to a 'lowland' and urban agenda"). But far more important is, surely, to discover that no such conflict essentially exists, and that it is one falsely contrived by our false economics. For the far truer picture (examined in those earlier articles) is that rural and urban areas share a decided *commonality of purpose*; to rid themselves of that landed interest which – built on the monopoly of land formed from capitalising community-created land rentals (underwritten by false human legislation), and thence gobbling up both capital and political power – now exerts that power nationwide (indeed globally), draining the life-blood from urban and rural communities alike.

If it be that towns at present have unsuitable humanly-structured command over rural areas, the Bioregional movement has a marvellously unifying solution to set on foot to that. In a chapter in Doug's book, by gene Marshall, *Step One: Mapping the Biosphere* we are re-located out of our world of institutional mappings – (councils and postcode areas, etc.) – into a world of ever-increasing *concentric* bioregional circles! – starting with "my neighbourhood – my community – my local bioregion," on to "my sub-biome – my biome", and ultimately "my planet – Earth". Thus the bioregional vision provides a practical basis for initiating a bonding between rural and urban areas even today, through the opening up of a shared bioregional concern; while we all work towards that saner day when – (the whole rotten system of taxation sent packing) – each community, urban and rural alike, is *in charge of its own affairs*, financed locally through its own revenues, sources from its own land rents.

This brings us to the great gift Scotland has to offer to the Bioregional movement – a gift that would end that "mystery" of which Doug Aberley speaks and which today confronts us, since it would at once remove its veilings from the scene.

There is one layer of mapping that is missing from the bioregionalists' arsenal – and in a way it is surprising; for they write so truly of the need to map all of the "extractions" from a bioregion – extractions which have led to such ensuing impoverishments. Thus they map the extractions of timber, ores, fish, etc. But the biggest extraction of all (because underlying all the others is the LAND – the ultimate source of power as well as money), is the extraction from a bioregion of its land's rental values – (those "juggernauts of development" a mocking later payback to us from this stealing). It is the mapping of *this* extraction – of land rents gone AWOL – that would make a unique gift indeed to the Bioregional movement from Scotland. (Nor is there any problem about such mapping, for it has been done already, without difficulty, in various parts of the world, where attempts have been made to set this just and radical reform on foot.)

Here then is something right to hand, and something of very great worth, which awaits the good attention of the UTDG and its partners: the mapping of the land rental values of our bioregion.* Moreover, I cannot but think what a fitting 'thank you' to Doug Aberley, for his inspiring work, this pioneering step would be – to Doug, who asks us at the end of his book to send to him in Canada our own experiences of local mapping. What a "first" for him to receive from Caledonia! The land to which his book is dedicated.

I checked, in the course of writing this article, on the availability of Doug's book. It would be hard to imagine such a manual for Bioregionalism as being out of print. It is indeed at work as ever, playing its part in the world – priced at a modest £6.99.

It could do with a few more readers in Caledonia!

*

---

* R ight to this point is the report in Comment (Jan 07, p.16) of the loss to Killin of some valuable land, for it is unlikely such apparent trickery would have been got away with, with an alert bioregional presence in the village armed with its maps – *including* that of the rental values.

War – and Peace

On making courteous enquiry of the Georgist Journal (USA), re the failure to appear of my response to X on the above matter of such import, I learned that it had been overlooked in error! – (at, I believe an exceptionally busy time). It was however subsequently published in Good Government (Australia), in Aug. 2008, for which I was very grateful. In placing it here, it may perhaps reach a wider audience – and even come into the hands of X himself!

*

I read with interest X's view that wars will always be with us, regardless of whether we live in a just society – because people will always be touting the superiority of *their* race, *their* religion, or *their* nation.

I believe that this view fails to take into account the extremely stultifying effects upon the human psyche of living in a society drastically out of gear with natural law. In such a society frustrations and resentments build up, and – (with the great mass of the people not understanding the profound effect upon them of their unnatural state) – easily strike at false targets.

There appears to be some evidence for my view from history itself. During the months of preparing material for my book "Birthright in Land – and the State of Scotland Today", there fell out of an old file, quite unexpectedly, an article I had not seen for twenty years and had quite forgotten – but was a thrill indeed to re-discover.

It concerned a small Georgist enclave founded, in extraordinary circumstances, in the first half of the twentieth century, on a small island called Gosaba in the Ganges delta. The pioneers of this amazing venture were a Scottish couple, the

Hamiltons; he – employed by a shipping company, and she – originally a daughter of the manse. The venture was extraordinary on account of the obstacles which had to be overcome in order to set this undertaking on foot, for when originally acquired, Gosaba was inhabited solely by wildlife such as tigers and crocodiles, while its soil was so saline as to be incapable of cultivation. Undeterred, the Hamiltons set about their task, displaying versatile skills – inspired by a determination, from what they saw around them, to "improve the terrible conditions under which the villagers of Bengal lived"; and aware of the essential basis of a just society, they founded it upon the Law of Rent. That they succeeded in their undertaking to the point where, in the disastrous famine of 1943, Gosaba was able to *export rice* to the mainland of India, surely testifies to the Hamiltons' remarkable accomplishment, (and of course tells us a good deal about 'famine' too).

All this is recorded in Part II of "Birthright ...", in the chapter "Gosaba – a Modern Miracle", (with a separate preamble noted in the List of Contents). But there is something further about Gosaba we would do well to ponder. On account of the extremely primitive conditions which prevailed on the island at the start, the Hamiltons were at first able to attract to their project only the 'dregs' of society, including ex-convicts; and it was, from the start, a mixture both of religion and race. Nevertheless it came about, in the course of time, that – (and I quote from the article) – "Hindus, Mohammedans, Christians live side by side so amicably that there is not a single policeman among the 22,000 population". (What does that tell us about the 'dregs' of society too? - !) Moreover, no internal disputes ever reached the mainland courts of India. All were successfully dealt with in the traditional Indian way of self-government by panchayat – the 'elders' in this case elected from amongst those managing the various co-operative ventures which the villagers themselves had set up.

No wonder that the inhabitants of Gosaba, enjoying a society founded on the strict tenets of justice and liberty, presented "an air of happiness and well-being ... (in) striking contrast to the misery and tension so evident elsewhere in Bengal". (Misery – and *tension*: the natural precursors of hostility.)

Reading the absorbing account of this community in Gosaba, it is hard to think of such crude sentiments having place in it as would ever wish to proclaim the superiority of one race, or one religion, over another. Indeed, it is impossible to imagine! Moreover, on Gosaba no one got something for nothing. Purposeful and satisfying work, freely entered upon by those who freely joined the community, made fruitful use of those energies which, in less fortunate societies – either unutilized, or engaged in frustrating, meaningless and boring tasks, usually under another's control – all too easily spill over, from suppressed rancour, into ugly posturing.

I could write more, but it is all in my book – and surely enough has been said here anyway. In conclusion: we stand so close up, in our society, to its various scenarios of selfish and arrogant outburst re race, religion, etc., that we fail completely to recognize their artificial grounding – that is, that they form part of the whole artificial structure and growth, *also in the mental realm*, of our hopelessly artificial, land-monopoly-based society.

24th January 2008

Addendum – 3rd June 2008

Of other societies I have come across presenting, as Gosaba, a picture of normalcy, an earlier, happier time in the history of Java is included in my book "Birthright in Land – and the State of Scotland Today" (ISBN 0 9535426 0 2), British rule this time playing an exceptionally positive part – on account entirely of the exceptional character of Sir Stamford Raffles, governor out there at the time.

Many are captured also in the writings of Dr Weston Price – (see the section on his work, in Part II of "Birthright ...". This normalcy always depends upon *the people themselves* having a sufficiency of power over their own lives – which to start with means, of course – over their own *land*; while we note that where there is a progression of centralized political power, (always founded upon the centralization of the fundamental *economic* power over land) – or where the corrupting influence of power-centralized societies is brought to bear upon more innocent peoples – this normalcy departs.

What huge lessons the whole saga carries for us!

*

Changing "the big picture" – at root!

This article was written in response to one which had appeared in a New Age publication. It was not published – which I understood, as it is a publication given to a rather gentler reach. However, sometimes sterner words are required to bring a matter fully to the light!

*

In your May issue, X bravely attempts to reply to one of your readers as to how we deal with "the big picture". Your reader, Y, is understandably rent by the widening gap between rich and poor in our society and the apparently irreversible position of its "wage slaves".

X's reponse, while mentioning once the term "our economy", actually confines itself to dealing with the environmental scenario – which does not really answer Y's concerns. This is because X does not herself understand that the calamitous environmental face of our times is really a huge mask and cover-up for our fundamental distortion, which is *economic* – and which re-shapes the environmental scenario in its own disastrous image.

The time has now come to break through this centuries-long cover-up. For not only will it open the way for us to deal with the environmental crisis effectively, but it brings us to the root of the ever-increasing divide between rich and poor (which so rightly cries out to Y for redress); in addition pointing us to the cause of the present economic crash, now further multiplying people's miseries – as multitudes are thrown out of work – thousands of home repossessions then take place – and the huge suffering of broken families follows on that. Hence it is vital that we at last break through the immoral silence on this great matter – which is so carefully excluded from our school and college syllabuses by an establishment founded on LAND MONOPOLY!

Thus, too, the new UK-wide Transition movement – (a book on which features on the same page in your May issue) – in declaring for the empowerment of communities while remaining silent upon the all-underlying *land question*, misses out precisely the bottom line. This, however, is brought into focus via the enclosed 40-page booklet, "The Land Question". This gives a useful overview of the whole matter, which turns upon society's implementation of the great natural social *Law of Rent*, pictorially presented on pages 26-27.

The crux of the matter is that, as land has no capital value (since it has no cost of production), but only an annual rental value (slyly multiplied up to appear as capital), and since furthermore this rental value is created entirely by the community from its need for land space and the differential value of sites – so, rent paid for land today (hugely involving those millstone mortgages) is paid *the wrong way round*. Communities need to wake up and demand that, instead, every holder of land in their locality pays, each year, the full annual rental value of his holding into the community's coffers. The scam of a pretended 'capital' value for land – (the casino games played with which non-existent entity have brought our economy to ruin) – thus vanishes back into its original thin air, while nobody then holds more land than he can use, as he must now pay society the annual rental upon it.

With the same stroke is ended the commoditising of Gaia including all her precious waters and forests, since the mechanism of her exploitation – the phoney 'land market' that had reduced her and all her gifts to us to saleable commodities – is now no more.

We can now readily see how the false capitalisation of land in the economy, instituted by a corrupt Establishment and tolerated by a deluded populace – with the rents stolen from the people going to line the pockets of an exploiter class – *could not but* have brought upon society, in turn, environmental ruin, since economic power swiftly buys its way into the political arena – and "he that pays the piper calls the tune". Thus it was inevitable that the long-standing exploitation of the people, practised by these falsely elevated mortals in our midst, would at once transfer itself to an equal exploitation of the environment – once the earth with all the riches of its resources fell into their grasp.

Finally, then – with the phoney 'land market' now no more – the floodgates of locked-up-for-centuries land are flung open to the people, with land available for all (down to its economic 'margin' where no rent is asked); while communities acquire their own revenue to boot.* Then will organic growing be brought readily within the reach of all, so answering Y's heartfelt plea on that score. Nor are there any more "wage slaves", since all men become perforce working men – and the wage slaves cast off at last those who have formerly ridden on their backs.

So long and assiduous has been the cover-up of the all-underlying *land question*, that few understand the root evil today

* See further the chapter "Community and Re-Empowerment", in "Birthright in Land – and the State of Scotland Today", ISBN 0 9535426 0 2.

is not environmental, but economic. *This*, then, is where genuine concern over the environment – (such as is felt by X and thousands like her) – needs focussing first; while the 'Ys' of this world take upon themselves the vital role of grasping and spreading the message of radical economic reform: that is, the bringing of society into conformity with the natural *Law of Rent*.

Finally, concerning the "cool detachment" advocated by X, this indeed has its place – concerning the fruits of our labour, just as Gandhi taught. But let us not deceive ourselves. Mere cool detachment would never have brought the outlawing of slavery; and in fact for the settlement of any great moral question, considerable 'fire in the belly' is most decidedly required. Nor is a fire of that nature one which ever (as X fears) burns out. Let us remember that Jesus, (whose mission embraced land justice – another big cover-up*), himself said "I have come to bring fire on the earth", while Ramana Maharshi – one of the great Eastern sages of our time – declared "it is possible to remain in a state of complete detachment, *while pursuing one's lifework like a madman*".

Beautifully stated paradox!

Plenty of room for 'fire in the belly' there!

May 2009

---

* See "Biblical Economics" by R. Archer Torrey III, 5th ed., 2005, ISBN 0-911312-99-4.

*

T he following contribution was sent to the Reform Scotland/Sunday Times Scotland Essay Competition in 2009, on the vexed question stated below, with closing date November. Although not acknowledged to me, I have always borne in mind the good assurance given me once, by someone who worked in the world of the press – that a good letter is never wasted in the Editor's office!

*

Dear Sirs – dear Friends! -

"Political Accountability in Scotland: how can we ensure our politicians are answerable and effective?"

Hopelessly strait-jacketed title!

"What new dreams do we have?"

- Michael Fry firing off on "pen your vision of Scotland's future". That's better!

Let us ponder, as a start, the wisdom of Thomas Jefferson, (1743-1816, U.S. President), as expressed in his following two statements:-

1) "... we are all aware that not only the wisdom of the ordinary man, but also his interest and sentiment, have a very short radius of operation; they cannot be stretched over any area of much more than township-size, and it is the acme of absurdity to suppose that any man or any body of men can arbitrarily exercise their wisdom, interest and sentiment over a state-wide or nation-wide area with any kind of success."

2) "I know of no safer repository of the ultimate power of society but the people themselves."

Hence, it is not "how to make our politicians more answerable and effective", but – how to get rid of the inherently corruptive structure of centralised power, and place power directly back into the hands of the people.

The "how to" is very simple.

There is a natural social law called the Law of Rent – (see pp.26-27 of green booklet enclosed) – which would take full care of the above. Suppression of its knowledge over centuries is all that has prevented its adoption and operation – to the liberation of the Planet as well as of its people.

The confining of your competition to the ages between 16 to 18, and 19 to 25, is, if I may say, somewhat unimaginative! There are old minds in young bodies, and young minds in old bodies. As the friend who sent me your article wrote, "I think it would be a much more interesting competition if it had those age ranges and then 75 to 82 year olds and 83 to 90 year olds. That would be quite fascinating I think – that juxtaposition." Hear, hear!

Being then, myself, of the latter brigades, I am not an official entrant to your competition – but in the hope that there are young minds in old/er bodies also among the judges, who genuinely seek to know what "new dreams" there are out there, I send you, as sufficient to set you on the track, this modest package enclosed.

Fortunately you will have plenty of time to study it, before the essays start coming in!

23rd June 2009

*

The Land for the People

When, in the spring of 2010, a friend sent me a newspaper cutting about an aspiring highland chieftain who, having acquired a coat-of-arms, then decided to attempt to reclaim the old clan lands via an approach to the Scottish Parliament's Petitions Committee – I could not resist the opportunity to plunge in and address the Committee myself with an alternative proposal!

*

A certain cutting from X newspaper has reached me, a copy of which I enclose. It concerns a claim by clan chieftain Y to certain clan lands, under the Ur Duthchas law of tenure.

I write therefore to alert you to a better, and prior, claim to the land of Scotland, by the people of Scotland themselves, which I hereby place before you.

The natural Law of Rent – (illustrated copy enclosed) – will, by its operations, not only return the land to the people but will secure to them a birthright in land for all time, and similarly to all succeeding generations. Since this law has existed since the beginning of time, being a natural law, it antedates, and supercedes, Ur Duthchas tenure.

Beyond this, the natural Law of Rent:-

1) Will bring the demise of the present embarrassing, and disastrous, situation whereby a body called the Scottish Government presides over an *enserfed populace* (see the Law of Rent), via the administration of a system of land tenure founded on a twofold robbery: namely, the robbery of the land from the people, and the sequential robbery from the community of the *community-created land rents*.

(See again the Law of Rent – generally attributed to Ricardo, but according to a footnote in "Progress and Poverty" by Henry George, first set out by Dr James Anderson of Edinburgh.)

2) Will do away with the present dominion of the WIZARD – conjuror-up of the entire global 'debt' fiasco. (See WIZARD enclosure – Comment, Sept 09.)

3) Will finally honour Scotland's preeminent part – for centuries kept hidden from us – in setting forth this great natural social Law. See contents of enclosed "Birthright in Land – and the State of Scotland Today".

The subordination of Scotland's land tenure to this natural Law of Rent will thus be a blessing beyond measure, both to the people of Scotland for far too long enserfed by a false land tenure law – spawning its plethora of social problems that become *intractable*; and to the land of Scotland, deprived of its true guardians – and similarly abused and languishing under false land tenure for shameful centuries.

Finally, it was the clan chieftains themselves who sold out to the feudal system – which led to the highland clearances. Thus our very history rises up against any return to Ur Duthchas land tenure. I therefore trust that you will thoroughly examine this communication, (including my letter enclosed to the Scottish Office, designating this reform as RENT, not tax); and I much look forward to receiving your reply to it.

Enclosures:
"Chief petitions MSPs ..."
Illustrated Law of Rent.
"The WIZARD ...", Comment, Sept 09.
Letter to The Scottish Office, 27 Sept 98, p.564 of the following,
"Birthright in Land ..." ISBN 0 9535426 0 2.

*

FOOTNOTE

The 'ethics' of today's land ownership – founded on a phoney capital value of land.

"My ancestors purchased all the lands I possess, with the exception of some commons, such as Cairngorms or Benmacdhui, acquired merely as their share of the spoil when the other landlords were having a general scramble for all the hills and glens of Scotland."

("Birthright in Land – and the Sate of Scotland Today", p.239.)

21st March 2010

*

The outcome of my approach was a happy surprise, since the copy of "Birthright in Land ...", sent in support of my letter, was finally placed in the Parliament's Information Centre – (which is "made up of professional researchers who ensure the provision of information ... to support MSPs and the business ... of the Parliament. They will be able to use your book for future background research.")

I was pleased with this gracious glad acceptance of my book, since I had not been at all certain, at the start, how my letter would be received by the Committee. But it is surely possible that it may have opened the eyes of some at least, of its members, for the first time, to the real depth of corruption of the land tenure system which currently holds sway – not in Scotland alone.

*

Drink and Drugs – Land Injustice
– and Foundational Morality

A meeting called at a certain local school last summer, to discuss growing problems with some of the younger generation today, provided an opportunity to go rather more deeply into the whole matter – and to touch on further areas of vital education which are tragically missing from today's syllabuses.

*

[Letter to a friend]

About the meeting at the school on Tuesday, concerning "drugs, drink, etc." – I just hope someone points out that the *root* trouble we are facing in all this is that young people today have nowhere proper, no space of their own, in which to deploy their – *basically creative* – energies!

When all they can use are bits of public ground which they are not allowed to touch – then what else *can* they do but congregate there, and get high, or drunk, or both? What could be more obvious? "We ain't got nothin' to do and nowhere to go", they tell us. So what then? The grown-ups wring their hands and rush forward with invented schemes – cafes – sport – whatever. How blind can we be? How deaf?

There is just *no* way of our escaping the fact that, to move them out of this culture, we must UNLOCK THE LAND!

These young people must have what is every young person's primary need – *and birthright:* a place of *their own* – a place where they can engage those CREATIVE ABILITIES which they were born to explore, and which require, as their basic need, the POSSESSION OF A PIECE OF LAND!

- A space of your very own, in which to dig, plant, build – create in whatever way. – To put up a hut on, or make a bender dwelling or tree house – something you can then *live* in – live in *independently*; to begin to shape your own adult life – not have others endlessly discussing and trying to shape it for you. Don't birds fly the nest when grown? – and don't animals turf out their young similarly, to fend for themselves? All primitive peoples recognised this need of their young. Our *perversity* in this simply backfires on us. Human nature won't stand it. And we think we have a problem with drink and drugs? The problem is – *ourselves!* It's the adults – not the youngsters!

And so – a piece of land, perhaps then to put up a shed on – to be a workshop – to discover/develop yet further creative skills. And to follow? Visiting each other's domains – seeing what others are doing on theirs. And so – exchanges of ideas, of skills – of hospitality. There is no end to it! And at some point inviting help, maybe, from some of the adults, others in the community – perhaps past school teachers? – people you feel you'd like to learn more from, as you explore further into these new horizons ...

What possible pull would that pathetic, knock-you-senseless drink and drugs scenario have on any young lad or lass, then? A real stand-on-your-own-feet start to adult life – no more just being treated on-going as children. The beginning of taking *real responsibility for yourself* – and a friendly vying with your peers as to who makes the best go of it.

In short, there is just no end to the degree to which young people could raise *themselves* up – BY THEIR OWN EFFORTS. Which is what they are actually crying out to do – because it's what they were BORN to do! And the whole of our youth's culture would then shift away also from another of today's huge 'social problems' – under-age pregnancies. For what more natural than to prepare a home, *first*, for the progeny you would bring into this world? Can't we finally see that it's our own blindness in *rendering impossible* this *natural order* for young people, which lies at the root of this yet further huge 'social problem'?

The first thing we need to do for today's youth is – GET OFF THEIR BACKS! That is – we need to UNLOCK THE LAND!

Could it be more simple?

NOR IS THERE ANY OTHER WAY OF TURNING THIS SCENE AROUND – let us be warned!

For drink and drugs are simply a last resort escape of the young today from what is intuitively recognised as an UNNATURAL AND INTOLERABLE scenario awaiting them on the threshold of adulthood – a state of prolonged childhood, offering *no rite of passage into adult life*.

I can hear the response of the adults: but how do we "unlock the land"? It's all held under title-deed.

Here is where we adults come face-to-face with our own shortcomings. These are *our children*. And we want to do our best for them? Then what are we doing standing by in a society that provides no place for our young?

We must WAKE UP! We must take hold of the fact which Lloyd George challenged us with a hundred years ago – that if you want to trace the original owner of a piece of land, you must *go back to the man who stole it*. Yes, indeed! – we must wake up to the fact that the system of land tenure we live under is one based on ROBBERY!

But does this not go down to the very roots of morality too? Something else that is not – *but should be* – taught in our schools today. So how about making a start where land justice and morality coincide? In the words of St. Chrysostom:-

"God gave the earth to be cultivated by all. Since, therefore, His bounty is common, how comes it that you have so many fields, and your neighbour not even a clod of earth?"

And how about twinning that statement with the most foundational of all moral teachings – the one given as elementary by all of the great religions of the world? All eight of them – see below. But just to quote two here:-

From Christianity: "All things whatsoever ye would that men should do to you, do ye even so to them."

From Hinduism: "... Do naught unto others which would cause you pain if done to you."

What clearer rebuke could possibly be turned upon the holder of all those fields? – or the holder of similarly extensive acreages in Scotland today? – both equally happy to ignore that "pain" we must not inflict. Here, the pain of a brother compelled to exist without "even a clod of earth". Heaven knows, are there not *thousands upon thousands* of these in Scotland today? – And the land a gift from a benevolent Creator, gifted to *all* of His children equally? In the matter of another's pain in which we are all involved, the question of land injustice meets us head-on. What kind of a moral code have we here?

Perhaps the heads of our schools could start to make good a huge twofold omission in today's curriculums:-

(i)   The teaching of that great moral code – fundamental to all the world's great religions – for the children to carry forward from their school-days, to be an on-going guide to them throughout their adult lives – (of equal benefit to society as to themselves); and in the *first* place to be of practical aid in resolving, at school, the day-to-day difficulties that arise, the children themselves exploring the way it relates to their lives and behaviour, *including* the ugly matter of bullying. As children enjoy learning by heart, why not get them to memorise that great code in all the eight forms we have come across? – alert to recognise any further expression of it.

(ii)   The teaching of this fundamental moral code in its particular reference to *the land question*, with accompanying research and discussion as to how best the gross land injustice of our society may be resolved. For heaven knows the "pain" in this sphere, involving whole families, and spreading to other victims too, which results from the young of today, denied their just birthright in the land of their birth, turning to drown their sorrows and despairs – (whether consciously or unconsciously held) – in *drugs and drink*.

21st June 2010

Extract from an issue of *Good Government* (Australia)

David Brooks recently brought to notice some surprising and striking similarities among the major religions and philosophies when it comes to the Golden Rule. Since this Rule, most often described by Henry George as the doctrine of equal rights, forms the basis of his philosophy, these similarities are set out below.

CHRISTIANITY: All things whatsoever ye would that men should do to you, do ye even so to them – *Matthew 7:12.*

HINDUISM: This is the sum of duty. Do naught unto others which would cause you pain if done to you – *Mahabharata 5:1517.*

CONFUCIANISM: Surely it is the maxim of loving-kindness: Do not unto others that you would not have them do unto you – *Analects 15:23.*

ISLAM: No one of you is a believer until he desires for his brother that which he desires for himself – *Sunnah.*

BUDDHISM: Hurt not others in ways that you yourself would find hurtful – *Udana Varga 5:18.*

JUDAISM: What is hateful to you, do not to your fellowmen. That is the entire Law; all the rest is commentary – *Talmud, Shabbat 31:a.*

TAOISM: Regard your neighbour's gain as your own gain, and your neighbour's loss as your loss – *T'ai Shag Kan Ying P'ien.*

ZOROASTRIANISM: That nature alone is good which refrains from doing unto another whatsoever is not good for itself – *Dadistan-i-dinik 94:5.*

*

IS NATURE INHERENTLY MORAL?
A perspective from Spirituality –
<u>not</u> Religion!

In the emerging world of the New Age we have come, happily, to a parting of the ways between religion – offspring of human institutions – and spirituality, born of no time or place.

A letter in Land and Liberty from a US reader, attempting to take Henry George to task on a question relating to this matter, drew from me the following response. It did not appear in Land and Liberty, but happily was published subsequently, slightly shortened, in both The Georgist Journal, USA and Good Government, Australia – (and has since drawn some warm responses from other readers).

*

W hilst I have much enjoyed elsewhere the Geoist writings of X, his contribution in your Winter 2010 issue on "Morality and Nature", - referring in part to Henry George – stems from a strangely constricted viewpoint!

By all means let us have "freedom from religion", for the religions of this world are all constructs of limited human thinking. But they having nothing essentially to do with *spirituality* – which was surely what Henry George was referring to, in, for instance, his deeply perceptive statement that to bring about land justice would require "nothing less than the religious conscience", "intelligent self-interest" alone being insufficient for the task.* The distinction between religion (as referring to humanly handed down bodies of teaching), and spirituality

---

* S ee "The Condition of Labour", ch. 2.

(immediate experience of the Unseen) has only received recognition since Henry George's day – whose writings are steeped in spirituality.

X deplores "faith in an afterlife" as a mode of escape from responsibility in this life – e.g., how we treat the Planet. But this is a view strictly *religion-bound*! Moreover – (since presumably X is speaking of Christianity) – stemming from a religion that, having sold its soul to the State at the Diet of Constantinople, had long ago become an extremely adept instrument of human politics! The Christian church emphasised an afterlife as an escape for itself from declaiming against the injustice and miseries that stemmed from land monopoly.

What we may call spirituality is something of an entirely different order. For some are born knowing that "not I live, but some force lives through me", and stemming from this inner knowledge – that "there is no death". This is not a mere intellectual knowing, but something far deeper, being the most certain identity of one's human self even in the here and now. Hence, instead of an *after*life, such see life as a *continuum*, in which we reap as we sow every step of the way – (an awareness which may be recognized at some point in our journey as what is called karmic law). This is of course at the other end of the spectrum from escapism!

"Belief in a conscious creator is humancentric" X writes. But how so, when this marvellous creation consists of myriads of other forms and forces which equally draw our wonder and awe? And what indeed could be more "humancentric" than the belief that the moral nature arises exclusively in man? - ! In fact evidence of a moral nature abounds in the animal world, as a whole library of books testifies, (and indeed my own experience of thirty-five years living in close contact with the wildlife here, including its winged creatures).

What, also of Tompkins and Bird's fascinating volume, "The Secret Life of Plants"? Or – to start at the very beginning of nature – what of the amazingly variant crystals formed by water, in response to the blessing or cursing over it of a human voice? The recent photographic recordings of these by the Japanese scientist, Masaru Emoto, reveals a profoundly responsive moral sense existent already in water ... which, come to think of it, makes up far the greater part of the human body! Furthermore, if the laws of nature are morally neutral, as X would maintain – then what is to be made of the blazing exception to this of the natural Law of Rent? – whose challenge to the human race lies precisely in our recognizing of its profoundly embedded moral code!

Finally, it is impossible to imagine – (and anthropology bears this out) – a people living in close contact with their soil, and partaking of its seasonal rhythms and productive powers, who are not profoundly aware of a Creative Intelligence running through all things, and existing far beyond the narrow boundaries of time and space. The growth of humanism today – (now *that's* "humancentric" if you like!) – is the signature of a people too long divorced from their land – this unfortunate dumbing-down of their life-experience no doubt playing a part in our movement's tendency today to reduce the land question to a purely fiscal measure. We need to remember that the final chapter of "Progress and Poverty" (preceding its "Conclusion") was the sounding of a great trumpet – "The Call to Liberty".

But what does a people dispossessed of their land and severed from the great Crestive Intelligence know of FREEDOM!

Easter 2010

*

Published Letters

and one other

"Where Talent Lies Crushed"

with Coda

*

Published under the heading "Reforms needed" – but more truly stated –

The one great essential reform

Sir, - I wonder that X, benign as his intentions may be about his great wildlife park (September 12), does not see how insulting it is to the people of Scotland that he should express himself as wishing to take "a little bit of land here, a little bit there, and end up with around 50,000 acres", when most Scots do not own a square foot of their own land, nor, as things are at present, have they any chance of doing so.

It is surely a staggering thought that the 5.1 million of Scotland's population live on only 3% of our total land area – and it is a disgrace. Need we wonder at our rising rate of drugs, drink, crime and suicides – our booze and blade culture as it is now being called – no superficial attempts to deal with which will ever succeed?

The Scots were always a people peculiarly hefted to their land, and the state of our society today but reflects (uncomprehending of its origins though it may be after so long a dispossession) the despair of those who, without a bit of land to call their own, feel bereft of identity – let alone that they are bereft of proper homes and work.

As Ron Greer says, what the land needs is sustainable human rehabitation. Where trees will grow, people can live and make their own lives – which will then be much too busy and satisfying to fall prey to these social ills.

But this cannot be if they live as tenants, it must be as free men that they repopulate the land.

Therefore, it is the reform of land tenure that needs addressing, with all occupants of land placed on an equal footing through paying the land rentals annually to the community.

But the call for such reform will need to come from the people, for it will not come from the Parliament.

Shirley-Anne Hardy
The Courier, 27 Sept, 2005

*

Published under the heading "Reverse is true" – or, as I would re-phrase it –

We see which way the 'filter' runs!

Sir, – "Estate hit by grouse decline needs windfarm cash: owner" – we read in your June 3 issue, re a Perthshire estate at the heart of a windfarm wrangle.

May I respond to that plea, and to the claim that the windfarm would benefit the area by generating "much-needed revenue" for the estate whose benefits would "filter down" to those living and working in the area.

It is time to point out that* these estates are in fact parasites on the communities they purport to serve, whose wealth "filters up" to them at present from below.

It is the need of ordinary folk for land – with its potential to produce everything from food to energy, besides sheer living-space – which generates the rental value of the land off which these estates presently feed.

Were these rental values returned each year to the community which generates them – as rightly should be – we would soon

* [Addendum]
however well-intentioned their incumbents may be,

"make poverty history" and lack of housing, too, right here at home (our example our best gift to the Third World).

I see the estate claims also to benefit the community by providing housing and "property". As distinct from housing, "property" must mean land. But as the land was here some while before these invented titles to it were set up, the situation is surely the reverse. These big estates actually cut ordinary folk off from that "property" which is their birthright equally!

It is not windfarms we need, but justice – and plain common sense!

Shirley-Anne Hardy
The Courier, 11 June, 2005

*

The Editor,
The Permaculture Activist,
U.S.A.

Dear Sir,

The Right to Food

May I comment briefly on the matter of the "right to food" cited as an article of the U.N. Declaration of Human Rights, quoted in "Community Food Security" in your issue 54, (an article otherwise full of good things).

If people in general in society have "the right to food", it follows that a certain element in that society has – for some mysterious reason – the ability (and hence bounden duty) to provide that food ... to the underdogs who, for some equally mysterious reason, are deprived of that ability.

This somewhat closer scrutiny of the matter presents, of course, a more problematical face to us, which obliges us to explore, to its depths and to its roots, the general DISEMPOWERMENT of whole populations world-wide today, regarding the fundamental human need for food – not to mention a number of other fundamental human needs as well.

I will willingly provide a copy of a fitting critique (conference paper of 1968) by Frank Dupuis, of this vaunted Declaration of Human Rights, to anyone sending an International Stamp Coupon to this address.

Yours truly,
Shirley-Anne Hardy
Published in Spring Issue, 2005

*

"The State will never house the people!"

I cannot let X's question on housing (August issue) *"Does one dare interfere with the free market?"* – pass without comment. There is of course **no** *"free market"* in housing, so long as land, its most essential component, remains locked up in monopoly.

"Ideas have been put forward to alleviate the problem", X continues. But he makes no mention of the simplest idea of all – (many times aired in these pages) – which is, of course, to remove from the scene that absurd monopoly.

Absurd? Surely! *"What more preposterous than that one tenant for a day of this rolling sphere should collect rent for it from his co-tenants or sell to them for a price what was here ages before him and will be here ages after him."*

But Henry George, whose words I quote here, did not merely denounce this folly – he pointed to its practical solution: that is, the collecting of the land's rental values, by the community annually, from every landholder; these rents belonging to the community by right, since they arise entirely out of its need for that land, and have nothing to do with the landholder.

Since land has no fall-back capital value (having no original production costs), so, with these rents annually collected, there is no monetary value left to furnish a land market. People hold only what land they can utilize for the annual rental required, and today's phoney 'land market' – with its fatal grip on the housing scenario – meets its demise.

Our persistent folly in looking to either local councils or the government to solve the 'housing' problem against the background of present monopoly, but testifies to the childish state of our thinking on many serious issues today. These ever-expanding centralist bodies – parasites upon an ever-dwindling base of actual wealth-producers – are in fact a huge additional part of the problem, not its solution! The State will never house the people! Rather, the land once freed from monopoly – (and of its great overload of building regulations too) – we shall find that the people will finally **house themselves**.

In a society where the great mass of the people can neither build their own houses nor grow their own food, we should long ago have grasped that there was something fundamentally wrong.

Shirley-Anne Hardy
Comment (Aberfeldy), Sept 2007

*

This letter was published under the title "Russia shows way forward", but its truer title is –

"The real future for food production is via land reform!"

Sir, - Re the letter, Matters Agricultural (January 21): the threat to our food security has fortunately nothing to do with the EU's regulations to limit – clearly half-heartedly! – certain pesticides.

Happily, re this whole matter, a new vision is now opening before us. For Russia's dacha movement is pointing the real way forward to food security, for any nation on Earth.

To boost food production during the second world war, millions of urban Russians were supplied with dachas in the country – usually modest wood-built homes, but with enough land for them to feed their families throughout the year – and often with a surplus. This dacha movement is gaining new momentum in the new century through the publication of The Ringing Cedars series of books by Vladimir Megre – which are now inspiring a movement worldwide.

Russia's official statistics reveal that in 2005 these Russian gardeners, using less than 3% of the country's agricultural land, produced over 53% of the country's agricultural output!

So we can safely put behind us our polluting, oil-based, EU-regulated agriculture. What Scotland – and the whole world – needs is radical land reform!

Shirley-Anne Hardy
The Courier, 13 Feb, 09

*

214

This letter was published in January 2011 issue of "New Leaves". Given no specific heading, I have placed my own one here.

The Great Primary Female

It is interesting to read of the evolution of the term 'man' since Norman times (your Oct-Dec 2010 issue).

However, I find my concern about the secondary female – the human one – swallowed up in a far greater concern about the **primary** female in our life: Gaia, the Earthly Mother of us all, yet so overlooked by society today that people – including vegans – buy and sell her, without batting an eyelid, with a market price attached to her as to any slave; indeed, as any slave, put up to auction and knocked down under the hammer.

It is my firm conviction that, were Gaia to be reinstated in our lives – recognised, as in earlier ages, as our Earthly Mother, forever beyond value or the shame of a monetary price ticket – that this resurrection of the Primary Woman from her present slave status would bring about, as a natural corollary, a total reconstruction of the relationship between her sons and daughters, between the human male and female (or female and male, daughters and sons, if you wish).

Need it be said that the Norman Conquest was a conquest by a **male-dominated people,** who had long placed the Earthly Mother under their heel, so it is small wonder if so many woes for the female human followed from that time. Merely to reassert the human female will not restore to us the vital Primary Woman, whom – crushed as ever under the Norman heel – we have done nothing to resurrect; not even to notice the slave status she occupies in our market-places, nor even the nonchalance with which we poison her with our thousand immoral inventions today.

The following final paragraph of my article in the Winter 2002 *Permaculture Activist* deals with the resurrection that is awaited also by the animal kingdom – the focus of vegans' concern – but will not come about until the focus of our concern becomes the Earthly Mother itself:

"Let us see that we catch up, then, with those thinkers who are truly of the New Age. For so shall we form part of today's most vital 'web of connectivity' – the movement that is dedicated to ending the buying and selling of our Earthly Mother, and which holds the essential key to achieving this. Let us do so not only for our own sakes – in our now visibly disintegrating Western society, reaping the terrible fruits of its immoral foundations. Let us do so also for the sake of all those other beings, and creatures, who exist on Earth today in a state of wretchedness, enserfed – within the ever-tightening noose of land monopoly – to those who are now their global masters ... That noose which, in the name of globalisation, holds in its grip the very Earth, having re-christened as 'commodities' both Gaia herself and all her bounteous gifts to us."

Yours truly,
Shirley-Anne Hardy

*

The following letter, (with minor editing for publication), written to the Convenor of a Scottish Local Council on 29 Sept 05, prompts the heading –

Where Talent Lies Crushed

Dear X,

You write, in your letter of September 18th, regretting the lack of talent produced by Scotland today. To me, having observed the scene carefully now, from a background of land economics, for several decades, the reason for the apparent lack of talent is very evident. I should think some of that talent is very likely sitting wrapped in a blanket somewhere on the chill pavements of Princes Street – sights today that I never saw in the Edinburgh I grew up in – or is simply, as T.S. Eliot put it, "living and partly living"; sapped, dragged down by the cost of the sheer struggle to survive ...

Then there are those whose talents will lie buried, not from lack of initiative as the ones Christ reproved, but buried simply under a crushing mount of DEBT: debt, which will dog their footsteps – all but the very luckiest – for all of their life's journey. Alas for the mountain of *talent* so buried, in such a society as ours!

When are we going to awaken to our real situation? See my enclosures here on this shameful matter.

As a Scotswoman myself, I would like to think that this letter is not written in vain, but that perhaps it may start to circulate, to set people thinking – and so help bring about a most necessary change in direction ere complete collapse arrives.

With all good wishes,
Yours sincerely,
Shirley-Anne Hardy

*

Stepping back from this depressive correspondence, and re-focussing: what do I myself know, and see, as to talent in Scotland – right now?

Why – an amazing band of people, who only need the freedom of their land to come to the full strength of what would be a marvellous flowering!

It is not talent that lacks – it's FREEDOM! – freedom which is crying out to us for its essential foundation-stone – JUSTICE!

I think of the throngs of 'green' people I know, only longing to set to work – only wanting land!

I pick up a card given me by one such. It reads:-

Artistic, Caring and Environmental

The Green Man

Garden Design, Planting & Maintenance

Wide Knowledge of Native Plants, Outdoor Art
Nature Gardens and low/no Maintenance

Here is someone of versatile skills indeed, for he is also a wide-ranging craftsman and artist. But he cannot grow his own wood, for his own work! Let alone all else that land will provide you with: your home – (a bender dwelling?), your food ...

I think next of an extraordinary soul, whom I have been privileged to meet – MAGI! ... Of another, whose visionary project is held in suspense – for the time being but not for aye! ... And yet another, who has just written me he has bought a piece of land in Bulgaria – because there was no room for him in the land of his birth!

No room? Just to pluck one random statistic: "We no longer question the evident iniquity of 350 families and institutions owning over two-thirds of the ten million acres of the Highlands and Islands of Scotland". So there's no space for this individual? Vast areas of habitable land in Scotland are empty! I quote

Charlie Pye-Smith in Undercurrents of June/July 1982. That's nearly thirty years ago – and we may be sure the monopoly has screwed considerably tighter since then, for that's how monopoly works.

So there is no room for someone who happens to be also a talented and widely experienced permaculturist! As if the land of Scotland was not crying out precisely for such! – to rescue it from aeons of over-grazing and other such ill-usages ... As Ron Greer is always reminding us, the true resource of Scotland's land is its soil-and-vegetation complex – the very thing which permaculturists have direct hands-on expertise in!

But the politicians who – (sitting at their desks in the 'upturned boat' that is the Scottish Parliament!) – oversee the present scenario of land-use via financial enticements and other manipulations, have no real interest in either the land of Scotland or its people.

It will take *the people themselves* to resurrect *their own land*!

*

So much for my Council Convenor correspondent!

But then – he's a politician too, of course!

*

Finally – on a lighter note!

Gorging Gastropods?

Dear Gardeners, plagued by Gastropods,
Would you defeat the little sods,
Grow you a bed of Garlic-Mustard* -
Its glorious pong soon has them flustered!
Your plants, in *this* GM's embraces
Wreathed, and sunned on by its faces,
The Gastropods won't bother you –
While joys gas*tric* await you, too!

For daily salads to embellish,
Garlic-mustard gives rare relish –
Chop the leaves to your delight,
A bounty both for scent and sight!
Perennial and evergreen,
With Dandelion a matching queen –
Such health and wealth of daily salad
Should well inspire a worthy ballad!

And those now gas*tricked* Gastropods?
Why, let us bless the little sods!

*Alliaria petiolata or Jack-by-the-hedge.

Shirley-Anne Hardy
Comment (Aberfeldy), May 2007

REVIEWS

*

The Land Question, (1981)

Birthright in Land – and the State of Scotland Today,
(Peregrine Press, 1999 ISBN 0 9535426 0 2)

*

Some extracts from reviews of "The Land Question"

A superb exposition of the centrality of the land question.
(Geoff Forster in *Progress*, Australia, Oct. 1981.)

...(I)ndispensable reading for those in the environmental movement who realise the impossibility of considering ecological matters in isolation from the social, political and economic context in which they arise.
(From FOE (Scot) Newsletter, Spring 1982.)

A truly inspirational and timeless read.
(P.R. in letter to the Author, 28 Dec. 2002.)

This 40 page booklet is available as a free download at http.//www.commentonline.co.uk/supplement/index.htm or send 9" x 6" self-addressed envelope with basic stamp, and £1.60 in payment, (stamps accepted), to The Peregrine Press, The Rocks, Pitlochry, Perthshire PH16 5QZ.

*

Some extracts from reviews of "Birthright in Land
– and the State of Scotland Today",
(Peregrine Press, 1999. ISBN 0 9535426 0 2.)

*

Land reform momentum is reaching a fevered pitch today in Scotland, but Shirley-Anne Hardy has been sounding the call for decades. Now she has collected and published her views, backgrounds and seminal influences in a tome that may well become a standard Georgist reference work.

(The Georgist Journal, USA, Aut. 1999.)

... As Hooton said in his introduction to *Nutrition and Physical Degeneration*, I will say to you, you have written what will be called "a profoundly significant book". I salute you with the sincerest admiration!

(Marion Patricia Connolly, Curator of the Price-Pottenger Nutrition Foundation, 2 Aug. 2001.)

... It may seem a difficult task to create a book which will set out in strict erudition the current scene of planetary – and social – destruction, and expose to the full the mechanism of land monopoly which lies at the root of both, but her writing style is such that every section is accessible to the reader, there is always the feeling that she is accompanying the reader in the style of the born teacher – her subject brought vibrantly alive ...

We must salute Shirley-Anne Hardy as one who can see, in the sense of Ruskin's observation, and who has shared that seeing in so vital a way:

"The greatest thing a human soul ever does in this world is to see something and tell what it saw in a plain way.

Hundreds of people can talk for one who can think.
But thousands can think for one who can see.
To see clearly is poetry, prophecy and religion all in one."

(Wm. Ruskin)
(Valerie and Peter Gould, in *Good Government*, Australia, Dec. 05.)

A review of a work of this scale cannot do justice to it by means of selective quotations. The only remedy is to urge anyone who reads this review to read the book in its entirely ... and thus do justice to a monumental work so relevant to Scotland today – and far beyond.

(Ian Lawson, in The Cairngorms Campaigner, April 2001)

A truly remarkable book by a truly remarkable woman.

(Mark Ballard, in Reforesting Scotland, Summer 2000).

*

Chapter 2

*

Reclaiming Our Language:
Imposter Terms

Imposter Terms

*

There is only time for a quick dive-in here, but it is a vital one, for the perversion of our language plays a major part in our on-going enserfment.

Let us take the first and most obvious imposter term: 'democracy'. How many people realize that the actual meaning of this word – (from the two simple Greek words, *demos* and *kratos*, that make it up) – is *people-power*? Our word 'democracy', therefore, as used, is not only a travesty of its true meaning, but a mockery of it. Unfortunately, we cannot fall back on 'de-MOCK-racy' – since the spoken word does not reveal it.

I can think of no word, in our present vocabulary, which properly describes the political power, sprung of land monopoly, which rules today – across the globe. 'Plutocracy', (the rulership of wealth), gives no hint of that wealth's *origins* – nor therefore of the necessary path to freedom from it. 'Territocracy' is too cumbersome. However, *grundocracy*, (using the Old English word *grund* for *ground*) seems possible. It has a useful earthiness about it, and would certainly bring home to us, at every utterance of it, the shameful root of that political power which we must rid ourselves of. Or perhaps readers can think of a better one? We should certainly launch some term alternative to the cover-up one of 'democracy'.

The second most obvious imposter-term is 'capitalism'/ 'capitalist' – as it is falsely used today, like 'democracy' to describe our politico-economic system. AJ Nock states the obvious, (if we give it a moment's thought), where he writes in *Our Enemy the State*, "there never has been an (economic) system, nor can one be imagined, that is not capitalist". For even the very simplest of tools produced in a society to aid work, are items of capital. The former Soviet Union was a full-blown capitalist society – only all the capital was in the hands of the State. This truer view of the matter offers us the truer term that we need: 'monopoly capitalism', or a 'monopoly capitalist' society. The West (to use a general term) – displays simply another form of monopoly capitalism, that based on *land monopoly*. On this both Karl Marx and Henry George agree: "Monopoly of land is the basis of monopoly in capital", (Karl Marx). "The concentration of capital is the child of land monopoly", (Henry George – revealing its powerful umbilical cord).

As for the description of a true capitalist society, freed from monopoly of any kind – it could, I think, hardly be more beautifully expressed than in the Biblical verses in I Kings: 4 and Micah 4; not surprisingly, as they speak of a society which had known life under the Law of Rent. They write of 'every man sitting under his own vine and his own fig tree, with none to make him afraid'. Your own secure home, with its produce to sustain you – and *no political power or bullying bureaucracy to oppress*! Socrates of course describes just such a society similarly - in fuller terms, albeit less poetically. (See p.116).

The third obvious imposter term that comes to mind is 'free trade' – taken over today to describe what is decidedly *not* free trade any more! Perhaps what I wrote re this matter in June 2001 to the International Union for the Taxation of Land Values – (term of anathema itself, it must be said! – see end of chapter) – will suffice re this imposter term:-

"May I make the following contribution to the FREE TRADE debate ...

Whether mankind is in the grip of a severe mental decline – (due to pollution, pesticides, etc., as convincingly argued, I am told, in a recent book, *Terminus Brain*) – with a huge decline in educational standards perhaps contributing too? – my first comment must be: I find it astonishing that the WTO's take-over of the term "free trade" should have been accepted by the public at large as it has – and not greeted with a howl of derision.

Clearly nothing that involves a contract (i.e. trade) can possibly be called 'free', unless it is freely engaged upon by *both* parties. Hence what the WTO advocates is *imposed* trade, and the WTO's imposed trade can no more be taken as 'free' trade than slavery can be regarded as a 'free' engagement of labour."

Readers may well think of other terms, similarly used today to obscure the perils of our society's false foundations and to maintain the present regime of serfdom. Here I will focus on just one more – (before the great final one!)

This is the term 'human rights', used freely towards just such confusion, in the *Declaration of Human Rights* produced by the United Nations. An excellent critique of this document was produced some decades ago by Frank Dupuis – who pointed out that most of the *rights* set down in it were such as might have been written for a society of serfs – looking for kindly keeping! And there was no place in it, of course, for any right to land! It is solemnizing to note, from the absence of any general outcry at this charade of a presentation of human rights, how deeply the *psychology of serfdom* is now embedded in us. My letter published in the *Permaculture Activist* of Spring 2004, "The Right to Food" (see under *Author's Writings* here) applies equally to many of the 'rights' put forward in this *Declaration*.

And now, finally: we must never allow the imposter term (if ever there was one!) 'tax' to oust the true term RENT in our efforts to bring forward, in Scotland at any rate, this vital fundamental reform. It is true Henry George occasionally used this term in his work – but we live in a different era, a great deal further down the road to the destruction he so clearly foresaw, and he would surely wish us to use our own 'nous' in today's scenario, as to what will, *and what will not,* aid us in our task.

On 27th September 1998, I had reason to address the (then) Scottish Office on this matter, (and received no further response from them). Later, in the summer of 2003, I had occasion to send a copy of this letter to the Australian publication, Progress, in Melbourne, and in autumn 2003 its editor sent me a copy of the following message they had received about it, addressed to the president of the movement in Australia:-

"I would ask you to pass on my congratulations to the Editor of Progress in his printing of that article by Shirley-Anne Hardy entitled 'Extract from the above-mentioned letter to the Scottish Office', p.15 of Progress July/Aug 03. That is the best article that has ever been written or published in Progress. It's absolutely spot on".

In the hopeful possibility that there may be others too who find it "spot on" – and hence that it may preserve us from a cauldron of confusions in our efforts to move this matter forward in Scotland – below follows that letter in full.*

*

Assistant Secretary to the Land Reform Policy Group,
The Scottish Office,
Pentland House,
47, Robb's Loan,
Edinburgh EH14 1TY.   27 Sept 98

Dear A..... M.....,

Land Reform for Scotland

Thank you for your letter of 22nd September, saying that "I understand your main interest lies in the subject of land value taxation ... discussed on p.21 of the consultation paper, that the "second paper contains the Group's emerging thinking and

---

* **P**laced also in "Birthright in Land ...", pp.564-5.

provisional view of all options discussed, including that of taxation", that the Group "will consider the responses" to this second paper in preparing its final document, and that you will send me a copy of that final document when it is published.

I must clarify a misunderstanding. I do not have any interest in the promotion of a reform by the name of "land value taxation". The reform referred to in my letter of April 29th is that of *land rent for revenue* – (sometimes also referred to as *community ground rent*). My letter makes no mention of "land value taxation".

The term "rent" – more precisely "rental value" – is the essential term descriptive of this reform. The reason is that rental values are community-created. The collection of *community-created values* to finance *the community's needs* is thus in accordance with natural law of an elementary kind. In the sphere of revenue-raising, natural law stands for those higher laws which are infallible and non-manipulative, as compared with human ones which are both manipulative and fallible. There can therefore be no questioning of the fact that these rental values, originating from the community, must be returned to the community from which they originate. To sum up:-

(1) The dedicating to the community's needs of the rental values it has itself created *meets a moral imperative as well as a practical one.*

(2) The applying to the community's needs of its own rental values *strengthens and empowers the community and every member of it.*

(3) The financing of the community's needs from its own rental values (as opposed to taxation), *promotes a background of stability* against which society can successfully operate – arbitrary human tax-devisings forming no part of that scene.

(4) The setting out of the question of revenue thus, in its correct terms, also *enlightens and educates the public* on a matter of

primary importance for their well-being – a matter upon which there has been a long and artful cover-up.

In contrast: I have come to recognize over the years that the term "land value taxation" – whether used mistakenly by its promoters (and I gather most have written to you under this term), or deliberately by its opposers – is essentially a term of *concealment*, since it places this reform within the brackets of a *tax*.

The nature of a tax is essentially as follows:-

(a) It is an *arbitrary* demand: that is, a demand which accords with the dictates merely of a collection of – entirely fallible – human beings. It is thus *the opposite of moral.*

(b) It is *imposed from above*, and is therefore essentially *contrary to the idea of community empowerment.*

(c) It has *no certainty of continued operation* – taxes change notoriously from one year, and from one budget, to another. This makes a ruinous background for human activity, including business activity, being essentially *de-stabilising.*

(d) It is *dis-educative* of the people as to a fundamental right – that of enjoying the values which they themselves create; and amounts (as stated above) to a term of concealment.

In short, by the term "land value taxation", the land rent reform is indeed *trivialised.*

Given (a), (b), (c) and (d) – with the stack of confusions that must follow therefrom – it is no wonder that your conclusion regarding "land value taxation", in your second paper ("Identifying the Solutions"), does not rise above: "Maybe, but not yet; a lot more study needed" - ! You will now be into that third study ...

Yours sincerely,
Shirley-Anne Hardy

Chapter 3

*

Scenes from a Tapestry

Panel 1:   Rooted Peoples

Panel 2:   Dispossession

Panel 3:   Fruitages of Dispossession

i.   The World Hunger and Population 'Crises'

ii.   'Work' – Fit for an Enserfed People!

iii. A Closer Look at Cities

iv.   The Environment: Gaia's Revenge
      on Globalization

v.   Who Are They? – and Brighter Pathways

Panel 4:   Rooting Back

Coda: The Loch Garry Project
             and its Vision

The ownership of land is the great fundamental fact which ultimately determines the social, the political, and consequently the intellectual and moral condition of a people.

(Progress and Poverty)

We cannot safely leave politics to politicians or political economy to college professors. The people themselves must think because the people alone can act.   (Social Problems)

Let no one imagine he has no influence ... the man who thinks becomes a light and a power.   (Social Problems)

*

Henry George:
Author of "Progress & Poverty" 1879
and other works bringing to light
the great lost <u>natural law of rent</u>

Scenes from a Tapestry

Panel 1: Rooted Peoples

*

In Tom Johnston's "History of the Working Classes in Scotland", published in 1920 – (a book of such interesting but grim content that I hastened to read through my borrowed library copy, that I might put it behind me) – there occurs in chapter 7, "The Reiving of the Common Lands", a beautiful and indeed moving description of life as it was lived formerly in the Highlands and Islands of Scotland, under the just Celtic system of land tenure. This was called 'run-rig' – "a corruption of Roinn Ruith – division run or division common", which was "the usual mode of agriculture all over the North until little more than a century ago" – (which would have been c.1820); vestiges of it lasting on until the time of publication of Tom Johnston's book.

What is of such particular interest concerning life as lived in those communities, was to read of the morality which pervaded them – the kindliness and care for one another which, along with care of the land, flourished among them.

Each township elects its own Constable, who, upon accepting office, "takes off his shoes and stockings. Uncovering his head, he bows reverently low, and promises, in presence of heaven and earth, in presence of God and man – Am fianuis uir agus adhair am fianuis De agus daoine – that he will be faithful to his trust." In some places, the elected Constable takes a handful of earth instead of uncovering his feet. The object is the same – to emphasis by bodily contact with the earth that he is conscious of being made of earth, to which he returns.

After the harvest is gathered in, he summons the people together for "Nabac" (neighbourliness). The meetings are held at night, and are "orderly" and "interesting" and at these meetings all the business of the township is decided by majority vote. What proportion of land will be put under green crop next year? That is settled. Then the Constable divides the arable land into rigs or divisions; lots are cast, what a man draws he holds and tills for 3-years (one-third of the soil being allotted every year); part of the soil is set apart for the relief of the poor, for "the kindness of the poor to the poor throughout these islands is wonderful".

A man must not allow his land to go to waste, since that would hurt the community; they have a Common Good fund, into which go all fines, and this is used by the Constable, after due resolution moved and carried at the Nabac, for the purchase of fresh stock, bulls, tups, etc.; they reclaim much moorland ... Should a crofter or his family fall sick, "his fellow crofters help on his work; if a man's horse dies, his neighbours bring his work concurrently with their own", and if necessary help him to buy another horse ...

(T)he houses of "tenants of the run-rig system are warm, good and comfortable. These tenants carry on their farming operations simultaneously, and not without friendly and wholesome rivalry, the enterprise of the one stimulating the zeal of the other. ... Compassion for the poor, consideration towards the distressed, and respect for the dead are the characteristic traits of these people. This is indicated by their saying, 'Succour to the poor and to the dead (in burying) and sympathy with the distressed are three things which a wise man never regretted', and "The division of the land is made with care and justice. This is in the interest of all."

At the front of this chapter – (which I have in its welcome republication by the Caledonia Centre for Social Development, June 2004) – I see I had put a note: "Pages 3-6 – bar some brief intermissions – utterly beautiful. The rest – recounts the doings of the devil" ... (as we shall see further, in *"Up-Rootings: its Various Devices*.")

In HJ Massingham's absorbing writings, "The Wisdom of the Fields", "Where Man Belongs", etc., which describe the lives of the last true survivors of the old English peasantry – (and what grand characters they were!) – I found the following account:-

> A letter to me from the local historian, Dr WG Hoskins, describes the Leicestershire village of Wigston Magna as an example of a free and self-governing cottager community. It was composed mainly of peasant proprietors without a resident lord since Doomsday "or even earlier". They made their own bye-laws for village and field, managed their own church and its finances, ran their own guild and "in short did everything themselves and were an absolutely independent community". Their mode of life, he added, was a "civilisation in the best sense of the word." ("The Wisdom of the Fields", ch.VI, Collins, 1945.)

I cannot help remembering this excellent summary of the matter by Tom Hodgkinson in "How To Be Free":-*

> Politics is not the art of running a country, it is the art of persuading people that they need a set of paid politicians to run the country ... they need to sell us the idea of themselves as our saviours and also to sell us the idea that we could not run things without them.
> Precisely!

---

* Discovered in a favourite book "Through the Eye of a Needle", by John-Paul Flintoff, (Permanent Publications, 2009).

In "Ujaama" (OUP, 1968), Julius Nyerere of Tanzania writes: "In our traditional African society we were individuals within a community. We took care of the community, and the community took care of us. We neither needed nor wished to exploit our fellow men." And he naturally had plenty to say about the *land justice* on which those African societies were built – before the false concept of land as capital was imposed upon them by the alien invaders of a decidedly inferior civilization!

I have never forgotten the words spoken by a Nigerian journalist, in exile at the time, who, giving a talk at the old Colonial Office, stated plainly that British rule in Africa "destroyed our life at family, village and tribal level". One thing is certain: had Britain not imposed on the foreign countries she occupied her own corrupt system of highly centralized political power, we would not have had the recent terrible events in the Congo.

For to impose – as Britain did upon all the territories she invaded – a political system which holds out but *one* glittering prize of power to be won, with its dominion extending over a vast area where disparate tribal loyalties are to the fore – *or* religious (*as in India* – with tragic consequence and horrendous loss of life) – is, with uttermost folly, to impose upon a people the surest recipe for strife. (Similarly re Rwanda – mentioned earlier.)

In fact, we all need to dissolve back into our 'tribal' communities – with their natural linkages to the bioregions of the earth; placing ourselves under the saner rulership of the natural Law of Rent. Perhaps Africa can help lead the way forward for us all by ridding herself of that alien political pattern of the *centralist State* – the 'black flower of civilization' – that we were so unwise as to impose upon her.

But to return: Dr Weston Price – (the Canadian dentist who travelled the world in the earlier decades of the last century, investigating the health of indigenous peoples before they had been contaminated by the West's deficient dietary or by its unjust land tenure) – gave a glowing account of the peoples of such communities wherever he found them as being, all, "open, friendly, generous, noble of character, totally to be depended upon and trustworthy in every respect".

In reviewing the lofty moral nature of these small self-governing communities rooted in their land and enjoying the freedom of it, let us appreciate what it means that the *first* community we belong to is not in fact the human one at all, but the community of *Nature*; the community of the great natural world, with all its trees, grasses, and marvellous array of plant-life, embraced within the further wonder of the conformations of hills, valleys and plains and the living waters that flow through them – along with the wild creatures of every kind which have preceded us here on earth.

For here we find ourselves in the hands of our *first* and greatest teacher on earth – Gaia herself; She, whose moral code is embedded at the very beginning in the natural world, although we may not at once recognize it.

Perhaps her most obvious lesson for us is in the familiar saying – (which must be in every language) – 'what a man sows, that shall he also reap'. Viktor Schauberger – who refused to go to university when he saw what it had done to his brother, and who learned, through long periods spent in solitude in the forests of Austria, to 'let his mind travel where eye cannot go' – tells us that, (as already quoted earlier) –

> The world is not subject to random accidents ... Left to herself Nature would have supplanted the earlier vegetation with newer forms, and not only would have transformed the world into a blossoming garden of immense fertility and stable temperature, but in addition would have renewed herself in cycles.

... Words which indicate clearly enough that the 'natural' disasters of this earth –- and are we not seeing plenty at present? – are not unlinked to the behaviour of 'natural' man.

Now the scientific findings of the Japanese Masaru Emoto are revealing to us the extraordinary effect of human thought upon the crystalline formations of water, as they respond to the words (or thoughts) pronounced over them of blessing or cursing, ranging from forms of stunning beauty to the hideous.

Since the human body is made up of 72% water, should we not guard carefully at all times the thoughts which we harbour? Moreover, two identical bowls of rice demonstrated the same startling effects – not surprisingly since rice too contains of course a fair component of water. Where in fact does this end, since a tiny component of water must surely exist in even the densest of objects that come into our orbit ...?

Do we not also have the teachings of the Essenes about the Earthly Mother – that great primary Mother of whose extraordinary love and care for her children they wrote so movingly, in the records they have left to us? The teachings of morality – from the most elementary to the loftiest – are encoded into our existence on this earth, as children of Gaia.

Finally, as illustrating how – for our additional blessing – behind yet the moral teachings of the Earthly Mother stands the great moral code of the mysterious Creator himself, let me place here as conclusion a favourite poem by Ralph Waldo Emerson, entitled *Brahma*:-

> If the red slayer think he slays,
>
> Or if the slain think he is slain,
>
> They know not well the subtle ways
>
> I keep, and pass, and turn again.

Far or forgot to me is near;
    Shadow and sunlight are the same;
The vanished gods to me appear;
    And one to me are shame and fame.

They reckon ill who leave me out;
    When me they fly, I am the wings;
I am the doubter and the doubt,
    And I the hymn the Brahmin sings.

The strong gods pine for my abode,
    And pine in vain the sacred Seven;
But thou, meek lover of the good!
    Find me, and turn thy back on heaven.

*

Scenes from a Tapestry

Panel 2: Dispossession –
by its Various Devices

*

When in the course of history we see the conquerors making chattel slaves of the conquered, it is always when population is sparse and land of little value, or where they want to carry off their human spoil.   In other cases, the conquerors merely appropriate the lands of the conquered, by which means they just as effectually, and much more conveniently, compel the conquered to work for them.

(Henry George, from chapter *Slavery and Slavery* in *Social Problems*.)

*

What follows is a collection of items that have come to hand on this great matter over time, placed in roughly chronological order.

I do not think it needs much commentary added!

The Diggers

In 1649 to St George's Hill
A ragged band they called the Diggers came
To show the people's will.
They defied the landlords, they defied the laws,
They were the dispossessed reclaiming what was theirs.

We come in peace, they said, to dig and sow,
We come to work the lands in common and make the
   waste ground grow,
This earth divided we will make whole
So it may be a common treasury for all.

The sin of property we do disdain,
No man has any right to buy or sell the earth for
   private gain
By theft and murder they took the land,
Now everywhere the walls spring up at their command.

They make the laws to chain us well
The clergy dazzle us with heaven, or they damn us
   into hell.
We will not worship the god they serve,
A god of greed who feeds the rich while poor folk starve.

We work and eat together, we need no swords,
We will not bow to masters, nor pay rent to the lords;
Still we are free, though we are poor,
Ye Diggers all, stand up for glory, stand up now!

From the men of property the orders came,
They sent the hired men and troopers to wipe out the
   Diggers' claim -
Tear down their cottages, destroy their corn,
They were dispersed – only the vision lingers on ...

(From the lyrics by Leon Rosselson – using the language of the
Diggers themselves. Acks to *Progress*, Australia, Nov.-Dec. 05.)

*

Forget Not The Enclosures

I t is a grim truth that all through the eighteenth century, all through the great Whig speeches about liberty, all through the great Tory speeches about patriotism, through the period of Wandewash and Plassy, through the period of Trafalgar and Waterloo, one process was steadily going on in the central senate of the nation.

Parliament was passing bill after bill for the enclosure, by the great landlords, of such of the common lands as had survived out of the great communal system of the Middle Ages. It is much more than a pun, it is the prime political irony of our history, that the Commons were destroying the commons. The very word "common", as we have before noted, lost its great moral meaning, and became a mere topographical term for some remaining scrap of scrub or heath that was not worth stealing.

In the eighteenth century these last and lingering commons were connected only with stories about highwaymen, which still linger in our literature. The romance of them was a romance of robbers; but not of the real robbers.   (G.K. Chesterton)

> The law indicts the man or woman
> Who steals the goose from off the common –
> But lets the greater felon loose,
> Who steals the common from the goose.
> > (Protest song from the time of the Enclosures.)

*

Scotland's Highland Clearances

Many of our readers have passed along Loch Lochy, and they have likely had the mansion of Auchnacarry pointed out to them, and they have been told of the dark mile, surpassing, as some say, the Trossachs in romantic beauty; but perhaps they were not aware that beyond lies the wide expanse of Loch Arkaig, whose banks have been the scene of a most extensive clearing. There was a day when 300 able, active men could have been collected from the shores of this extensive inland loch, but nothing is now to be seen but the ruins of their huts, with the occasional bothy of a shepherd, while their lands are held by one or two farmers from the borders.

(*The Depopulation System of the Highlands* – Rev. Dr Maclauchlan, (Edinburgh, 1849.)

*

The evictions of the Clan M'Lennan from Strathconnan by the Balvour trustees were carried out in a most barbarous manner, and to this day the spot is shown where the dispossessed men and women crouched together, praying rather for a merciful death than that they should be driven farther from the strath of their birth ...

(History of the Working Classes in Scotland – Tom Johnston.)

*

In 1843, the Chief Government Relief Officer for Scotland reported: "The aim of the highland landlords is the extermination of the people".

The Highland Clearances stemmed from the Act of Union ... Contrary to (Professor X's) statement that the Union has been tremendously beneficial ... (the) Union bounty (of the Highlanders and Islanders) was to be used as front line troops in war only to be evicted from their land in peace time. The depopulated and deserted Highland glens are cenotaphs to the evicted and exiled as a direct result of the Act of Union.

(Donald J. MacLeod, Scotsman, 14 Mar. 2011.)

From the lone shieling on the misty isle,
    Mountains divide us and a waste of seas,
But still the blood is strong, the heart is highland –
    And we in dreams behold the Hebrides.
(*The Canadian Boat Song*, 1829. The words of an exile from Lewis
to Nova Scotia in the migrations of the 19th century.)

*

Let us not forget either the vast, wanton destruction of wildlife
that accompanied these Clearances – furred and feathered of
every description. Recorded in the book *Mountains and Moorlands*
by WH Pearsall, D.Sc., F.R.S., Quain Professor of Botany at
University College, University of London. Published by Collins
under *The New Naturalist* series, 1950.

*

The History of Common Land in Scotland

Few burgh commons survive in Scotland today. However,
a clear indication of their former great extent is given by the
reports of the House of Commons Select Committee on the
Royal Burghs of Scotland for 1793, 1819, 1820 and 1821 and also
in the 1832 report of the Commission into the State of Municipal
Corporation in Scotland. These investigations were all
prompted by the growing concern and scandal of the
disappearance of burgh commons, and resulted in the Burgh
Reform Act 1833.

The reports showed how the loss of the burgh commons
stemmed in large part from an Act of the Scots Parliament in
1469. This Act had suppressed the popular election of Councils

and led to the dominance of burghs by local landowners and wealthy merchants. The evidence in the reports shows how these landowners and merchants, with their relations and allies, had appropriated the burgh commons to themselves through generous land grants and cheap feus. By the early nineteenth century, when the new legislation was brought in, they had already stripped the Scottish burghs of nearly all their common land and other associated rights.

(From "The History of Common Land in Scotland" by Robin Callander – Caledonia Centre for Social Development, Jan 2003.)

*

In America ...

In the pages of "Our Enemy the State", AJ Nock gives a colourful description of the main 'economic activity' which followed upon America's War of Independence from Britain:-

> The primary monopoly, fundamental to all others – the monopoly of economic rent – was sought with redoubled eagerness. The territorial basis of each (State) now included the vast holdings confiscated from British owners ... land grants were sought as assiduously from local legislatures as they had been in earlier days from the Stuart dynasty. Professor Sakolski observes drily that 'the early land-lust which the colonists inherited from their European forebears was not diminished by the democratic spirit of the revolutionary fathers' ...!

*

Further Parliamentary Skulduggery

Richard Cobden (of Anti-Corn Laws fame), in his speech to the House of Commons on 14th March 1842:-

"Hon. Gentlemen claimed the privilege of taxing our bread on account of their peculiar burden in paying the highway rates and the tithes. Why, the land had borne these burdens before corn laws were thought of ... For a period of 150 years after the Conquest, the whole of the revenue from this country was derived from the land. During the next 150 years it yielded nineteen-twentieths of the revenue. For the next century, down to the reign of Richard III it was nine-tenths. During the next 70 years to the time of Mary it fell to about three-fourths. From this time to the end of the Commonwealth, land appeared to have yielded one-half the revenue. Down to the reign of Anne it was one-fourth. In the reign of George I it was one-fifth. In George II's reign it was one-sixth. For the first thirty years of George III's reign, the land yielded one-seventh of the revenue. From 1793 to 1816 land contributed one-ninth. From that time to the present one-twenty-fifth only of the revenue has been derived directly from land ..."

... Until today, when of course it is none at all. What an account of the gradual stealing from a people of their sustenance (both the land and its rents) – with the gradual anaesthetising of their sense of it alongside!

*

Evidence given before the Native Labour Commission, Kenya, 1912-13

"Settler after settler came before the Commission and demanded in the most precise terms that the natives should be forced out of 'Reserves' to work for wages by cutting down their land so that they should have less than they could live on. Lord Delamere, himself owner of 150,000 acres, said: 'If this policy is to be continued that every native is to be a landholder of a sufficient area on which to establish himself, then the question of obtaining a satisfactory labour supply will never be settled.' The process of reducing men to unemployment and poverty is here stated in all its nakedness and simplicity."

(Extract from *Unemployment and the Land*, by WR Lester, 1936, published in Progress, Australia, July 1992.)

*

Britain's Legacy to India

Extracts – made with some freedom of abbreviation, from Dr GT Wrench's *"The Restoration of the Peasantries"*.

The imposition of the English land system upon India was fortunately limited ... (owing to stout) opposition from Sir Thomas Munro (1761-1827), the governor of Madras ... throughout the forty-seven years of his service ... That which has gravely affected ... the Indian ryots has been the imposition upon them of the English view of debt ...

Before British rule, the communal ownership of land made mortgage difficult. Money could not be raised on the security of land, because land was not private, (except) in a few parts of India ... Mortgage, the raising of money on land, awaited a new conception, that of private property in land. This conception of land the ruling British brought. All land in England at that time

250

was private property; upon all English land money could be raised with the land as security. So debt, which was common enough in India, came to have a different effect and influence upon men from that which it had had in the pre-British period ... The rigid application of the law which ensued put the ignorant peasant entirely at the mercy of his creditor ...

As the Royal Commission on Agriculture in India reported of the peasant: "Where the land has passed into the possession of his creditor, no legislation will serve his need; no tenancy law will protect him". Mr Boys, of the Bengal Civil Service, writing in 1892, referred to "the fatal gift of proprietary right (in land) with which, while striving to bless, we have so effectually cursed the soil of India".

*

How Land Monopoly ... Spawns Monopoly Capitalism

The following are extracts from "History of the Great American Fortunes", by Gustavus Myers, (Published by the Modern Library, N.Y., 1907. Subsequent reprints.)

(T)he landowner occupied a superior position which neither political conditions nor the flux of changing circumstances could materially assail ... Furthermore, the landowner had an efficient and never-failing auxiliary. He yoked society as a partner, but it was a partnership in which the revenue went exclusively to the landowner. The principal factor he depended upon was the work of collective humans in adding greater and greater value to his land ...

Under such a system land was the one great auspicious, facile and durable means of rolling up an overshadowing fortune. Its exclusive possession struck at the very root of human necessity ... A more formidable system for the foundation and amplification of lasting fortunes has not existed ...

The invariable rule ... has been to utilise the surplus revenues in the form of rent, in investments in a great number and variety of corporations. The rent-racked people of the City of New York ... have sweated and laboured and fiercely struggled, as have the people of other cities, only to deliver up a great share of their earnings to the lords of the soil, merely for a foothold. In turn these rents have incessantly gone toward buying up interests in railroads, factories, utility plants, and often more and more land.

*

Extracts from
The Bankers' Manifesto of 1892

Revealed by US Congressman Charles A. Lindbergh,
SR from Minnesota, before the US Congress, sometime during
his term of office between the years 1907 and 1917,
to warn the citizens.

"We (bankers) must proceed with caution and guard every move made, for the lower order of people are already showing signs of restless commotion. Prudence will therefore show a policy of apparently yielding to the popular will until our plans are so far consummated that we can declare our designs without fear of any organized resistance ...

The courts must be called to our aid, debts must be collected, bonds and mortgages foreclosed as rapidly as possible.

When through the process of the law the common people have lost their homes, they will be more tractable and easily governed through the influence of the strong arm of the government applied to a central power of imperial wealth under the control of the leading financiers. People without homes will not quarrel with their leaders ..."

"As long as the land monopoly is maintained, the few can take possession of what Nature free of charge has granted to everyone, and usury will penetrate the whole society, and we will have banks which, instead of being servants for the exchange of goods, will become powerful extorters."

(Pierrre Proudhon, 1809-65. Emphasis added.)

*

It is of more importance to the community that regulations should be imposed on the proprietors of land than on the proprietors of money.
(The wisdom of our own William Ogilvie, 1736-1819 – whom the so-called Scottish Enlightenment deigned not to notice!)

... (Banks) have raised up a monetary aristocracy that has set the government at defiance. The issuing power should be taken from the banks and returned to the government, to whom it properly belongs.

(Thomas Jefferson)

The important thing about Henry George from the viewpoint of the American Monetary Institute is that George understood the monetary problem, understood that money was an abstract legal power, not a commodity, and understood that it belonged in the province of government, not private banks, to issue and control the money system. George was in fact a knowledgeable greenbacker.

(Stephen Zarlenga, acks. to *Progress*, Australia.)

*

Extracts from
"Why the German Republic Fell"

By Bruno Heilig, an Austrian, and leading journalist of his time,
who recorded Hitler's rise to power as foreign
editor/correspondent of various papers in Eastern Europe,
and later survived Dachau and Buchenwald to write his book
"Men Crucified".

G ermany, it seems to me, has provided a striking example
supporting the theory that the private appropriation of the
rent of land is the fundamental cause of industrial depression and
of distress among those who labour in the production of wealth –
the theory expounded by Henry George in his *Progress and
Poverty* ...

Was there a link between the economic and the political
collapse? Emphatically, yes. For as unemployment grew, and
with it poverty and the fear of poverty, so grew the influence of
the Nazi party, which was making its lavish promises to the
frustrated and its violent appeal to the revenges of a populace
aware of its wrongs, but condemned to hear only a malignant
and distorted explanation of them.

The wall painter and corporal was not of course to the taste of
the German landlords, but in the most important problem he has
not betrayed his sponsors. He did not touch the land problem ...

Similar conditions will be of the same effect everywhere ... The
Nazi regime is not Hitler's, the man's, achievement. Nazidom
has grown organically out of a rotten democracy, and the
rottenness of that democracy is the natural consequence of
unequal economic conditions; and unequal economic conditions
obtain all over the world owing to the instituted private
appropriation of the rent of land. Therefore every country is
potentially a Fascist country. Germany is but the type of a
development which no country can escape except by the

establishment of the equal right to the occupation and use of land.

Therefore also there can be no lasting peace even after the defeat of Nazism if the present economic structure of the civilized countries remains. The private appropriation of the rent of land is the deadly enemy of mankind.

*

The "deadly enemy of mankind" indeed! – and some words captured from Nye Bevan (Labour politician of the last century) give us the curtain-raiser on its latest deadly exploits:-

> "In practice it is impossible for the modern State to maintain an independent control over the decisions of big business. When the State extends its control over big business, big business moves in to control the State."

But – lurking under today's hugely inflated parasol of the "black flower of civilisation", the State itself – that old monster, land monopoly, now sporting its more modern monopoly-capitalist hat, surely cannot fool us longer! For this charmingly pretended two-some dance, dear Nye Bevan, put on for our distraction, is simply the *one-some winsome* dance of *land monopoly* – playing all the different parts in this tangle by rapidly exchanging one hat after another!

It is this same old ugly monster that we catch up with again in today's scene – now sporting its decidedly grander 'State' hat – carrying on the same old cruel game of the clearances; but dispossessing today not merely hundreds or thousands, but tens and hundreds of thousands, millions even, in its extended global ride facilitated by monopoly-capitalism's monster-suiting giant technologies:-

> "In March, China announced it was adopting private property (in land). With a true Orwellian flourish it said

that Communism would be preserved. In fact of course it was laying one of the bases for (monopoly) Capitalism.

Unannounced reports circulating a few days earlier showed that China was busy laying the other basis of (monopoly) Capitalism as well, by vast evictions of peasants. These were estimated by one specialist to be between 40 and 80 millions."

(Richard Giles, in *Good Government*, Australia, Apr 07.)

Need one quote further from the countless reports of similar tragedies overtaking peasant peoples across the globe, under the aegis of today's sacred 'State'?

It is a sound saying that a problem cannot be solved in the same dimensions as those within which it arose – or, as Schauberger was always reminding us, we need to "think an octave higher". It is a report from Mali of similar tragic happenings (The Guardian, 28 Dec 2010) which brings us slap up against this piece of wisdom. In Mali, a foreign so-called 'development' company, with a huge water scheme to re-sculpt a massive area of Nature, is threatening the lands and livelihoods of the peasant farmers there. "The government are bandits", proclaims Ibrahim Coulibaly, leader of the opposing peasant organization: "Even if the land does belong to the government, the people living on it still have rights". As background information, the article tells us that "Mali has almost no private land titles and land is owned ultimately by the State".

BUT IS IT?

The education of her peasant peoples – by the State of course – is being stepped up in Mali – but it will not include the wisdom of an earlier indigenous tribal spokesman of North America: "Some of our chiefs make the claim that the land belongs to us. It is not what the Great Spirit told me. He told me that the land belongs to Him, that no people owns the land; that I was not to forget to tell this to the white people when I met them in council."

(Kaneku, Kickapoo prophet. Acks. to Progress, Jan 2006.)

"No people owns the land." The statement is plain – and it goes, of course, for bodies of humans just as for individuals. This wisdom is so clear and elementary that it is equally laughable to think that a humanly-concocted 'State' can own the land as that single members of the human tribe should do so. The same elementary wisdom is encapsulated in the words of the renowned commentator on law, William Blackstone, who pointed out: "There is no foundation in nature or in natural law why a set of words upon parchment should convey the dominion of land".

It is Henry George who puts the obvious corcollary to this so well:-

> "No one can bargain away what is not his; no one can stipulate away the rights of another. And *if the newborn infant has an equal right to life, then it has an equal right to land. Its warrant, which comes direct from Nature, and which sets aside all human laws or title-deeds, is the fact that it is born.*"

(Emphasis added.)

"Sets aside all human laws or title-deeds!" But who is to instruct the peasant peoples of Mali in the wisdom of Henry George – from which their State-sponsored education is tragically moving them ever further away ...?

It is surely time that the Geoist (Georgist) movement addressed this matter – with global State powers allied to State-sponsored educational systems now wrecking the lives of increasing global millions.

Is the movement clear on this itself? For to discern, through its many masks, the actual nature of the State today – that is, to recognise beyond all trickery, its ancient and unreformable *land monopoly face* – is surely to warn us, once and for all, off any attempts to bring in this reform via the machinery of any State-constituted body – whether local or central, or indeed any of those supra-State bodies that dot the world today.

Far wiser would it be for us to ally ourselves with the inspired, earth-sprung and earth-oriented Bioregional movement – the movement which offers us the only sane patterning for a society of the New Age, and a movement waiting, as I have already pointed out, for its Geoist land reform embrace!

*

Uncivilized

An ancient ape, once on a time,
Disliked exceedingly to climb ,
And so he picked him out a tree
And said, "Now this belongs to me.
I have a hunch that monks are mutts
And I can make them gather nuts
And bring the bulk of them to me,
By claiming title to this tree."

He took a green leaf and a reed
And wrote himself a title deed,
Proclaiming pompously and slow:
"All monkeys by these presents know!" –
Next morning when the monkeys came
To gather nuts, he made his claim:
"All monkeys climbing on this tree
Must bring their gathered nuts to me,
Cracking the same on equal shares;
The meats are mine, the shells are theirs."

 "But by what right?" they cried, amazed,
Thinking the ape was surely crazed.
"By this", he answered; "if you'll read
You'll find it is a title deed,
Made in precise and formal shape
And sworn before a fellow ape,
Exactly on the legal plan
Used by that wondrous creature, man,
In London, Tokyo, New York,
Glengarry, Kalamazoo and Cork.

"Unless my deed is recognized,
It proves you quite uncivilized."
"But", said one monkey, "You'll agree
It was not you who made this tree."
"Nor", said the ape, serene and bland,
"Does any owner make his land,
Yet all of its hereditaments
Are his and figure in the rents."

The puzzled monkeys sat about:
They could not make the question out.
Plainly, by precedent and law,
The ape's procedure showed no flaw;
And yet, no matter what he said,
The stomach still denied the head.

Up spoke one sprightly monkey then:
"Monkeys are monkeys, men are men";
The ape should try his legal capers
On men who may respect his papers.
We don't know deeds; we do know nuts,
And spite of 'ifs' and 'ands' and buts'
We know who gathers and unmeats 'em,
By monkey practice also eats 'em.
So tell the ape and all his flunkies
No man tricks can be played on monkeys."

Thus apes still climb to get their food,
Since monkeys' minds are crass and crude
And monkeys, all so ill-advised,
Still eat their nuts, uncivilized.

(Edmund Vance Cooke, 1866-1932)

*

Scenes from a Tapestry

Panel 3: Fruitages of Dispossession

*

i. The World Hunger and Population 'Crises'

I f there is anywhere we should hear, and rejoin to hear, the sound of "fetters breaking" – fetters that have for too long chained our thinking to false pathways – it is concerning the above two 'crises' which so haunt us today. For both are a deliberate creation by the political element in society – which indeed, as we have seen, touches no sphere of our life but to bring confusion and ruin upon it.

To tackle first food production: my discovery of a specific political ploy, which was deliberately introduced into the scene nearly half-a-century ago in order to confuse it – (briefly mentioned in my *Beauly-Denny Folly* article) – is of dramatic memory!

While living in London I attended, in 1971 (or thereabouts) the A.G.M. of a certain organic agriculture organization, at which – being kindly allowed onto the platform (as it was not on the agenda) – I made a strong speech against the organization's policy of silence on the Common Market which we were then about to enter.

The suppressed chagrin of those on the platform at my unexpected words was more than compensated for by the eager welcome they received from those on the floor, many of whom came up to speak to me afterwards. Among these was a Cornish small farmer, Mary French, who decided to miss her last train home and stay the night at my flat instead. I thus had the privilege of spending the evening with this remarkable and fondly remembered woman – and what an experience of enlightenment it proved! For Mary had had published, just two years earlier, her book entitled "Worm in the Wheat" – and here was revealed the extraordinary ploy which I now learned from her at first hand, (recorded on p.67 of her book).

In 1965, the government had 'changed the goal-posts' concerning agricultural productivity, and instead of measuring this in the only rational way, *per acre*, suddenly switched to assessing it *per man unit*. This naturally favoured a further lot of clearances from the land and the replacing of people with big machinery – (land monopoly wearing its second hat) – which brought with it all the paraphernalia of oil-based production, health-depleting both to soil and to man. I should add that it is plainly recorded also in Mary French's book – quoting the government's own figures – that the annual production per acre of Britain's *small* farms had greatly exceeded that of her large ones. Thus – could the folly of this change-over have been exceeded? But the 'three-hatted one' of course ruled.

What really amazes me is that, in all the nearly fifty years since Mary French's book came out – (published by Collins in 1965) – with its clear and unequivocal statement on this matter, through all that time I have never come across a single writer – among so many passionate champions of our landscape, wildlife and health – who has pointed out this truly Alice-in-Wonderland scenario of our agriculture today. WHERE ARE THEY? And this – not as to Britain alone of course, since the same 'mad-hatter' has ensured its global reach. No wonder then if a 'global food shortage' now thunders at us! Talk about the human race having shot itself in the foot!

The answer to our *real* situation is of course to bring people back onto the land via the Law of Rent – with grass-roots empowerment built into the reform, (see my article 'The Unsuspected Lynchpin'). Meanwhile we can cite the splendid evidence from Russia, from the new *Ringing Cedars of Russia* movement there – (see letter on this under 'Author's Writings') – that it is indeed the *gardeners of the earth* – the people re-inhabiting their own land – that we must look to, to solve the 'food crisis' we are so panic-ed about today!

The above findings happily wash over onto the second 'crisis' that causes us so much concern – that of the explosion of the earth's population since industrial times. This matter I have already dealt with in the round in my book 'Birthright in Land ...' (listed among its Contents, towards the end), where I applied to it Krishnamurti's splendid saying – which might have been coined for it – that "order imposed from without breeds disorder". *Breeds disorder!* No truer word could have been spoken of this population matter, since the explosion of the population world-wide has taken place strictly in conjunction with the economic enserfment, under land monopoly, of what is virtually now the entire global population – (with Britain having much to answer for, for that). *Disorder* - "imposed from without". Precisely!

I could cite instances from various reports of where increase in population has reversed itself where that economic enslavement has been lifted. But let us rather bring to bear upon the scene, and learn from it, the profound statement on this matter by Dr Hasbach of Kiel University, which is quoted by Dr Wrench in his book 'Reconstruction by Way of the Soil':-

> "The English labourers of the early part of the 19th century had lost all courage. They were an unprotected proletariat. In the times of their prosperity and independence, they had avoided early marriages, and abstained from multiplying as a mere proletariat does; whereas now all such evils appeared. This ... is the answer to Malthus, who failed to recognize the psychological elements – despair of the future and of freedom – in the rapid increase of population. The error was immense."

Hasbach's words strike home at once. We need no second telling. For there lingers in our ears still that cry whose sorrow cannot be obliterated from the memory – the cry of the peasant people to Richard II when he asked them what they would: "that we be never held nor named for serfs". Their dreadful fate being presently to be held and named as *slaves*, it is no wonder if that cry, put forth in all its piteousness, carried with it a sense already of their premonition of a lost cause, a cause that had meant to them more than life itself – FREEDOM!

Freedom! – man's unquenchable thirst ...

O Enslaver of men across the globe – is there any sin not to be laid at your door?

*

The country road from Pitlochry to Strathardle in Perthshire takes you through some of the most desolate and barren countryside in Scotland. Winding through Glen Brerachen, it follows the river between the high peaks of Ben Vrackie and Creag Dubh on the southern slopes of the Grampian Mountains.

A less promising place to grow good crops would be hard to imagine. This glen was once covered in forest. Now the land is exposed to the full might of the Scottish winter. With many of its nutrients washed away, the soil has grown acid and sour. Coarse upland grasses clothe the hillside that once grew good potato crops.

But a remarkable couple – Cameron and Moira Thomson – have made this desert bloom again. They've found a way to grow superb vegetables – large cabbages and onion, while their greenhouses and polytunnels grow crops of tomatoes, cucumbers, sweetcorn, squashes, courgettes and marrows.

The secret of the Thomsons' gardening success is simple – so simple that it's hard to grasp the importance of what they've done. There among the heathers and the tussocky grasses they have recreated a fertile soil. And in doing so they've proved it's a good soil – not chemicals – that grows healthy crops.

As you walk up the farm lane from the little car park at Ceanghline, Straloch Farm, Enochdhu, you know you're witnessing something remarkable. Even on a rainy day the terraced gardens stand out like oases in the desert. Amid the drab green of the upland grassland, they are filled with tall, brightly-coloured flowers and healthy-looking vegetables.

The soil they're growing in is dark and slightly gritty to the touch. The Thomsons mix it themselves before spreading it onto their garden terraces. It's made from fine rock dust hauled from a nearby quarry, and compost made from green waste by Dundee City Council. Together the two ingredients produce ideal conditions for healthy crop growth. The dust – from the volcanic rock basalt – supplies minerals that rainfall and chemical farming have stripped out of many soils. Compost provides organic matter for microbial activity, the prerequisite of a fertile soil.

With their rock an 'instant soil' – fertility on tap. And they've done it by copying nature. They have effectively reproduced post-glacial conditions on their worn-out twenty-first century hillside. They have shown that on a soil rich in minerals, and well endowed with organic matter, it's possible to grow large, healthy crops without the arsenal of chemical fertilizers and pesticides used by commercial farmers today.

*

Mineral depletion!
Just one of the ravagings of our health wrought by phoney – CUCKOO agriculture! (Acks. to Gavin Putland for this inspired term from the heading to his article 'Cuckoo Economics'!)

Just another of the *grim fruitages of dispossession.*

On the other side of the picture: let us appreciate how fortunate we are to have the wonderful work and demonstration garden of Cameron and Moira Thomson, right here in the heart of Scotland, to show us how these mineral deficiencies can be *reversed*. (www.seercentre.org.uk)

And on a whole wider scale of course, once the people are able to repossess their land!

*

ii. 'WORK' – fit for an Enserfed People!

To lose your birthright in land is a heavy business.
It means to lose control over your life
... to lose control over your work
... to lose control over your health.

*

1. ZUCKERMAN PESTICIDE REPORT unearthed again,
and again. Thousands condemned to chronic disease.
Government prefers not to know.

In the late 1940s the UK Government commissioned leading scientists to explore the risks of using organophosphate (OP) pesticides in agriculture. The resulting 'Zuckerman Report' was completed in 1951 but never released to the public. Presumably considered too damning, it was 'filed away' in the House of Commons library. The report was apparently rediscovered in the 1990s but to no avail. Perhaps, now that the report has come to light once again, action will be taken and those whose lives have been ruined by exposure to OPs will be properly compensated.

The Zuckerman Report:

- warned that exposure to OPs "could lead to more than 30 symptoms, including giddiness, tinnitus, loss of memory, depression and schizophrenia"

- strongly advised the UK Government to label products containing OPs as a "deadly poison" in large clear type and to warn users that, while death could result from a single exposure, repeated exposure could result in cumulative poisoning leading to chronic toxicity.

- warned that the principal routes of absorption were the skin, the respiratory tract and the eyes, and that OP formulations based on organic solvents could penetrate the protective clothing

- Recommended weekly medical exams for anyone using OP products, and training doctors to diagnose and treat OP poisoning.

This lack of Government action, and the attempted suppression of another earlier 'inconvenient truth', has robbed tens of thousands of farmers, shepherds and agricultural workers worldwide of their health and many hundreds worldwide of their lives, including many suicides.
(13914) Brenda Sutcliffe, Environmental Issues Forum 1.6.08, p.19. Republished in Green Health Watch Magazine 2008, Issue 35.

2. 'DISASTER LOOMS' ON CANCERS RELATED TO WORK.

A Scots scientist said yesterday that urgent government action must be taken to avert a "major public health disaster" caused by occupational cancer.

Professor Andrew Watterson, of Stirling University, says that more people die in Scotland from occupational cancers than from road accidents, murders and suicides combined.

With over half a million Scottish workers still exposed to workplace carcinogens, he has called for the government to implement a range of prevention measures that have been shown to make a difference in other countries.

Professor Watterson, chairman of the Occupational and Environmental Health Group, said, "The high toll taken by occupational cancers has been neglected, and UK regulators have been silent on this subject for a quarter of a century.

"Approximately 539,172 Scottish workers are exposed to workplace carcinogens. Each year new carcinogens emerge, and more people are exposed to them."

It is believed that between 10% and 12% of all cancers are estimated to be work-caused or work-related.

(The Courier, 8 Mar 08)

3. TOXINS BLAMED FOR EYE DEFECTS

In every 4,000 to 5,000 births, one baby will either be born with a tiny eye (microphthalmia), or virtually no eye at all (anophthalmia) ...

The question is not just what can be done to improve the baby's sight ... The important question is: why are babies born with anophthalmia! ...(I)t is thought that they are (possibly) the result of a vulnerable foetus being exposed to an environmental toxin ... the accusing finger of the green movement has pointed at fungicides and pesticides.

Those opposed to widespread chemical farming claim that the incidence of anophthalmia is more common in areas where there is widespread arable agriculture ...

(Daily Telegraph, 25 June 98)

4. WORK – Cancer Wafers

The computer ship (semiconductor) industry is probably the largest industrial expansion in history ... However, this £150 billion industry brings its own toll on human health. Semiconductor workers lose twice as many workdays through occupational illness as workers in other manufacturing sectors.

The huge amounts of toxic materials the industry uses – many known or suspected carcinogens – include hydrochloric acid, arsenic, cadmium, lead, methyl chloroform, toluene, benzene, acetone, trichloroethylene and arsine gas ...

There are now three major lawsuits running against semiconductor manufacturers ... Scientists predict that there will be a significant rise in the cancer rate in the computer chip industry ...)

(Environment and Health News, 2000, Issue 15)

5. SUPPRESSED DATA: WE'RE BEING MICRO-BLITZED!

Planet Earth is being "microwaved" into a high-tech holocaust by a cell phone-crazy, personal computer-dominated, cable TV-influenced, electromagnetic gadget-frenzied human society, which is virtually unaware of the extreme biological – as well as psychological – perils of low-intensity but high frequency electromagnetic fields (HF EMF). (Lifeforce, May 02)

"It can be proposed that the current increase in electro-magnetic pollution of the environment exceeds human adaptation capabilities, warn Ukrainian researchers ..."
(International Council for Health Freedom Newsletter, Vol. 5, No. 2)

6. NANOTECHNOLOGY

Now, for the first time, a scientific study has established a clear and casual relationship between human contact with nanoparticles and serious health damage.

According to an article in the *European Respiratory Journal*, by a group of Chinese researchers headed by Huguo Song from the Department of Occupational Medicine and Clinical Toxicology at Beijing Chaoyang Hospital, seven young female workers fell seriously ill after working in a paint factory that used nanotechnology. The workers suffered severe and permanent lung damage, and face and arm eruptions. Two of them died, while the other five have not improved after several years.

Around 500 studies have shown nanotechnology toxicity in animal studies, in human cells and in the environment. Although Song's article finds evidence of clinical toxicity in human beings for the first time, this finding could be only the tip of the iceberg of an extremely risky industry ...

Personal products that you may use daily – cosmetics, suntan lotion, socks and sports clothes – and think are harmless may all contain atom-sized nanotech particles ... Until now, few adverse effects have been found (in the marketing of) this virtually unregulated technology. Yet that may simply be due to the relatively few studies that have been done in the rush to find ever more and profitable nanotech applications ...

(NEXUS, Dec 2010-Jan 2011)

Excellent sources of such information are:-

The monthly WDDTY (What Doctor's Don't Tell You). From Autism to Alzheimers. Access to their website helps avoid an unfortunately high sub. rate. www.wddty.com

The quarterly Green Health Watch magazine, Muir of Logie, Forres, Scotland IV36 2QG. Or www.greenhealthwatch.com "It is simply the best and most informative magazine on health and the environment in existence" – LN, Carmarthen.

*

To repeat:

> To lose your birthright in land is a heavy business,
>> It means to lose control over your life
>>> ... to lose control over your work
>>>> ... to lose control over your health.

In the light of the above category of disasters owed to those who have "created" jobs for us, and the conditions of those jobs – is it not high time we rid ourselves of the mantra that begs "the creation of jobs"?

If we are born onto this earth with a mouth to feed, we are born to a task that awaits us. And if we are deprived of the means of accomplishing it then it is high time we woke up to the fact that there is *something fundamentally wrong with the society we were born into.*

As someone once put it: "If only the jobless could see what is in front of their noses! What they need to go after is – *LOST PROPERTY!*

*

From *Protection or Free Trade* by Henry George

The Gift of Reason

Near the window by which I write a great bull is tethered by a ring in his nose. Grazing round and round, he has wound his rope about the stake until now he stands a close prisoner, tantalised by rich grass he cannot reach, unable even to toss his head to rid him of the flies that cluster on his shoulders. Now and again he struggles vainly, and then, after pitiful bellowing, relapses into silent misery.

This bull, a very type of massive strength, who, because he has not wit enough to see how he might be free, suffers want in sight of plenty, and is helplessly preyed upon by weaker creatures, seems to me no unfit emblem of the working masses ... Bitterly conscious of injustice, feeling in their inmost souls that they were made for more than so narrow a life, they, too, spasmodically struggle and cry out. But until they trace effect to cause, until they see how they are fettered and how they may be freed, their struggles and outcries are as vain as those of the bull. Nay, they are vainer. I shall go out and drive the bull in a way that will untwist his rope. But who shall drive men to freedom? ... Under all forms of government the ultimate power lies with the masses ... But what avails this? The little finger of aggregated capital must be thicker than the loins of the working masses so long as they do not know how to use their power.

*

iii. A Closer Look at Cities

We humans, born onto a multi-sensory planet, are multi-sensory beings. But the sensory world we were formed to inhabit is the world of Nature – the world of the terrene man.

In the city-scapes in which most of us now live on account of land dispossession, our three more 'etheric' senses, of sight, hearing and smell, having lost their essential field of play, cannot bring us satisfaction. If only the cruder senses of taste and touch are then left to us to explore, is it surprising if they become overwhelming in their demands?

Obesity and abuse of various kinds are the natural outcome of life lived unnaturally. They mirror the profound disorientation of a creature born to a different world, and trapped in an alien one. Was it Thoreau who said, "the great mass of men lead lives of quiet desperation"?

To read WH Murray's description, in his book "Rob Roy MacGregor", of the highlander of old, his every sense engaged to the full with the beloved, challenging environment in which he must survive – is to gain some understanding of how estranged we have become from that original terrene state, and no more to wonder at how indigenous man could "hear the grass grow".

The bleakness of the city-scape for the multi-sensory creatures we were born to be, we no longer recognize. Our sense of it, through long acclimatisation to the abnormal, has become numbed. Nor can those valiantly doing their best to help in this scenario, succeed, for they too are sufferers from the same deprivation – and so are unable to recognise it in the vital first place.

Alcohol and drug addiction, obesity, abuse of all kinds and sex-without-love, on such a scale as exists today, is a signal to us, if we could only see it, of a multi-sensory deprivation as painful as it is profound – if only we could feel it any more ...

J. Symonds, in "Sketches from Italy", writes of how – when the senses of sight, hearing and smell are deeply engaged in the world of nature, it renders to man the utmost happiness. Truly – for when, on a warm day, the ravishments of scent are added to sound and sight, one may sometimes enter a kind of ecstasy. For unlike sounds and sight, which issue to us more immediately, scents as they come over us may have scanned on their way far-off lanes of memory, carrying intimations even of other lifetimes.

What does this multi-sensory deprivation do to the mind?

The indigenous peoples of America, on being dispossessed of their land and put into reservations, felt that to be taken out of their place (i.e., their land) was to be *taken out of their mind*. "The dome of the sky above is your skull", (Radio 4 prog. 7 Dec 08). ... Recalling the line "the grass beneath, above the vaulted sky", from his poignant poem, by John Clare, 'poet of the Enclosures'.

"One in seven adults in Britain suffers from a diagnosable mental health problem in any given week." (Samaritans.) "One in ten Scots children suffers from severe mental illness ... this figure is set to rise to one in five by 2020." (The Big Issue in Scotland, 20 Mar 03)

"The grass beneath" counts too. For there has recently come to light the dramatic healing effect that can be experienced from walking barefoot on the earth, on grass - (as indeed I can bear witness). By this practice, our bodies become "naturally charged with the earth's free electrons ... Current research is showing that inflammation, including oxidative stress and autoimmune disease, is the direct result of a shortage of free electrons in the body ... (and) that conditions ranging from chronic pain to cancer, and perhaps all diseases, may be linked to one common cause – chronic inflammation ..." (See leading article in Vol.30 No.1 of the Price-Pottenger Nutrition Foundation Journal, 7890 Broadway, Lemon Grove, CA91945, USA.) And what may this not also do for the mind, the emotions, the soul? – since "all things are connected" (Chief Seattle.)

Is this more etheric experience from our Earthly Mother, of the sense of touch, something else that our city-scapes deprive us of? Perhaps it is just as well if we are indeed – "approaching ... the twilight of the Great City civilization" – (Revolutionary Socialism", by Arnold Lunn). One look at the cover, merely, of "Planet of Slums" by Mike Davis, is quite enough.

If we would enjoy once more the healing power of Gaia in our life, we know what it is we must do. We must confront, in full, the ruthlessly magnetizing power of *monopoly capitalism* – in its cruel requirement for a work-force crowded onto concrete terrain:-

"As the land in the cities becomes more valuable, more and more goes to rent. The bigger the city, the deeper the poverty; the bigger the city, the more the degradation. It is better for the men who own the earth to have big cities – but for no one else.

(Charles Darrow)

"Behold and ponder
    Yonder
Skyscrapers'
    Incomparable capers!

Read the inviting
    Sky-scrawled writing:
"Skywards stack us –
    And then pack us!"

PIE-IN-THE-SKY
    - For real!
Great recipe –
    Grand deal!

But the 'vaulted sky' above even such skyscrapers will not do.
For where, in all this grandiose scenario, is the Earthly Mother –
precious healer of her terrene child?

*

"Burying our hands in the earth, and turning the turf ...
was an amazing experience. I know of no restorative of
heart, body and soul more effective against hopelessness
than the restoration of the Earth. Like childbirth, like the
giving and receiving of gifts, like the passion and gestures
of the various forms of human love, it is holy."

(Barry Lopez, in Earth First magazine)

*

iv. The Environment:
Gaia's Revenge on Globalisation

You'll pay for the worst sin ever committed, a sin that
more than anything else is dreadful in its consequences.
The natural source of life for all you've treated as
merchandise! And trying to escape the outcome, of the
world you've made a chaos.

(Johannes Bouma, Wageningen University, The Netherlands)

*

Monopoly capitalism has come a long way since the time of
the Industrial Revolution.   Today, modern technology
holds the world as its oyster. Or does it? Suppose Gaia does not
like modern technology? Who knows who the ultimate oyster
may then turn out to be!

The computer chip (semiconductor) industry comes at
enormous environmental cost ... According to the May/June
1997 issue of *E – The Environmental Magazine*, just one 8"
computer wafer containing hundreds of chips requires, on
average, 27lbs of chemicals and 29 cubic feet of hazardous
gases to manufacture, and produces 9lbs of hazardous
waste and 3,787 gallons of waste water ... More than 100
different contaminants have been measured above safety
levels in some drinking water in Silicon Valley (which)
houses 29 US Environmental Protection Agency 'disaster
sites'.

(6071-74 Environmental Health Perspectives, 1.9.99 pA453.
Republished in Environment & Health News, 2000 (15) –
now Green Health Watch magazine.)

A silly con called silicon? - !

*

The environmental turmoil we are now experiencing is assuredly the result of land monopoly's intolerable dispossession of the Earth's *rooted peasant peoples* – who alone understand how to care for their Earthly Mother. Hence, it may well be summed up as 'Gaia's revenge on globalisation'. (See article on Globalisation under 'Author's Writings'.)

Of one thing we may be certain – Gaia holds up her sleeve the last laugh!

*

Regarding today's World Water Wars over the life-giving rivers that flow across this planet, I would like to ask: what of that *other* river, which has so far escaped their attention – the river of RENT, which – stolen from the peoples of the Earth, has achieved, with that stealing, the further stealing from them not only of their rivers but of their *land* – which *encompasses* those rivers?*

*

Time does not allow any further embroidering of this part of the Tapestry – but perhaps this book contains enough on this matter anyway!

---

* The river of Rent has so far escaped the notice also of the Permaculture movement – a movement close to my heart. By giving its attention to the natural Law of Rent, its long puzzlement over how best to 'share the surplus' would be at an end. For under the natural Law of Rent, that 'surplus' over which they at present puzzle flows naturally to the community, leaving to its individual members simply the fruits of their own labours – good to share with family and friends, or as wide a circle as one chooses.

Whom better, then, to give the last word to, than to Viktor Schauberger, renowned Austrian forester, guru of energy and 'Water Wizard' of the last century – and still leagues ahead of ours!

But firstly – some reminders from his work, which we can do with today.

(1) We can provide ourselves with all the energy that we need, from the sea – and at practically no cost. The books by Callum Coats (published by Gateway Books in the late 1990s), on Schauberger's work, reproduce in one of them – (so wisely and so well, in order to prevent any attempts to patent it) – the illustrated model of Schauberger's design, showing how this may be done. We have no need of industrial windfarms or of giant pylons deforming our landscape – (but just see the 'Mad Hatter' heeding any such common sense!)

(2) Victor Schauberger's work reveals that we should not be taking oil out of the earth at all, since its purpose in remaining underground is to remineralize the waters that are stored in the bowels of the earth, which eventually return to us as our drinking water, thus properly remineralized for our health.

Since our civilization devours oil, not only for its agriculture and transport, but also for a huge range of its manufactured products (including computers, as I have read) – this certainly invites a big rethink on our part! For supposing Gaia does not appreciate our thwarting of the plans she has so carefully made for us ...?

(3) Our conversion of water's natural Full Hydrological Cycle to a Half one, through our denuding the earth of its essential forest cover, and the loss in addition of water into the upper atmosphere, and equally too deep into the earth

– likewise from human misbehaviours – has placed us in a parlous position regarding climate change:-

"In the long term all of these effects act to reduce the general ambient temperatures and the presence of atmospheric water, and while initially the temperature in parts of the Earth will rise, in the end it will inevitably cool off dramatically as the precursor to a new ice-age".

The above is an extract from "Living Energies" by Callum Coats, ch. "The Earth's Atmospheric Envelope". I cannot recommend too highly Callum Coats's brilliant presentations of Schauberger's work in his several books on this. (For briefer consultations, my own "Birthright in Land ..." contains a roughly 40-page section on Schauberger, which Callum Coats has most kindly approved.)

Further on climate-change: Peter Taylor's book "CHILL" warns of the blunder of today's warming theory, as being constructed chiefly upon the superficial left-brain technology of computer modelling which is unable to take proper account of such phenomena as vortexes and spirals, so readily recognisable to the intuitive feminine right brain as vital factors in the climate-change scene. As he points out in brilliant metaphor – that the "green economy" now being planned for us "will be wearing a black shirt is not yet obvious, as such things seldom are at the outset." ...!

*

And so – back finally to Viktor Schauberger! Some of my favourite words from this extraordinary genius, as he sighed over his contemporaries' ambitious plans to carry out large-scale re-sculpturings of Nature, warning them ever against these absurd and fruitless attempts to – **"control the eternal woman"**!

Ah Gaia – our blessed Gaia!
(And blessed Schauberger too!)

*

v. Who Are They?
- and Brighter Pathways

"For the animals shall not be measured by Man; in a world older and more complete than ours, they move finished and complete, gifted with extensions of the senses we have lost or never attained, living by voices we shall never hear. They are not brethren; they are not underlings; they are other nations, caught with ourselves in the net of life and time, fellow prisoners of the splendour and travail of the earth."   (Harry Beston)

*

"The suffering of an animal like a fox or a badger trapped in an illegal snare, or of a majestic bird of prey after consuming an illegal poison, doesn't bear thinking about."

(OneKind – Edinburgh)

"Every year, in Europe alone, millions of cattle, sheep, pigs and horses are carried by lorry and ship, on journeys that may span three or four countries and cover many hundreds of miles ... Live exports are a cause of needless suffering ... in the worst cases many animals die ... We must stop this recurring nightmare."

(CIWF – Compassion in World Farming)

"Our investigation at X Laboratories ... uncovered the cruel use of rabbits and mice ... Home Office review finally confirm that mice ... died routinely *in extremis* ... Approximately 115 million animals are used annually in global research ... The UK is one of the biggest animal researchers."

"In September we launched our 'Stop the Baby Trade' campaign, to end the cruel trade in monkeys for research ... (and) in June our appeal about the terrible explosion experiments carried out on pigs at Porton Down ... 119 live pigs blown up ... in animal warfare experiments ...

(BUAV – British Union Against Vivisection)

"Our investigations have revealed appalling illegal brutality ... in slaughterhouses."

(Animal Aid – campaigning for the use in all slaughterhouses
of CCTV systems.)

"Every year, 30-40 million ... male chicks ... are killed at just a day or two old. They are either suffocated in great gas chambers or dropped alive into electric mincers."   (Viva!)

*

"Cruelty is barbarism, whether it is inflicted on humans or on other species." (Peter Tatchell, Patron of Animal Aid)

"The morality of a nation can be judged by the way it treats its animals."   (Gandhi)

Let us remember also – "all those other beings, and creatures, who exist on Earth today in a state of wretchedness, enserfed – within the ever-tightening noose of land monopoly – to those who are now their global masters ..." (See more fully under III: 1 Letters.)

"When Elephants Weep"
by
Jeffrey Masson & Susan McCarthy

Brighter Pathways

"My eyes became progressively photosensitive. As time went on, it became so much worse that seeing a bright sky, even for a few seconds, was enough to leave me prostrate and vomiting for the next 48 hours. Eventually, I became imprisoned in a darkened room throughout the summer.

Then, in autumn, someone told me about Eyebright herb. I started taking teas made with it every day. By the following spring, my photosensitivity was cured."

(P.... K...., WDDTY, Feb 07)

"A year ago I was diagnosed with Parkinson's Disease and cannot tell you how hard life has been since then. Just recently, the organist at church gave me an article extolling the virtues of asparagus in controlling this disease. I pureed a can of it, stored it in the fridge and took 4 tablespoons night and morning. The article said results appeared in between 2 to 4 weeks. After a month, I could walk again and reduce my daily tablets from 6 to 2. Its effect has been to give me a second chance. Before, I could hardly walk to the post box. Now, I can walk anywhere. I can write again, hold a book steady and sit still in an audience. Absolutely unbelievable relief. Apparently the asparagus contain Glutathione, something which is a free radical scavenger that protects the cells from further damage. It has certainly worked for me!"

(Mrs W. Lancashire, with acks. to Grace Magazine – in its invaluable section, "While the Kettle Boils"!)

"I would like to pass on something that happened to my grandmother many years ago. She had a poisoned hand. It did not respond to the doctor's treatment, but got steadily worse. It got so bad that she was to go into hospital to have the hand removed. My grandfather, going home one day, met an old countryman who begged him to collect Ragwort and make a poultice of it. This he did. They applied it and kept it on for a few days. When the time came for the operation the hand was healed.

My grandmother used to show me her hand and tell me this story when I was a small child. She always remembered how nearly she lost her hand, and felt grateful all her life for the 'mircale' that saved it.

(Mrs E.L., Surrey, by courtesy of Grace magazine)

"The flowers of Ragwort have important forces which magnetize and remove deep seated impurities and which also dissolve swellings."
(Juliette de Bairacli Levy, in "The Illustrated Herbal Handbook")

See also the profound and moving book
"The Lost Language of Plants"
By Stephen Buhner.

See further the remarkable work of Dr F. Batmangelidj "Water & Salt: Your Healers from Within". (The reference is of course to *original fully mineralised* Salt.* As Dr B. Points out, commercial salt is a poison to the body. *Enquire at your local health food store, or obtain from Lifeworks, Muir of Logie, Forres, Moray, IV36 2QG.)

Also: "Laetrile vs. Cancer: An Australian Story", published in Nexus magazine, Feb-Mar 2011.

*

"The Doctor of the Future will give no medicine, but will interest his patients in the care of the human frame, in diet, and in the cause and prevention of disease."   (Thomas Edison)

"We must look for hope, not to doctors, but to those, whether or not they are medically qualified, who see the need to create a new society, of which health will be an integral part (as ill-health is of ours)."

(In Session Eighteen of the court proceedings, Dr John Bradshaw sums up his verdict, above. From Introduction by Ivan Illich to the book, "Doctors on Trial", by Dr John S. Bradshaw, published by Wildwood House, London 1978 – an indictment of modern technological medicine.)

*

284

Scenes from a Tapestry

Panel 4: Rooting Back

*

Land is kinship, family and clan. It is the basis of life,
identity and spirituality. Land is home.

(Aboriginal saying)

*

In this final panel of the Tapestry, I revert to the term 'rooting'
– and so, 'rooting back'. For the restoration to us of the
original terrene man's sanity can come only with his actual re-
rooting in the earth again – in Gaia; that is – the end of his
physical displacement from the land.

However, if we would truly find our way back home – a word
of warning here at the beginning.

The institution of the natural Law of Rent will make available
for the people's re-occupation an abundance of land formerly
locked away from us. But a warning awaits us at the start of this
new adventure. For *unless* the people bestir themselves to set up
their own small community organizations (wardships in the
towns), with full powers to assess, collect and disburse the rental
fund, (besides managing all their other local affairs)* - they will
assuredly find themselves no better off.

---

* Re how to link up with other grass-roots communities for the
undertaking of more joint affairs – see article "The
Bioregional Movement and Scotland", under "Author's Writings".

We need only remind ourselves of Voltaire's words – that "the art of government is to make two-thirds of a nation pay all it possibly can for the benefit of the other third" – to be sure that the *first* outgoings from this temptingly abundant new rental source, *if administered by a centralising power,* will be for the propping up precisely of those same quangos and other 'authorities' which so persecute and disempower us today – while a multitude of political regulations and outright embargoes will be placed upon the people's freely re-occupying their own land, we may be sure ... hence throwing us once more back into the State's arms for its familiar 'creation of jobs' – to the on-going impoverishment of our lives – (for we should as good as have lost our rental fund again) – and of course to the on-going destruction of our health. "Plus ça change ..." would be our own fully deserved indictment.

Henry George observed the fundamental law of economics as being that 'man seeks to satisfy his desires with the least possible exertion'. Let us be warned of the mental application of this law – and remember the fate of the Children of Israel when, flourishing under the rental law of their Jubilee Year, they began to whine for a 'father figure' to look after them ... And let us have more gumption!

If we truly wish to redeem ourselves by honouring Gaia and instituting the natural Law of Rent – the 'black flower of civilization' *must go*!

*

It was to my great delight that I learned last year, from a friend, of a new initiative in precisely this great journey of the re-rooting of ourselves back in Gaia. In Europe there has arisen a new movement calling itself Reclaim the Fields, while there has recently come into being also a sister organisation – a peasant movement of more world-wide reach, La Via Campesina. What is of special interest is that these movements are not just sudden upshoots of today, but represent the resurgence of a long-lost – forgotten – suppressed – Green smallholder and peasant movement of our not-so-far past!

It was some 25 years ago, in 1985, that I first made discovery of this movement, from a letter of quite absorbing interest which was published in April of that year in Green Line, (Oxford).

I cannot do better than reproduce it here in full, for what an education it is in revealing to us a certain long tradition of radical opposition to the ruling political 'grundocracy' in Europe – and an opposition that was not Socialist.

Green peasant tradition

Dear GL,

David Pepper is wrong to assert (GL 30) that opposition to multinationals, and an approach which places dual emphasis on social justice and ecology, must be 'by definition talking about some form of socialism.' Andrew Ferguson is equally wrong to assume that ecology without socialism leads to 'an eco-fascist state entirely lacking in social justice.'

They are both assuming that socialism (and David adds anarchism) are the only traditions with a record of fighting for social justice. They both imply that Green ideals can only thrive conscientiously along with a commitment to socialism.

It is not their fault that they have apparently not heard of a different tradition and philosophy which did have the social concern they equate only with socialism, and which put it into workable practice.

I refer to the 'Peasant', 'People's' and 'Agrarian' parties of south and eastern Europe, between the wars. Their history is given in D Mitrany's work 'Marx against the Peasant: a study in social dogmatism' (1951).

These parties achieved quite wide popular support and political influence. Amongst their policies were: land reform and redistribution, collective and cooperative projects in agriculture, food processing, road building, irrigation and export management, cultural and literacy programmes amongst rural communities which often had no educational facilities at all, opposition to massive industrialisation, state collectivisation, urbanisation and bureaucracy, etc. etc. As their title suggests the Peasant Parties began as outlets for newly emergent political consciousness in rural areas; but they later developed a specific philosophy which saw the virtues of small-scale, self-supporting communities united by certain co-operative foundations; and wished to protect the rural environment against urban depredations.

If these policies sound familiar, I need only add that at one point the various national Peasant Parties tried to set up a federation to rival the Socialist International – it was to be called the Green International!

No one who looks at the ideals and practical achievements of these Peasant Parties could seriously suggest they were without a sense of social justice and a deep commitment to social reform. Yet they were not socialists – they came from a different tradition, had a philosophy with a distinctive perspective, and participated in political activity as rivals to socialist and communist parties.

Neither were they insignificant. They participated in several governments in Eastern Europe while a form of democracy prevailed; their organisation of co-operatives and cultural initiatives was another solid achievement.

Were their supporters free to speak today, there is little doubt they would have much to say about whether socialism is the sole route to social justice!

Mark Valentine, 35 Grafton Way, New Duston, Northants.
Green Line, 34 Cowley Road, Oxford – April 1985.

*

The Green Line article was not quite the first that I had heard of these peasant and agrarian parties – but it was the first I learned of its extent - and of the splendid concept of a Green International. For already in 1972 and again in 1981 articles had appeared in Land & Liberty on this matter. The earlier was a moving article by the Hungarian, Charles Ravasz, recounting the part played in the resistance to Germany's invasion of 1944 by a group of keen young students of Georgism, and mention is made in it of the Smallholders' Party. Hungary had already achieved a remarkable assessing of Budapest's town sites for this radical land reform, carried out by Dr L.L. Pikler in 1919 – a great character, whose report on this had appeared in Land & Liberty at the time.*

---

* It is easy for us today, nearly 100 years on, to see that, re Dr Pikler's tremendous achievement, it was in fact a mistake to place the assessments as he did on the (*so-called*, but in reality of course non-existent) 'capital' values of the land. For as the 'capital' values reduced each year with the reduced selling power of the land under this reform, so the basis of the assessment was being continually eroded. The only method of assessing land is of course according to the only real value that it ... not *has*, but carries, as we have seen in Part I. For the *annual rental* value will never erode.

This but illustrates another huge stumbling block the movement for this reform has created for itself, by fastening on the quite erroneous term 'land value', which would indicate that land has an actual capital value, when it has none – and with it, of course, in the first place, the hopelessly erroneous term 'tax'!

'Land value' should, in fact, have been included as another 'IMPOSTER TERM' in 'Reclaiming our Language' (Pt.III ch.2), for it should never appear without the word 'rental' in the middle. So why not simplify and just say 'land rent'? [The ultimate horror of a term: 'land tax'!]

The Sept-Oct 1981 article was prompted by the publication in Spain of a book recounting the long struggle of the Andalusian peasants for land rights, and is of such interest even beyond that, in describing the very same economic serfdom – continuing of course in Spain – that we ourselves equally 'enjoy', that I am republishing practically the whole of it here, and it will surely be of particular interest to those in the Reclaim the Fields and La Via Campesina movements. (My only editing of it has been to replace the term "land tax supporters" with "land rent supporters". See footnote re Dr Pikler's work.)

Andalusia: Physiocracy & the fight for autonomy

La Tierra: Physiocracy & Autonomy in Andalusia, by J.M. Santos, M.R. Lagos and E.L. Ortega, Jerez: Centro de Estudios Historico Jerezanos, 1980.

By German Lema

The more favourable political climate in Spain has made possible the publication of this book (in Spanish), which in a concise form presents the historical facts that created and maintain the economic slavery in Andalusia and also the struggle for liberation.

Santos Lopez recalls the situation at the beginning of the 19th century when the liberal ideas of the French revolution spread through Spain and caused a decline of the feudal system which would soon disappear altogether, giving way to new methods of production.

The land, which up to that time was largely administered by the nobility or by co-operative bodies like hospitals, the church, municipalities, etc., in a very short time became private property, being sold at public auction at very low prices. This put an end to serfdom but introduced the economic slavery that still remains.

The nobles and rich merchants, in acquiring what was previously communal property, thereby became also owners of the non-proprietors. Both capital and labour fell under their power of monopoly: the capitalist had to pay a maximum price for the use of a locality or for access to raw materials, and the labourer had to accept a minimum wage, just enough to remain alive.

The value of land increased with the increase in productivity brought about by technology, or as a result of public investment, or because of an increase in demand due to the increase in population. That is, land increased in value without any effort from its proprietors.

When the effects of this modern slavery began to show, people reacted in various ways, with uprisings, protests, strikes. This was the situation in 1913 when the first international conference of land rent supporters took place in Ronda. By then Henry George's ideas were already pointing at land monopoly, created by the law, as the source from which emanated the Andalusian evils: poverty, fear of temporary or permanent unemployment, emigration.

But to be able to do away with the evils, it was necessary to extirpate their cause. The Physiocratic postulates of the Ronda conference became known and accepted by political leaders like Blas Infante, thus adding a new dimension to their movement for Andalusian autonomy, the Georgist solution to their land problem.

The history presented by Santos Lopez is the history of social transformation in Spain: the conversion of serfs with limited rights into dispossessed labourers. And that is the present situation under both dictatorship and democracy.

Manuel Ruiz Lagos is a keen researcher who continues to present the Spanish speaking world with evidence, facts and figures that could very well have disappeared during the forty years' duration of the latest Spanish dark age.

He analyses the Physiocractic activity in Andalusia. The manifesto, 'Land and Liberty' (1911), opened the door to the international conference at Ronda (1913), followed by the manifesto of Blas Infante (1916), the Ronda Assembly (1916) and the Cordoba Assembly (1919). The formation of the Juntas Liberalistas, a political body, gave backing to the Georgist ideology that shaped the project for agrarian reform during the short-lived Second Republic.

Ruiz Lagos points out this peculiarity of the Andalusian movement in contrast to the Catalonian autonomy movement backed by protectionist interests and with the merely political autonomy movement of the Basque country. Free trade and land reform still inspire the Andalusian leaders of today.

When reading the step-by-step programme drafted by Blas Infante for the legal removal of land monopoly, which would enable the Andalusian people to obtain their economic freedom, one does not need to look further for the reasons for his political murder in 1936.

La Tierra includes appendices giving details of the Physiocratic manifesto of 1911, Blas Infante's proposals to the international conference in Ronda (1913) and to the Andalusians of the Cordoba Assembly (1919), and of the agrarian reform project for the solution of the problem of latifundi (1931).

All three documents were destroyed by fire, but repression has not been able to weaken the resolution of those who stood and stand by the Andalusian ideals: Physiocracy & autonomy.

*

There is a coda to this.

In the early 1980s there was a demonstration in Glasgow against the Falklands war, and I went to join in. There I ran into a friend I had not seen for some time – Kay Blackstock, on account of whose splendid educational work at Barlinnie Prison, a wing there has been named after her.

Kay was just back from a trip to Spain, to Andalusia, and while there she was intrigued to notice how many streets and other public places were named after someone called 'Blas Infante' – and asked me if I could throw any light on this. I replied that indeed I could, adding that, apart from readers of Land & Liberty north of the Border, there were probably few in Scotland able to, (for it is hard to think of so radical a soul as Blas Infante entering into any of our courses of Spanish studies!). When I had recited his history, and especially his presence at that international conference in 1913 at Ronda on radical land reform, she said – "That's interesting! Because when Franco invaded Spain with his troops, it was from North Africa that they came, and Andalusia that they landed in". Franco no doubt realized that he had a great deal more to fear from the spread of the gospel of *land justice* than from mere Communism.

Some time ago – probably in the early 1970s – I recall reading in a chance copy of the Financial Times a most interesting article about Spain, telling how the Spanish people had a vague awareness of suffering some kind of "amnesia" about a chapter of their history lost to them. Some of us certainly know what that "lost chapter" is likely to be! – and often have I wished that I had kept that article.

"Blas Infante perez Andalucia
Por si" (for Andalusia) "por Espana
y la humanidad hijo ilustre de cesares"

(It is not hard to translate into English.) Such are the words inscribed on the placard below a bust of Blas Infante, a photograph of which, sent me by another friend in Spain, I much treasure.

Upon reading the Green Line article, I sought out a copy of Mitrany's book, and in it was most interested to read of how the peasant peoples of Eastern Europe – (true to the original terrene nature of man) – invariably found common ground with one another, remaining free from that nationalistic bias upon which the political element depends. For allegiances to Statehood, in fostering among different peoples suspicions of one another, divert their suspicions away from where they should more properly rest – namely, upon that political element which parasitically lives off them:-

> With rent and with taxes abuse 'em,
> And with sport to distract still amuse 'em.
> Peace or war? Nought to choose –
> Heads we win, tails they lose –
> But there's nought like a war to confuse 'em!

Discovered recently on an old piece of paper – hard to tell from it whether by HG Wells or by SAH! But beside it is a note as to which there is no uncertainty: "The political movement for land rent reform died out with the Second World War".

*

Gaia has her own ways of emasculating that political element, and bringing Earth back to its springtime again. In his absorbing book "The Black Sea", Neal Ascherson writes of the many different peoples who live on the periphery of that great inland water, their lives flourishing or declining according to its well-being or otherwise. Now, in more recent times, as various ecological crises threaten that great sea from man's misdemeanours, the peoples of the Black Sea are converging with one another in their ecological plight. Those of us who know of the Biogregional movement easily recognize in this how a naturally all-embracing *bioregional* awareness is beginning to supercede the old, inherently divisive *political* one.

How much must this process have been hastened since the disaster to the river Danube of last autumn from a huge onslaught of toxic red sludge, the output of waste from aluminium manufacture! For after flowing through seven countries – which it provides with much of their drinking water – it is into the Black Sea that the Danube empties.

*

"The storm is here. From the clash of these two winds a storm will be born. Its time has arrived. Now the wind from above rules, but the wind from below is coming." (Subcomandante Marcos)*

From another part of the globe comes dramatic news of the defeat of the political element by direct peasant power. The Zapatista movement in Mexico has proved the truth of its communiqué that "it is possible to govern and to govern ourselves without the parasite that calls itself government."*

Mitrany's book speaks of the peasant as one whose real power lies in resistance – "he is the greatest passive resister in history", who will "wait ten, twenty or fifty years" to bring about the change he wants. They have waited longer than that in Mexico, where the movement for "land and liberty" goes back a very long time – but it seems that that time has indeed now come.

"Zapatistas, unlike most revolutionaries, don't want to seize power at the barrel of a gun. In fact they don't want to seize power at all. They did once march on Mexico City, but did so without guns. They have guns, but rarely use them. Zapatistas don't want power for themselves, they want power for the people to govern themselves. This they have put into practice in Chiapas where large areas have been declared autonomous zones, and all government influence and officials eradicated. The government did once try to reclaim one of these autonomous zones. They were beaten back by the people and have never tried again."*

---

* With acknowledgements to http://www.heureka.clara.net/gaia/democracy.htm (11.03/04)

Chekhov is recorded as saying once, as he tended the garden he loved at his country home in Yalta: "In three or four hundred years, the whole world will be a beautiful and flourishing garden."

With the peasant, the bioregional, and the land rent movements, now all part of that "wind from below", perhaps it will not take three or four hundred years after all. ...?

"Truth is on the march and nothing will stop it."

(Emile Zola)

*

The Acres and the Hands

"The earth is the Lord's and the fullness thereof,"
Said God's most holy Word:-
The water hath fish, and the land hath flesh,
And the air hath many a bird;
And the soil is teeming o'er all the earth,
And the earth has numberless lands,
Yet millions of hands want acres,
While millions of acres want hands.

Sunlight and breezes and gladsome flowers
Are over the earth spread wide;
And the good God gave these gifts to men,
To men who on earth abide;
Yet thousands are toiling in poisonous gloom,
And shackled with iron bands,
While millions of hands want acres,
And millions of acres want hands.

Never a foot hath the poor man here
To plant with a grain of corn;
And never a plot where his child may cull
Fresh flowers in the dewy morn.
The soil lies fallow – the weeds grow rank;
Yet idle the poor man stands!
Oh, millions of hands want acres,
And millions of acres want hands.

'Tis writ that "Ye shall not muzzle the ox
That treadeth out the corn;"
But behold, ye shackle the poor man's hands,
That have all earth's burdens borne.
The land is a gift of a bounteous God –
And to labour His Word commands;
Yet millions of hands want acres,
And millions of acres want hands.

Who hath ordained that a few should hoard
Their millions of useless gold,
And rob the earth of its fruits and flowers,
While profitless soil they hold?
Who hath ordained that a parchment scroll
Shall fence round miles of lands,
When millions of hands want acres,
And millions of acres want hands?

 'Tis a glaring lie on the face of day,
This robbery of men's rights;
'Tis a lie that the Word of the Lord disowns;
'Tis a curse that burns and blights.
And 'twill burn and blight till the people rise,
And swear, while they break their bands,
That the hands shall henceforth have acres,
And the acres henceforth have hands.

Reprinted from The Beacon, September 1894
by Augustine Duganne (Acks. to Progress, Australia)

Coda

*

The Loch Garry Project and its Vision

(See photographs overleaf)

One magical day last autumn, Ron Greer took me up to Loch
Garry on a long anticipated excursion.

I was eager to see the planting of trees in that landscape,
which he had initiated and then carried forward with the help
of the others he had gathered round him in the Loch Garry Tree
Project.

What I saw was quite beyond my expectations. A new
landscape was coming into being – and a whole new vision with
it; for "where trees will grow, people can live" and as Ron says
"what the land needs is sustainable human rehabitation", (letter
in The Courier of 27 Sept 05).

Tragically, due to the bungling political element in our society,
the promised funding needed to carry this work on to a further
stage – was abruptly halted. What can one say but that, in a
society founded on the many corruptions of land monopoly,
there are those who *do not wish* it to be discovered, what a
marriage of the land and the people of Scotland could achieve.
But one day – in the day when we have come to our senses, and
have done away with the imposter political element in society –
in that day the vision will be realized!

Meanwhile the trees are growing on, clothing the land with
ever increasing beauty and shelter, and welcoming in ever
greater numbers those earlier denizens of the natural world,
furred, feathered and finned ...

*

Changing landscapes up Loch Garry

Chapter 4

*

Other Scenarios

Other Scenarios

*

i. WATER – A Certain Saga!

Those of us who have been in the opposition to the Fluoridation of water supplies for the past half-century have been able to watch, during this time, the unfolding of a certain 'dance sequence' – which, for the sleights-of-hand within it accomplished, must be reckoned remarkable!

Going back some 35 years, the public domain, in its sphere of local government, underwent a dramatic transformation. All of the small town and rural councils were abolished in one of those *strides towards centralization* to which a society founded on monopoly – originating of course from the monopoly of land, the all-underlying – is ever prone. (For who is really going to think anything special about it – amidst all the upheavals?) And nobody really did – except for just a few, of course ...

But – wait a moment! That wasn't quite *all* that happened. For somewhere along the way there was achieved a very strange 'tweak'. Of *all* the former spheres of governance that fell to be placed with the newly devised 'regional' bodies, there was for some reason singled out – HEALTH! Instead of accompanying all the other spheres of social responsibility which became the province of those now more centralized (but still elected) regional set-ups, HEALTH took a different turning ... and fell into the hands of a newly invented phenomenon in this sphere: *boards*. Non-elected, *appointed* Health Boards!

It certainly invites reflection as to who – or perhaps, what 'interest'? – proposed this somewhat remarkable step in re-patterning. All that one can come up with is that – it certainly achieved a remarkable 'field day' for a certain *pressure group* in

the *field* of *big business*! Nought now to fear from pretence
'consultations' – for these Boards now held the whip-hand.

But – wait another moment! In organizing into being this
good new set-up – hadn't something been overlooked? Those
dratted Water Boards! For, with these Water Boards operating
still under the *councils*, the final say on Water still came under an
electoral vote ...

But – never mind!

Next step: the regional councils have after all proved too
'cumbersome'. (The people will readily agree to *that!*) So – let's
now simplify by abolishing them – and devolving their powers
back to the *local* councils instead!

So it was done. And strangely enough, during this further
step-in-the-dance there was accomplished – *another 'tweak'*! This
time – WATER! Still boards – but this time of a very different
kind! ... And so, this time: "GOTCHA! – right into our laps!"

And again – nobody really did notice it either. Except of
course just for some ...

There is a rather striking quotation attributed to one, Gaius
Petronius, around AD60:-

> "We trained hard – but it seemed that every time we were
> beginning to form up into teams, we would be re-organised.
>
> I was to learn late in life that we tend to meet any new
> situation by re-organising, and a wonderful method it can
> be for creating the illusion of progress while producing
> confusion, inefficiency and demoralisation."

(Acks. to Craigie's Column in The Courier – date unknown)

And perhaps a unique
Opportunity to tweak?

For there has since been achieved at Westminster, for England
and Wales at least, (Scotland's powers in this being devolved), a
certain ... what one might call *big-business-enabling* Act. Despite
the fact that –

"Children under three should never use fluoridated toothpaste – or drink fluoridated water. And baby formula must never be made up using fluoridated tap water."
> (Dr Harry Limeback, DSc, PhD in BioChemistry, head of Dept. of Preventive Dentistry, University of Toronto.)

"Fluoride and Bone Cancer." (Report in WDDTY, Feb 07.)
Etc. ... Etc. ... Etc. ...!

*

"The greatest medical fraud of the century" – describing Fluoridation.   (U.S. scientist Dr John Yiamouyiannis.)

"The sheer irresponsibility of the medical and dental profession about this problem is frankly frightening."
> (Ivan Lawrence, QC, MP. *Hansard*, 12 June 78.)

Those fluoridistas! ... But – GOTCHA!

THE "BLACK FLOWER OF CIVILIZATION" HAS SEEDED AGAIN!

*

ii. WORK – in Tune with a <u>Free</u> People

I heard on Radio 4, in May 2010, an interview with Matthew Crawford about his new book, "The Case for Working with Your Hands, or Why Office Work is Bad for Us and Fixing Things Feels Good" (published by Viking, 2009), and was inspired to acquire a copy. Here are some notes made from its most interesting and extremely apposite contents.

He goes right to the heart of the matter of work: the fatal step of separating *thinking* from *doing* – making for the dumbing down of jobs, computers leading us in the same direction.

He tells most interestingly how, when Henry Ford started up the mass manufacturing of cars, he had to hire 963 people to fill finally 100 places. People loathed the factory work, as they came from places like bicycle repair shops, where their *minds*, equally, were engaged fully in their work.

How in the manual trades you are dealing with things resistant to your will, which ask for real learning and careful judging – faculties we were made to develop.

How it is important to see the direct effect of your work in your life, including that danger could be involved – to yourself or another – if something is incorrectly done.

That it is "infantilizing" – not to have a direct effect on your environment.

Young people 50 years ago were involved with motor bikes and other mechanical things – and so learned how to take them apart and assemble them again, thus gaining real pride in their work and in themselves.

By contrast today they engage with mobile phones – things which are just a kind of 'magic', as you can't take them apart or mend them. (*Very* few people can.)

Also – how the need for concentration on your work means that time flies by.

What a wonderful gift of a book – made for this day and age!

In short – man was made for CRAFT work, not factory work! Incidentally, the effect upon the brain of today's intensively computerized workplaces may make for some vivid discoveries. Looking recently at an instruction manual provided for one of today's complex telephone machines ... *Gobbledygook!* And Matthew Crawford and his hands-on colleagues found *just the same* when they tried to cope with the manuals provided for the latest models of today's motor-bikes!

Being highly qualified also academically, Matthew Crawford recounts his experience of employment in the higher echelons of mental work. You should just read his account of that! No wonder he returned thankfully to the scene of hands-on repair workshops!

I do not feel I can leave this scenario of WORK without quoting from Gandhi's hardly surpassable summary of the matter, from ch. "Wardha", in Lanza del Vasto's "Return to the Source":-

"(T)he object of work is not so much to make objects as to make men. A man makes himself by making something. Work creates a direct contact with matter and ensures his precise knowledge of it as well as direct contact and daily collaboration with other men; it imprints the form of man on matter and offers itself to him as a means of expression; it concentrates his attention and his abilities on one point or at least on a continuous line; it bridles the passions by strengthening the will. Work, bodily work, is for nine-tenths of humanity their only chance to show their worth in this world.

But in order that work itself, and not just payment for it, shall profit a man, it must be human work, work in which the whole man is engaged: his body, his heart, his brain, his taste. The craftsman who fashions an object, polishes it, decorates it, sells it and fits it for the requirements of the person he intends it for, is carrying out human work. The countryman who gives life to his fields and makes his flock prosper by work attuned to the seasons is successfully accomplishing the task of a free man.

But the worker enslaved in a serial production, who from one second to another repeats the same movement at the speed dictated by the machine, fritters himself away in work which has no purpose for him, no end, no taste, no sense. The time he spends there is time lost, time sold: he is not selling his creation but his very lifetime. He is selling what a freeman does not sell: his life. He is a slave."

(Acknowledgements to the Publishers, Rider & Co., 1971.)

Precisely!

And we know now the path by which we can finally break out of that slavery – that *enserfment*.

It will be better not only for our physical health, but for our mental health as well!

*

iii. Another Kind of Vet!

It was certainly a radical book – but happily the buyer for that range, in a northern Scottish town, was keen on it and welcomed the idea of a flyer – (a suggestion from a friend) – to place by it for those who entered the bookshop.

Presently – after the flyer had been in place for some days – she decided to ring the buyer and find out how things were going, but the person who answered the phone said "I'm sorry, she can't talk to you – she's with the vet". The author of the book was flummoxed – all she could think of saying was, "What – is her dog ill?" There was a roar of laughter at the other end of the line: "No – the *book* vet!"

Well!

After that it was never possible to speak to the buyer again. And then one day a letter arrived from the friend who had suggested the flyer. He had been in the town that morning, and as he was passing by the bookshop he suddenly noticed – amidst a motley pile set out on the pavement of obviously get-rid-of-quick-and-cheap items – HER BOOK!

Well!

"But then", she thought – "let's look on the bright side of things! *Excellent* that the book had been regarded as RADICAL!"

*

iv. Street Theatre!

We need *street theatre* – or dance? – here in Scotland – and plenty of songs of protest, of course! – to tear the veils away from the centuries-old suppression of *the land question*.

As the simplest way to do it at the last moment – an extract from the chapter "Community and Re-Empowerment", in "Birthright in Land ...":-

"Something else fell out of that serendipity file. With joy I pounced on a faded cutting about the Italian 'street' actor, Dario Fo – a performance once seen, never forgotten! 'Unique in world theatre, playwright, actor, clown, teacher and philosopher ... and great hero of the Italian Left' – (Radio Times of 25 Feb 83).

Fo revived the *Comedia dell'Arte* of Italy of the Middle Ages – that street theatre which had in it a strongly satirical element; its purpose being – in that age of something-less-than-free speech – to allow the ordinary people, labouring under the cruelties of a land feudalism that held all of Europe in its thrall, (the real cause of the Peasant Wars), in this safe 'comedy' way to denounce those social structures under which they felt and knew themselves *trapped*.

When I say that Dario Fo revived this old *Comedia dell'Arte*, in fact it was still very much alive and flourishing in the Lucania of Carlo Levi's exile; and his account of it there, in his book – with the people's mysterious borrowing of his doctor's accoutrements for their performance! – is one of its most unforgettable passages ... as we share in how brilliantly-bitterly through their acting the inside story of their lives is revealed.

We can do with some street theatre right here in Scotland – right now! The Scots can do it as well as anyone. I could hardly tear myself away from the performance I stumbled on, so deliciously unexpectedly, on leaving Glasgow's Garden Festival one evening in 1988. I know little about the Scots' equivalent of the *Comedia dell'Arte,* for I confess I have never seen *The Three Estates.* But the old Morality Plays had their Seven Deadly Sins, did they not? – which no doubt might approximate to the Seven Wise Masters! ..."

Over to you!

*

v. A Matter Metaphysical?

It has long struck me that the natural Law of Rent, while it is in its outer manifestation a social law, in a more innerly sphere manifests with a profoundly personal face.

For the primary field in which we operate is the field of consciousness.* It might well be asked then: to whom in *that* field are we payers of rent – knowingly or unknowingly? Might an investigation of this sphere of our life not yield equally valuable fruitage ... re a somewhat subtler area of our possible freedom – or enserfment? - !

*

Heart of all happening,
Below as above –
Thou: touchstone of sanity,
Wellspring of love!

---

* Today's quantum physics has added some beautiful insights into this primary field of our linkage – a vastly superior *'internet',* or *'web'!*

Pithy Pieces

A brilliant contribution from Colin Spencer includes an encapsulated analysis of the *collapse of British dietary health* resulting from the Enclosures (18th – early 19th C): 'Rural life was radically altered and partially destroyed and whole villages were abandoned. Within a generation cooking skills and traditional recipes were lost forever, as the creative interrelationship between soil and table (the source of all good cuisine) had been severed." (Emphasis added.)
(From the Introduction to the Cambridge World History of Food.)

The Lord giveth and the landlord taketh away.
(John W. Raper, 1870-1950, Acks. to Progress, Australia.)

"Sasine Register" – these words clearly seen on a TV programme on "Whose Land is it anyway?" on 10 Mar 96. More recently changed to "Land Register". (The word "sasine" means "seizings". Another clue we must erase from the scene!)

If women landowners wish to retain their land rights, they should not marry. The Marriage Act is fraudulent because it does not declare that women lose their land rights on marriage. It has a severe impact on women farmers: divorce results in their being ousted from their farms, dispossessed and impoverished. Resistance has led to loss of life, increasing the culture of fear experienced by many women in the farming industry.
(Ann Mallaby, courageous founder of Women's Land Reform Group. info@womenslandrights.org)

Land monopoly has created the class of the dispossessed, and from them the monopolists of capital recruit their slave-gangs ...

The wage-slaves not being allowed to consume what they produce, the capitalist employer seeks markets abroad.

(From ch. "The Origins of War" in "Land or Revolution" by R.L. Outhwaite.)

We did not conquer India for the benefit of the Indians ... that is cant. We conquered India as an outlet for the goods of Great Britain ...

(From a speech by Lord Brentford, Tory Home Secretary 1924-28. Acks. to Peter Cavanagh, in The Courier, 10 June 1999.)

'The first object of any tyrant in Whitehall would be to make Parliament utterly subservient to his will', the great legal jurist Lord Devlin wrote.

The next, he said, was 'to overthrow or diminish trial by jury, for no tyrant could afford to leave his subject's freedom in the hands of twelve of his countrymen.

'So that trial by jury is more than an instrument of justice and more than one wheel of the constitution: it is the lamp that shows that freedom lives.'

(Marcel Berlins, commenting on an article "British Justice: Shadow of the tyrant falls on our freedom", Daily Mail 7 July 93.)

What good is our intelligence to us, if we won't use it in the greatest issues?   (D.H. Lawrence)

*

Without economic freedom, no other freedom can endure.

(Benjamin Franklin)

There will be no settlement of the land question for us, until the whole of the rents are taken for the country.

(The Skye Crofters, in their Resolution of 1885, at the height of the Highland Clearances.)

There are a thousand hacking at the branches of evil to one
who is striking at the root.   (Thoreau)

One does not need a college education to see that the Trade
Union Movement has become part and parcel of monopoly
capitalism.   (James MacMurchie)

It is no measure of health to be well adjusted to a profoundly
sick society.   (J. Krishnamurti)

*

The City of London pledged last night to continue to support
India's efforts to transform its financial sector to benefit all
citizens "rich or poor".

The lord mayor of London made the commitment at a
Guildhall banquet in honour of Indian president Pratibha Patil
and told the head of State "we offer you our experience".

(Apt comment on the above: I once read in Progress – "I don't
make up funny stories. I just report what the Government does."
Or says? (The Courier, 29 Oct 09)

"Every child should have the best possible opportunity, which
begins with education."

(Minister of Education, 14 Nov 06)

Education in the Law of Rent?

The fiftieth anniversary of the signing of the Treaty of Rome
has not been seen as a cause for celebration by Lord Stoddart of
Swindon, when stepping down this summer as Chairman of the
cross-party Campaign for an Independent Britain ... Instead, Lord
Stoddart has described the last half-century as "fifty years of
deceit".

He said: "It began with a deception as the signatories to the Treaty all signed a pile of blank sheets because only the cover had been printed in time."

(Published in Get Britain Out, Spring 2007)

If you want to make God laugh, tell him about your future plans. (Woody Allen)

Dear Editor, - Before any Westminster candidates open their mouths to expel air on the topic of wind power, could I point out to them that at 9.30am this morning (Friday, April 23) the 2800 wind turbines in the UK, of which 1190 are in Scotland, were producing just 30 megawatts of electricity? Further, in the previous 24 hour period these turbines only produced 0.4% of UK energy. Perhaps it's time to eat more beans.

(Ron Greer, Blair Atholl, The Perthshire Advertiser, 30 Apr 10)

Sooner or later we sit down to a banquet of consequences.

(Robert Louis Stevenson)

*

The rich sin and the sackcloth and ashes are handed out to the working and unemployed classes. The rich sin and the poor get the hangover. (Diana Forrest)

Giving power and money to government is like giving whisky and car keys to teenage boys.

PJ O'Rourke, Civil Libertarian, Progress, Sept-Oct 2005)

Bureaucracy is the art of making the possible impossible.

(Javier Salcedo)

Dear Sir, - You are so twisted up in knots
        Of your own invention,
    That my quill to make response
        Has no further intention.
(SAH – in response to a letter from a Scottish Government
                                Minister, 20 July 08)

5% who see the cat will have their lives forever turned upside
down, and will spend years of wrecking dinner parties fruitlessly
trying to explain what it's all about.
                    (Karl Williams, in Editorial, Progress, Jul-Aug 06)
                            (Memories – memories! SAH)

    A college professor once planned
    To live without access to land.
        He nearly succeeded,
        Then found that he needed
    Food, clothing and somewhere to stand.
                                    (Author unknown)
                        *

When the bank manager sent me a new bank card, he
explained that I must have been waving the old one near a
television: that would account for the power having gone out of
it. I mentioned this in some amazement to a friend, but she
merely added that 'because of radiation' I had better keep eight
feet away from any colour set myself or the power would go out
of me too. After this I began to feel differently about television.
        (Part of an old torn-off sheet from The Observer, 10 Jan 82)

Mobile telephones are the most radioactive appliance we have
ever invented apart from the microwave oven, and people are
putting them to their heads ...
                    (Price-Pottenger Journal, Summer 08)

Microsoft PowerPoint and the Decline of Civilization. A tale of extraordinary opposition to this icon of communication and all it stands for. There are thought to be 30 to 40 million PowerPoint presentations a day. DJ Taylor discovers a fierce rebellion against the world of bullet points and the auto-content wizard.

(Radio 4 programme, 12 Oct 04)

The logical end of mechanical progress is to reduce the human being to something resembling a brain in a bottle.

(George Orwell)

(It's already begun – those instruction manuals!)

*

To counter the Surgeon's belief in God, the Astronaut says, "In none of my travels throughout the Universe have I encountered any evidence indicating the existence of God, and so I think you are wrong."

"Funny that", replies the Brain Surgeon. "In all my neurosurgical experience, I have yet to encounter any evidence proving the existence of a thought."

(Sent me by a friend. From a letter in The Independent.)

Know what is in front of your eyes. (Gospel of St Thomas)

Three great mentors – especially amidst nature: stillness, silence and solitude ... (having little truck with the twitter-twatter of today!)

Blessed are those who can laugh at themselves:
   they will have no end of fun.
Blessed are those who can tell a mountain from a
   molehill: they will be saved a lot of bother.

Blessed are those who know how to relax without
    looking for excuses: they are on the way to
    becoming wise.
Happy are you if you can take small things seriously
    and face serious things calmly: you will go far in life.
Happy are you if you can appreciate a smile and forget a frown:
    you will walk on the sunny side of the street.
Blessed are they who think before acting and pray
    before thinking: they will avoid many blunders.
        (Some of the Smaller Beatitudes, from an issue of the Edgar
        Cayce Newsletter.)

The majority believe that everything hard to comprehend must be very profound. This is incorrect. What is hard to understand is what is immature, unclear and often false. The highest wisdom is simple, and passes through the brain directly into the heart.   (Viktor Schauberger)

Viktor Schauberger (1889-1958)
"If I were to be asked what statement of
Viktor Schauberger's in my view most clearly reflects the
grandeur of his mind, and gives insight into the force of his ideas
and thinking, it would be (the above)..."
(Quoted from my Tribute to him in "birthright..,"⁎, P.438.)

Tribute to Henry George

A ll his life George was seeking the one (social) formula that would prompt individuals to adhere to the eternal justice of the Golden Rule. He assailed the "new" study of economics because it taught that there were "no eternally valid natural laws".

"Compared with the solar system", George exclaimed, our earth is but an indistinguishable speck; and the solar system itself shrivels into nothingness when gauged with the star depth. Shall we say that what passes from *our* sight passes into oblivion? No; not into oblivion. Far, far beyond our ken the eternal laws must hold their sway." (Land & Liberty, Sept-Oct 1979)

*

Henry George did of course succeed in his life's aim – that of discovering the great social formula which "would prompt individuals to adhere to the eternal justice of the Golden Rule".

For as the highlanders of old put it, in a statement worthy of the Scots' intuitive grasp of the matter – "The division of the land is made with care and justice. This is in the interest of all." That is: in the most fundamental of all social matters, the sharing of the earth, it is in every man's best interest that the Golden Rule of life is obeyed.

The achievement of Henry George – (one of whose grandfathers was "a Glasgow body") – was to discern the formula, in *the natural Law of Rent*, which gives expression to this Golden Rule in the sphere of our social life –and blesses us all. See Part I ch. 5. Thus he at the same time exposed to the full the folly of the 'new' economics which declared that there are *no* eternally valid natural laws – (that false economics which rules to this day, is taught in all our highest institutes of learning – and has brought us to such disaster!)

318

"It would require less than the fingers of the two hands to enumerate those who, from Plato down, rank with Henry George among the world's social philosophers."

(Professor Dewey, Columbia University, USA)

"People do not argue with the teaching of George: they simply do not know it. The teaching of George is irresistibly convincing in its simplicity and clearness. He who becomes acquainted with it cannot but agree." (Leo Tolstoy)

"Men like Henry George are rare, unfortunately. One cannot imagine a more beautiful combination of intellectual keenness, artistic form, and fervent love of justice." (Albert Einstein)

"Henry George was one of the great reformers of the world. His conscience was active, his sympathies broad, his purpose indomitable, his courage unfailing, his devotion to principle absolute ... but with these were united the passion of a great ideal, the perception of a primal truth unrecognised, and the genius of language to move mankind." (William Lloyd Garrison)

"The purity of his motives, the integrity of his character, the power of his intellect commanded universal recognition. As a thinker, a philosopher, a writer, he was great; but he was greatest as an evangelist carrying the doctrines of justice and brotherhood to the remotest corners of the earth." (New York Herald)

"Of all modern prophets and reformers, Henry George is the one whose arguments are absolutely unanswerable and whose forecast is sure." (Elbert Hubbard)

*

My Favourite Cartoon!

I am told that a photograph is obligatory - so this one is slipped in here! A favourite taken in 1986. Tom and I, and our beloved Juniper did not know we were being snapped in another corner of the garden! Owed to Janie Morrison of Pitlochry.

Chapter 5

*

Amazing Grace

and

The Music of the Spheres

Amazing Grace

*

The Tablecloth

True Story submitted by Pastor Rob Reid

*

The brand new pastor and his wife, newly assigned to his first pastorate, arrived in suburban Brooklyn in early October excited about their opportunity to reopen a church. When they saw their church, it was very run-down and needed much work. They set a goal to have everything done in time to have their first service on Christmas Eve.

They worked hard, repairing pews, plastering walls, painting, and whatnot. On December 18th they were ahead of schedule and just about finished. On December 19th a terrible tempest – a driving rainstorm – hit the area and lasted for two days. On the 21st, the pastor went to the church. His heart sank when he saw that the roof had leaked, causing a large area of plaster about 20 feet by 8 feet to fall off the front wall of the sanctuary just behind the pulpit, beginning about head high. The pastor cleaned up the mess on the floor, and not knowing what else to do but postpone the Christmas Eve service, he headed home.

On the way he noticed that a local business was having a flea market type sale for charity so he dropped in. One of the items was a beautiful, handmade, ivory-coloured, crocheted tablecloth with exquisite work, fine colours and a cross embroidered right in the centre. It was just the right size to cover up the hole in the front wall. He bought it and headed back to the church.

By this time it had started to snow. An older woman running from the opposite direction was trying to catch the bus. She missed it. The pastor invited her to wait in the warm church for the next bus 45 minutes later. She sat in a pew and paid no attention to the pastor while he got a ladder and hangers to put the tablecloth up as a wall tapestry. The pastor could hardly believe how beautiful it looked and it covered up the entire problem area. Then he noticed the woman walking down the centre aisle. Her face was like a sheet. "Pastor," she asked, "where did you get that tablecloth?" The pastor explained. The woman asked him to check the lower right corner to see if the initials, EBG were crocheted into it there. They were. These were the initials of the woman, and she had made this tablecloth 35 years before, in Austria.

The woman could hardly believe it as the pastor told how he had just acquired the tablecloth. The woman explained that before the war she and her husband were well-to-do people in Austria. When the Nazis came, she was forced to leave. Her husband was going to follow her the next week. She was captured, sent to prison and never saw her husband or her home again.

The pastor wanted to give her the tablecloth; but she made the pastor keep it for the church. The pastor insisted on driving her home, feeling that was the least he could do. She lived on the other side of Staten Island and was only in Brooklyn for the day for a housecleaning job.

What a wonderful service they had on Christmas Eve! The church was almost full. The music and the spirit were great. At the end of the service, the pastor and his wife greeted everyone at the door and many said that they would return.

One older man, whom the pastor recognized from the neighbourhood, continued to sit in one of the pews and stare, and the pastor wondered why he wasn't leaving. The man asked him where he had bought the tablecloth on the front wall because it was identical to one that his wife had made years ago when they lived in Austria before the war and how could there be two tablecloths so much alike?

He told the pastor how, when the Nazis came he forced his wife to flee for her safety, and he was supposed to follow her, but he was arrested and put in a prison. He never saw his wife or his home again all the 35 years in between.

The pastor asked him if the man would allow him to take him for a little ride. They drove to Staten Island, to the same house where the pastor had taken the woman three days earlier. He helped the man climb the three flights of stairs to the woman's apartment, knocked on the door and he saw the greatest Christmas reunion he could ever imagine.

(With acknowledgements to Grace Magazine, 2009.)

*

On a lighter vein –

The Kitten

A true story from the newsletter published by St. Mary Church, Greenhithe.

*

W ho says the Creator doesn't have a sense of humour?

A pastor had a kitten that climbed up a tree in his back garden and then was afraid to come down. The pastor coaxed, offered warm milk, etc. to no avail. The kitten would not budge. The tree was not sturdy enough to climb, so the pastor decided that if he tied a rope to his car and drove away so that the tree bent down, he could reach up and get the kitten.

He did all this, checking his progress in the car frequently, then figured – if he went just a little further the tree would bend sufficiently. But as he moved a little further forward the rope broke. The tree went "Boing" and the kitten instantly sailed through the air – out of sight! The pastor felt terrible. He walked all over the neighbourhood asking if they'd seen a little kitten, but nobody had. So he prayed "Lord, I just commit this kitten into your keeping" and went on about his business. A few days later he was at the grocery store and met one of his church members. He happened to glance in her shopping trolley and was amazed to see some cat food. Now this woman was a cat hater, and everyone knew it, so he asked her "Why are you buying cat food when you hate cats so much?"

She replied "Well you won't believe this" and told him how her little girl had been begging her for a cat, but she kept refusing. Then a few days earlier the child had begged again so the mother finally told her. "Well if God gives you a cat I'll let you keep it," she told the pastor. "I watched my child go out in the garden, go down on her knees and ask God for a cat. And really Pastor you won't believe this but I saw it with my own eyes, a kitten suddenly came flying out of the blue sky with its paws outspread, and landed right in front of her!"

Never underestimate the power of God!

(With acknowledgements to Grace Magazine, Autumn 2004.)

*

Lighter still! –

The Double-Decker Bus

*

She was on her way back from a rewarding session of the Alexander Technique with a practitioner in Montrose. It had been arranged that her husband would wait for her in Perth at the Station Hotel, until her train got in, and they would then drive home together. But the train for some reason was not running that day. There was a bus – but it would get to Perth far too late.

Climbing aboard – "I'm *not* giving up!" she said fiercely. "Dear Lord, you can do anything!"

Arriving at Perth, she sped straight for the Station Hotel. "Have you seen my husband?" she asked at Reception – "a man with a little black dog?"

"Oh yes, he *was* here", the Receptionist replied, "but he left some time ago".

Straight she sped across the hall and out through the back door to the parking area. ... And there he was, just backing out from a parking-space ! "Damned double-decker bus!" – greeted her as she reached the car door. "Had me completely pinioned – I've been sitting here for ages". And indeed, sure enough, a large double-decker bus could still be seen, disappearing down the road!

"Come on – hurry up and get in, and for goodness sake let's get going!"

Hiding a jubilant smile, she climbed meekly in beside him!

*

The Music of the Spheres

*

Hidden Music

As I stood on the mountain-top at sunset, looking below and beyond, great masses of cumulus clouds were turning to pink and gold as they silently assembled in the valley. All petty thoughts ceased, gazing in wonder and silence. Without warning, the mountain commenced to play itself in magnificent music, first as on a mighty organ and then a symphonic sound. All the way down the mountain the music was playing gloriously, and then ceased. Had I been a musician, it might have been recorded, but it faded from memory. It was so real while it lasted. I had never heard it before or since.

Dr. D. H. Andrews, a scientist, has said: "We are making the startling discovery that, in a word, the basic reality of the universe is not matter but music ... All atoms give off music, vibrations that are rather like light. Each of us is giving off vibrations all the time, something like super-symphonic radiations! Whence came that music on the mountain, from without or within? The mind cannot explain or grasp it. One can only say, "Like God, it IS." .... The inner harmony of all things which seems to our sense imprisoned, even as the flower and perfume lie imprisoned in the seed and the bulb, will reveal and unfold hidden splendours as we are ready to receive them.

(By Bernard C. Thune. With acknowledgment to Grace Magazine).

*

Hidden Splendour

... The teacher of music had sat for some time looking at the familiar view in the green countryside, feeling at a very low ebb, when suddenly – "it seemed as if the world had been turned inside out. The grass, trees and sky took on a new intensity of light and colour as if the whole vista represented a glittering crystal in the process of formation. It came to him that all his life he had been looking at the wrong side of a work of art and that he was seeing the right side of the canvas and the true picture for the first time; that by means of this shimmering scene he was being offered an explanation of all things and a hidden meaning, just beyond his power to grasp ..."

(From "Garden Thoughts", by Michael Donnelly, published in the Science of Thought Review, (a 1997 issue). Quoted in "Birthright in Land ...", concerning Gosaba.)

*

The Unseen and the Unheard

If I could wave a magic wand before you and give you the power to perceive all the invisible sights and inaudible sounds around you at this moment, what would you see and what would you hear?

Shall we try it? Close your eyes for an instant. I wave the wand. Now look around you. The room is ablaze with dazzling light. The chairs, the tables, the floor, the ceiling and the walls are prismatic crystals, sparkling with a thousand shades of red, yellow, green and blue such as you have never in your life seen before. Your clothes are on fire with a million microscopic rainbow flames. Your nose, your cheeks, your hands are shining ruby, emerald and sapphire. You open your mouth and a shaft of amethyst light beams out before you. The air itself sparkles as if millions of miniature meteors are darting all around you, as if a cluster of skyrockets had just exploded. There is a swift rain of tiny incandescent bullets shooting down from the ceiling, shooting through the table, through the chairs, right through your body, and disappearing into the floor.

Almost blinded by this strange blaze of light, you shut your eyes in bewilderment. I now press the magic wand on your ears. Suddenly you are aware of a hurricane of sound beating upon you, as if a thousand symphony orchestras were magically squeezed into the room and all playing fortissimo. For every object near you is resonating with its own strange, peculiar music. The table booms like a hundred big bass fiddles doing a bolero. The lamp is trilling like a dozen flutes. The carpet is carolling. In this very book you hold in your hand, you hear a chorus of a thousand voices. And your body is vibrant with the most complex music of all. You hear a super-symphony resounding within you – melody, harmony, counterpoint – canon and fugue intermingling in a tapestry of sound with tones millions of times more varied, with texture millions of times more complex than any symphony ever dreamed of by a human composer.

This is the realm of the unseen and the unheard that shines and pulsates around you and within you unperceived during every moment of your life ...

(Opening paragraphs from "The Symphony of Life", by Donald Hatch Andrews, Distinguished Professor of Chemistry at Florida Atlantic University. Published in USA, 1966.)

And there are some who believe this creation is just a collection of random molecules, with no design, purpose or intelligence beyond what we humans have contributed to it!

*

... All at once, without warning of any kind, I found myself wrapped in a flame-coloured cloud ... I knew that the fire was within myself. Directly afterward there came upon me a sense of exultation, of immense joyousness accompanied or immediately followed by intellectual illumination; impossible to describe ... I saw that the universe is not composed of dead matter, but is, on the contrary, a living Presence; I became conscious in myself of eternal life. It was not a conviction that I would have eternal life then; I saw that all men are immortal; that the cosmic order is such that without any peradventure all things work together for the good of each and all; that the foundation principle of the world, of all worlds, is what we call love ...

(Richard M. Bucke in an issue of *The Science of Thought Review*.)

Chapter 6

*

Of The Spirit

To love is to feel the anguish of the poor and dispossessed and to seek remedies for their plight.

(Marie Busch)

Dearest of all to me, O Beloved, is he who feels for another, whether in joy or in sorrow, even as he feels for himself.

(Words of Krishna – as remembered, from once reading.)

What is the value of freedom? What is the real worth of life other than to give hope to those who have none? There are worse things than prison bars. The real incarceration is a life without principles. The worst prison is apathy.

(Cecilia of the Philippines, who started the Visaya Forum Foundation there, and won Anti-Slavery International's 2005 Anti-Slavery Award.)

*

Only those who see the invisible can do the impossible. *(Richard Sipe)*

Steadfast imagination can achieve all things.

(Paracelsus)

I have learned this at least by experience: that if one advances in the direction of his dreams, and endeavours to live the life he has imagined, he will meet with a success unexpected.   *(Thoreau)*

To love, and bear; to hope till Hope creates
From its own wreck the thing it contemplates ...
(Percy Busshe Shelley)

What lies behind us and what lies before us are small matters compared to what lies within us.
(Ralph Waldo Emerson)

In the depth of winter, I finally learned that within me there lay an invincible summer.   *(Albert Camus)*

*

There is no difficulty that enough love will not conquer; no disease that enough love will not heal; no door that enough love will not open; no gulf that enough love will not bridge; no wall that enough love will not throw down; no situation that enough love will not redeem ...   *(Emmet Fox)*

He drew a circle that shut me out –
Heretic, rebel, a thing to flout;
But Love and I had the wit to win –
We drew a circle that took him in.
(Author unknown)

My friend Antonio is a spiritual healer in Angola. During the terrible civil war that tore his country for 30 years, he at one time sought to flee the capital that was being attacked by rebels. He had been praying non-stop for three days. On the outskirts of the city, the truck of civilians he was in was stopped by the rebels, who separated the women and children from the men, who were taken to the nearby football ground to be shot.

Antonio, who practises a non-dualist spiritual teaching based on the understanding of the complete supremacy of these spiritual laws, was just knowing (not hoping) that 'God, the one Life, is one and all. He was my one and only life, and that of the so-called rebels. This Life, which is One, could not menace itself.' (I am drastically shortening his spiritual affirmations.)

The officer told his men to shoot but not one bullet came out of the rifles! For 15 minutes the rebels checked their rifles, but not once did a single rifle function, and the officer finally released the civilians saying 'Deus esta com vosco' (God is with you).

(Pierre Pradervand, with acknowledgements to Cygnus Review.)

As above, so below –
As within, so without.
(The Emerald Tablet. Circa 3000 B.C.)

*

Does the fish soar to find the ocean,
The eagle plunge to find the air –
That we ask of the stars in motion
If they have rumour of Thee there?

Not where the wheeling systems darken
And our benumb'd conceiving soars! –
The drift of pinions would we harken
Beats at our own clay-shuttered doors.

The angels keep their ancient places –
Turn but a stone and start a wing!
'Tis ye, 'tis your estranged faces
That miss the many-splendour'd thing.

(Francis Thompson)

I stay my haste, I make delays,
    For what avails this eager pace?
I shand amidst eternal ways,
    And what is mine shall know my face.

(John Burroughs)

Far, far above your thought
    My purpose shall appear,
When fully I the deed have wrought
    That caused your needless fear.

(Author unknown)

Man is not alone in the universe – he is
surrounded by infinite powers of love and wisdom.

(Leo Tolstoy)

Universally heralded as messengers of God, angels
are known in different cultures, religions and
spiritual traditions. It is said that angels visit us as
thoughts, visions, dreams, animals, and even as other

people who may cross our path at just the right moment, moving easily between the seen and unseen worlds ... carriers of divine grace.

(Hannah, P.O. Box 6126, Cranston, Illinois 60204.)

*

The secret of life awaits him that is free of desire.
Eyes that are filled with longing see only the outer container.

(Source unknown)

Never the spirit was born; the spirit shall cease to be never;
Never was time it was not; End and Beginning are Dreams;
Birthless and deathless and changeless remaineth the spirit
forever;
Death hath not touched it at all, dead though the house of
it seems.   *(The Bhagavad Gita)*

Just before lying down to sleep last night, I was reading in W.E. Butler's book about the aura – more particularly about the 'light' body of the astro-mental aura, and how this is built by the individual.

It thrilled me deeply, revealing to me something further of the underlying laws which had been at work during that string of apparent 'miracles' of healing in 1978 – connecting with those words about the advanced yogi "rearranging at will the light atoms of the universe", in "Autobiography of a Yogi", (which I had been reading at the time).

In the early hours of the morning I awoke from a vision of the working of these light laws which was deeply thrilling to me.

As I lay there, I began to recollect about the book I had been reading before lying down to sleep. It was then that the real thrill of the vision came over me, for it had related – not to the structure of the forms of the universe, but to some heightened level of perception of the workings of the *underlying social law relating to land tenure* – (as expounded especially by Henry George in our time, but glimpsed and put into practice with blessing for man through the ages).

I lay there trying to take in the profundity of the revelation of the burning land question to me in this way.

All I could remember was the indelible writing of it amongst these laws of light. The specific features of the vision were beyond my recall by then, for upon first awakening the unusualness of it had not struck me at all – just the concepts of the *law of light* and *holy* remained with me.

(*SAH, 12th February, 1980*)

The light of the world comes and goes, it is unstable. The Light that is eternal can never be extinguished. By this Light you behold the outer light and everything in the universe; it is only because It shines ever within you, that you can perceive the outer light. Whatever appears to you in the universe is due solely to that great Light within you, and only because the Supreme Knowledge of the essence of things lies hidden in the depths of your being is it possible for you to acquire knowledge of any kind.

(*From "Words of Sri Anandamayo Ma", published by Shree Shree Anandamayee Sangha, Varanasi, India, 1961.*)

I brought with me the thirst for the Infinite, and have come for the meeting with him.

(*Kabir, 14th century Indian tentmaker and mystic.*)

Our divine beginning lives is us and strives perpetually to return to its origin. (*Seneca, c. 5BC-AD65.*)

*

Chapter 7

*

In Farewell

"It is more blessed to give than to receive"
is a special equation in economics
in the sphere of *the land question!*

*

But how? For – what have we to "give"?
The first and most precious of gifts – the gift of *attention!*
Attention? Where? How?
A focussing on the fact that the land, given to us freely, being the very source of our life here on Earth, and so, being our very *Mother* – is a gift truly 'beyond value and beyond price'.
How could we so long have remained blind to it? – something so simple and so beautiful!

> Gaia, our Earthly Mother – beyond all value and price:
> How could we ever have reckoned You a piece of merchandise?

No monetary value has ever, in reality, attached itself to Gaia – for she has none. No one has ever actually *bought land*. The surplus product which, in a community, flows from the land – (surplus to the return the labourer would have received back from it as a lone settler) – is but the glad reflection of the simple fact that, joined in community, each works for all as well as for himself; and all for each.
This surplus – which by a beautiful law cannot be prevented from arising where a community gathers, and which reflects the different advantages to be enjoyed from differing sites – asks, then, scrupulously to be removed from every site, annually, and placed in that common sibling fund where it clearly belongs ... so, by this simple act ensuring that the world of commerce taints never the Sacred Mother.

344

Such is the measure of her reward to her children – to those who give to Her that first essential of caring – attention: a communal fund that *cannot be stopped from arising!*

What mortal could possibly have thought up such a magical thing?

How blest was that first 'giving' indeed!

Just so! "Give, and it shall be given unto you, good measure pressed down and running over ..." Likewise – "Seek ye first the kingdom of heaven and its righteousness, and all these things shall be added unto you". For what else is that "righteousness", in the realm of the land question, save that same primary acknowledgement that *the land is a sacred gift to us from a mysterious Creator?* And what human being could possibly have reckoned the marvel of the blessing which would be added to *that!*

As the great Austrian soul, Viktor Schauberger, sought repeatedly to instill into us – "man thinks an octave too low"!

That which outwardly appears as a fiscal matter holds a great secret within. By concentrating his attention upon the fiscal, man continues to miss it. For as the poet said:-

The world is too much with us, late and soon
Getting and spending we lay waste our powers.

The fiscal question is not the heart of the matter. For the land question is not a fiscal affair – it is an affair of the heart.

So if we will withdraw awhile from the confusion of this world of our creation, to a place of stillness and silence – who knows but that some of the old sanity of the man rooted in the soil will return to us, and give us back our vision again!

*

Modern civilisation is enveloped in a rising crescendo of noise, which can only be pierced by the soul-illumined mind in unison with the open heart devoted to the good of mankind. Modern man has to discover the note of the soul, the voice of the silence, and the silence that sounds in the noise of the world. But when he does so, his words will gather power and his thought will resonate throughout the planet. The world is transformed by the power of thought conforming to the livingness of great spiritual ideas and humanitarian principles brought down to earth by men and women of goodwill and applied to human living.

(Triangles Bulletin, 1965)

*

Not for silver, as a trinket,
　Shall our land fore'er be sold,
For the soil that gave us Wallace
　Means far more to us than gold.

Nor fore'er shall people-power
　Be usurped by yonder brood
Whom we foolishly reward
　For ruling us from Holyrood.

Oh yet may Scotland's Saltire waving
　Cry our voice across the sea,
Earth and people blessing, saving –
　Land where dwell the truly free!

*

346